W9-AWC-394

ISRAEL
and the
ARAMAEANS
of
DAMASCUS

ISRAEL
and the
ARAMAEANS
of
DAMASCUS

Merrill F. Unger

Introduction by Kenneth L. Barker

BAKER BOOK HOUSE
Grand Rapids, Michigan

PHOTOLITHOPRINTED BY CUSHING - MALLOY, INC.
ANN ARBOR, MICHIGAN, UNITED STATES OF AMERICA
1980

INTRODUCTION

IT is a pleasure to recommend this work of careful scholarship. After surveying the Aramaean city-state of Damascus in the earlier periods, the author brings the light of archaeology to bear on the history of Damascus from the time of its rise as a rival of Israel in approximately 900 B.C. to its fall to Tiglath-pileser III, king of Assyria, in 732 B.C. The book is thoroughly documented, but some of the sources should be updated. This can be accomplished if the reader will supplement Unger with more recent studies such as (1) B. Mazar, "The Aramaean Empire and Its Relations with Israel," *The Biblical Archaeologist* 25 (1962):98-120; (2) A. Malamat, "The Aramaeans," *Peoples of Old Testament Times,* edited by D. J. Wiseman (Oxford: Clarendon Press, 1973), pp. 134-55 (see particularly the Notes and Bibliography on pp. 149-55); and (3) W. F. Albright, "Emergence of the Aramaeans," *The Cambridge Ancient History,* edited by I. E. S. Edwards *et al.* (Cambridge: University Press, 1975), II/2, pp. 529-36.

Fortunately, however, not much of the material requires correction. Some of the matters that call for special comment are these (most are in the early chapters):

1) The treatment of Mari should be augmented by reference to A. Malamat, "Mari," *The Biblical Archaeologist* 34 (1971):2-22.

2) There is now a more cautious attitude toward the use of certain isolated Nuzi customs to illuminate patriarchal social practices. See M. Greenberg, "Another Look at Rachel's Theft of the Teraphim," *Journal of Biblical Literature* 81 (1962):239-48; C. J. M. Weir, "Nuzi," *Archaeology and Old Testament Study,* edited by D. W. Thomas (Oxford: Clarendon Press, 1967), pp. 73-86; M. J. Selman, "The Social Environment of the Patriarchs," *Tyndale Bulletin* 27 (1976): 114-36; and K. A. Kitchen, *The Bible in Its World* (Downers Grove: InterVarsity Press, 1977), p. 70.

3) The information on the Habiru should be supplemented by at least Mary P. Gray, "The Habiru-Hebrew Problem in the Light of the Source Material Available at Present," *Hebrew Union College Annual* 29 (1958):135-202 (an oft-neglected but valuable study), and F. F. Bruce, "Tell el-Amarna," *Archaeology and Old Testament Study* (see above), pp. 3-20.

4) *Dawidu(m)* does not mean "leader" but "defeat" and is merely a variant spelling of Akkadian *dabdu*; cf. I. J. Gelb *et al.*, editors, *The Assyrian Dictionary* (Chicago: The Oriental Institute, 1959), III, pp. 14-16. This alleged etymology of the name David must now be abandoned. Actually, the traditional meaning assigned to his name ("beloved") is probably correct.

5) There was no Solomonic copper refinery at Ezion Geber. N. Glueck retracted this identification in his article, "Ezion-geber," *The Biblical Archaeologist* 28 (1965):70-87. The structure involved was most likely a storehouse and/or granary.

6) There may have been three rulers of Damascus bearing the name Ben-Hadad instead of two as Unger (following Albright) maintains; see, for example, R. K. Harrison, "Ben-Hadad," *The International Standard Bible Encyclopedia,* edited by G. W. Bromiley (Grand Rapids: William B. Eerdmans Publishing Co., 1979), I, pp. 458-59.

7) Finally, it is too early to ascertain the extent to which our understanding of the most ancient periods of Aramaean history may have to be revised in the light of the new Ebla (= Tell Mardikh) tablets. See, provisionally, the steady stream of articles that have been appearing in the recent issues of *The Biblical Archaeologist, Biblical Archaeology Review,* and *The Month*; cf. also K. A. Kitchen, *The Bible in Its World,* pp. 37-55, and his bibliographical references on pp. 140-42. No definitive conclusions can be reached, however, until all the texts have been published and then analyzed and interpreted by specialists.

Baker is to be commended for reprinting this classic. May it encourage evangelicals to produce comparable works of scholarship today.

KENNETH L. BARKER

CONTENTS

FOREWORD

As a contribution to evangelical scholarship, one of the ministries of the Evangelical Theological Society is to publish outstanding, scholarly monographs of its membership. As the second in a series of volumes selected for this purpose, the dissertation of Dr. Merrill F. Unger, submitted as a part of his work toward the degree of Doctor of Theology at Johns Hopkins University, has been chosen. The original study has been revised by the author himself in preparation for publication.

Though the author is responsible for the opinions expressed in this volume, the conservative scholarship which characterizes the work is representative of the Society as a whole and serves to focus the light of archaeology upon Biblical history. In presenting this important material in book form to the public, the Society hopes to offer the benefits of the scholarly research of its membership to a wider circle and thereby extend the borders of Biblical interpretation.

The Evangelical Theological Society wishes to express its grateful appreciation to publishers who have granted permission to quote respective authors.

John F. Walvoord, EDITOR
EVANGELICAL THEOLOGICAL SOCIETY
Dallas, Texas

LIST OF ABBREVIATIONS

AASOR, *Annual of the American Schools of Oriental Research,* (New Haven, Conn.).

AfO, *Archiv für Orientforschung* (Berlin).

AJSL, *American Journal of Semitic Languages and Literatures* (Chicago).

ARAB, *Ancient Records of Assyria and Babylonia,* Vols. I, II (Chicago).

BASOR, *Bulletin of the American Schools of Oriental Research* (Baltimore).

EA, *Die El-Amarna-Tafeln,* Vols. I, II (Leipzig).

ICC, *The International Critical Commentary* (New York).

JAOS, *Journal of the American Oriental Society.*

JBL, *Journal of Biblical Literature and Exegesis.*

JEA, *Journal of Egyptian Archaeology.*

JNES, *Journal of Near-Eastern Studies* (Chicago).

JPOS, *Journal of the Palestine Oriental Society* (Jerusalem).

JSOR, *Journal of the Society of Oriental Research* (edited by S. A. B. Mercer, but now extinct).

OLZ, *Orientalistische Literaturzeitung* (Leipzig).

PJB, *Palästina Jahrbuch.*

RA, *Revue d'Assyriologie.*

Syria, *Revue d'art oriental et d'archéologie* (Paris).

ZA, *Zeitschrift für Assyriologie* (Leipzig).

ZAS, *Zeitschrift für Agyptische Sprache und Altertumskunde* (Leipzig).

ZAW, *Zeitschrift für die Alttestamentliche Wissenschaft.*

ZDMG, *Zeitschrift der Deutschen Morgenländischen Gesellschaft* (Leipzig).

ZDPV, *Zeitschrift des Deutschen Palästina-Vereins* (Leipzig).

CHAPTER I

DAMASCUS IN THE EARLIEST PERIOD

COMMONLY considered to be the oldest continuously occupied city in the world, Damascus has a place of unusual prominence in the Bible, particularly in the Old Testament period. As the capital of a powerful Aramaean state which came into ascendancy during the political disintegration following the death of Solomon about 922 B.C., eventuating in the division of the Hebrew Monarchy, the city grew so formidably in strength that it became a continual threat to the life of the newly-formed Northern Kingdom of Israel. The incessant clash of Israel with the Aramaeans of Damascus for over a century and a half, from about 900 to 750 B.C., constitutes one of the most important, and until quite recently, one of the most misunderstood epochs of Old Testament history, which is now, however, happily illuminated by archaeology.

Although the ninth and eighth centuries B.C., extending to the fall of Damascus to the Assyrians in 732 B.C., mark the era in which the city exerted its greatest influence on biblical history, its fortunes go back far beyond the advent of the Aramaeans to its earlier Egyptian overlords, and to its still earlier pre-Semitic inhabitants. These early founders, establishing it in a fertile spot on vital international trade routes, played a significant part in preparing the city for its later Aramaean conquerors, who as clever tradesmen and able warriors, in turn lifted the ancient commercial emporium to the apogee of its influence as the hub of a powerful city-state.

However, the actual origin of Damascus is unknown. Yet this much can be said. Since the triangular uplands of North Syria between Adana, Damascus and Mosul do not seem to have been glaciated at all during the Ice Age in the Near East,[1] occupation of this exceedingly choice district in the fertile Ghutah (the Arabic name for the Damascene) doubtless goes back to a very early period, perhaps to the Neolithic Age, or earlier. As the site has been continuously inhabited for millennia

1

and has never been excavated, and since there is as yet no clearly established reference to the city in contemporary documents before the late Bronze Age (15th century B.C.),[2] the problem of origins is wrapped in almost complete obscurity.

I. THE NAME OF DAMASCUS

It is uncertain whether the name of Damascus, ancient *Timašgi*, *Dumašqa*, etc., is Semitic or not. In 1930 E. Speiser traced the beginnings of the city to the Hurrians, whom he related to the Lullu, and whom he regarded as the pre-Semitic inhabitants of the land.[3] However, excavations at Nuzu in 1930–31 reaching to the lower levels of earlier Gasur, dating to the middle of the third millennium B.C., compelled Speiser to abandon his theory of a Hurrian substratum for northern Mesopotamia and Syria and to admit in 1933 that " the Hurrians were clearly new-comers, who made their appearance at a comparatively late date ".[4] On the basis of the new archaeological material he places the Hurrian migrations in their entirety in the second millennium, and maintains that upon overrunning the new territories the migrants " faced for the most part populations of Semitic or semitized stock ", while still holding that the Semites did not form the earliest ethnic group in those areas, at least not within historical times.[5] Although it is now known that Semites preceded Hurrians in Palestine-Syria, place names of the early Bronze Age in these areas (according to Speiser), testify to the early occupation of this region by non-Semitic elements.[6] Among such place names he lists Damascus, whose suffix Dumaš-gi, Dumaš-qa, he says, points to a non-Semitic origin in the East.[7]

With our present sources of knowledge we must despair of arriving at a decisive or even satisfactory etymology for Damascus. It is possible, on the other hand, that the name is of Semitic provenience and attributable to the period when Semitic or semitized stock was dominant in this region from about the middle to the end of the third millennium B.C., or earlier.[8] Biblical indications take note of the presence of Semites in the West at a remote date and mention their very early migration eastward to the " plain of Shinar " where they made Babel a permanent centre.[9] Shamash was recognized as the great solar deity of the Babylonian Semites, and this god[10] with certain other Babylonian deities[11] was of western importation. The name *Mash*, which figures prominently in the eastern as well as the western Semitic cultures, and which may possibly be an element of the name of the solar deity, may point to the early occupation of Syria and northern Mesopotamia by Semites. *Mash* is specified as one of the sons of Aram in Genesis x, 23. Mâshu in the Epic of Gilgamesh, the solar hero, is the mountain where the gates of the setting sun were found. Upon very tenuous evidence Clay would locate this mountain at Hermon in the region of Damascus, and offers an ingenious theory to explain the origin of the city's name in a supposed connection with the abode of the solar deity Shamash.[12] This hypothesis, however, involves philological difficulties and contains too many assumptions to be taken seriously.[13] The same may be said of Haupt's theory which presupposes a form *Dar-mashqi* as original, and renders the meaning " a settlement in a well-watered region ".[14]

It is difficult, if not impossible, to ascertain the original form, which may have been Arabic *Dimashqu*, appearing in the Old Testament as Dammeseq[15] and composed of the elements *di* and *mesheq*.[16] Kraeling prefers to regard the variant *Darmeseq* as a later Aramaic form which was already coming into vogue at the time the Aramaeans began occupying the region during the thirteenth century B.C.[17] According to his theory the new population fortified the city and proudly called it *dar* or *fortress* rather than merely " place of Mesheq ".[18]

The Assyrians employed the term (*al*) *Sha-imeri-shu* for the city, which Haupt construed as meaning " city of asses ".[19] An interesting parallel is to be found from the stele of Shilhak in Shushinak. Among a group of towns in the Zagros region preserved on the monument occurs *Sha-imirê*, " city of asses ".[20]

To judge from the much-vexed passage, Genesis xv, 2, 3, in the light of the evidence furnished by the Septuagint, *Mesheq* is apparently a more ancient name of Damascus than *Dammeseq*, or is perhaps to be regarded as a shorter poetical designation.[21] It is obvious from the Greek that Eliezer was called *ben Mesheq*, as the Massoretic text correctly preserves the tradition,[22] but it is also at the same time patent that the Greek translators completely misunderstood the term, arbitrarily rendering the expression as a feminine proper name, and interpreting it as the mother of Eliezer. However the significance of the Semitic

idiom is now well attested. "Eliezer ben Mesheq" is tantamount to "Eliezer of Mesheq" (Dammeseq, Damascus) or
"Eliezer, the Damascene".[23]

The passage as commonly treated is regarded as having
suffered considerable corruption,[24] despite the fact that the
general sense of the Massoretic tradition appears to be clear.[25]
Accordingly, various ventures have been made to emend the
text.[26] Of these, Albright's efforts seem to be the most felicitous
in clarifying the obvious meaning intended as it has come down
to us in the Hebrew. His rendering, following an easy emenda-
tion,[27] runs thus: "And the 'son of my house' is the 'son of
Mesheq', which is Damascus . . . and behold the 'son of the
house' shall be my heir". The "son of the house", like Aramaic
bar baitâ and Accadian mâr bîti (prince), has reference to the
heir presumptive. The "son of my house" would therefore be
"my heir". The passage tersely paraphrased would read
"And my heir is a Damascene", or following the reconstruction
which assumes only the haplography of one of the bens, without a transposition, "And an inhabitant of Damascus is my
heir".[28]

The Nuzu Tablets, which so brightly illuminate biblical
customs of the Patriarchal age, remove any singularity which
might be attached to the circumstance that at first Abraham's
heir was a slave. At Nuzu childless people were accustomed
to adopt a son to serve them as long as they lived, to bury and
mourn for them when they died, and to inherit their property.
Should the adoptor beget a son after the adoption, however,
the adopted must relinquish any claim of being the principal
heir.[29] This situation gives the legal aspect of the divine word
to Abraham. "This slave shall not inherit thee, but he that
shall come out of thy inwards shall inherit thee".[30]

II. THE LAND OF DAMASCUS IN THE PRE-PATRIARCHAL PERIOD

About two centuries before the land of Damascus first emerges
into the light of history, the kings of the Third Dynasty of Ur
(c. 2070–1960) ruled in lower Mesopotamia. Scattered documents indicate the expansion of their power toward the north
and east. They not only extended their sway up the Tigris to
Asshur, whose governor Zariqum declared himself to be the
servant of Bur-Sin,[31] but they appear to have controlled the

Middle Euphrates also. The princes of Mari, Tura-Dagan, Puzur-Ishtar, Ilum-Ishar and Idi-Ilum were contemporary with the last kings of Ur and likely their vassals, although doubtless enjoying a large measure of independence.[32] Although there is no evidence to indicate that their domination extended farther than this, the éclat which they gave to Sumerian culture radiated beyond their frontiers to North Syria. The region of Damascus must have shared in the commercial activity of the period. Peoples of Asia Minor and North Syria went to Lower Mesopotamia for business transactions, as the numerous economic tablets from the Ur III era show.[33] Archaeology bears witness to the same influences. In the region of Carchemish and in the Orontes Valley certain vases and bronzes derived from Sumerian types have been found.[34] Cylinders of this period have been discovered at Hamath,[35] at Qatna[36] bordering on the land of Damascus, and as far as Byblus.[37] The flourishing traffic of Syria with Southern Mesopotamia suffered evident disaster in the period of Elamite and Amorite invasion (c. 1960–c. 1830) which put an end to the Third Dynasty of Ur.

Meanwhile the Twelfth Dynasty in Egypt extended its influence in Palestine-Syria. While evidence for actual Egyptian domination in extant records is not extensive,[38] it is definite. Sesostris III (c. 1876–1838)[39] conquered Sekmem (Shechem) in Retenu (Syria),[40] and although this is the only military campaign mentioned, there must have been other and older expeditions, for on the day after the death of Amenemhet I the political refugee, Sinuhe, did not escape the surveillance of the pharaoh until he had reached a region situated to the east of Byblus, probably in the lower Biqaʿ or in the region to the north of Damascus.[41] In addition to the story of Sinuhe and the biography of Sebek-khu, the execration texts presuppose Egyptian rule not only in Palestine but also in Syria.[42] Further evidence is afforded by Syrian seals which belong to the period of the Twelfth Dynasty.[43] Byblus appears to have been an Egyptian dependency from the time of Amenemhet I.[44] At Qatna a sphinx inscribed with the name of Ita, a daughter of Amenemhet II, was found.[45] Egyptian statuettes and other objects at Ras Shamra indicate that the city was dominated by Egypt at least from the reign of Sesostris II (c. 1890–1877, Edgerton) till the reign of Amenemhet III (c. 1837–1789, Edgerton).[46] Alalakh, too, was under Egyptian influence during the same general period if we may judge from the seal impression of Shamshu-Adad.[47]

We, therefore, seem justified, in the light of the general evidence for the Twelfth Dynasty in Syria, in concluding that the land of Damascus passed for a protracted period under pharaonic control until Egyptian power collapsed just before Shamshu-Adad I's Syrian expedition.[48] Precisely during this era of Egyptian power in Palestine-Syria during the Middle Kingdom the land of Damascus emerges into the light of actual history. The first mention of the district in which the ancient city was located occurs in the historically important execration texts deciphered by M. Posener.[49] These priceless documents shed much light on south-western Asia in the last half of the nineteenth century B.C., and, according to Albright,[50] belong more precisely to the period 1850–1825, in the first half of the reign of Amenemhet III. The names of the Brussels figurines which have been identified[51] cover approximately the territory embraced by Egypt's Asiatic Empire under Amenemhet III,[52] including western Palestine and Phoenicia as far as Ullaza and 'Irqata in the Eleutherus Valley, Transjordan from northern Gilead through Hauran to the region of Damascus, and the Biqa' as far as Ras Ba'albek, some forty miles south of Ḥums in Middle Syria.[53]

The most important place name for our study occurring in the Brussels texts is *Apum* (spelled *a-p-w-m*), which, as Albright first noticed,[54] is well-known *A-pi* (*U-pi* or *U-pe*) of the Amarna Letters, the designation of a land (mâtu) in which Damascus was located.[55] This region was so extensive it was divided into two districts, a southern and a northern. Although the name of the town of Damascus has not yet occurred before the campaigns of Thutmose III in Syria almost three centuries later,[56] the city was doubtless in existence, and may reasonably be expected to turn up in future excavations of records belonging to this era. However, along with other Syrian geographical sites, the name *Âpum* occurs some three generations after the Brussels texts in the famous Mari tablets from Tell el-Harîri on the Middle Euphrates. As we would expect, the name also appears in the old form *Apum*, rendered in the genitive *A-pi-im* (*ki*), as well as *ma-a-at A-pi-im* (*ki*), "the land of Âpum".[57] The Mari letters thus agree with the Brussels figurines and the Amarna correspondence in presenting *Âpum* as a district and not as a city, although the possibility is, of course, not precluded that there might have been a town by the same name called after the district, or the district called after the town.

The etymological significance of the ancient designation of the Damascene region is suggestive and appropriate. The name apparently comes from the Accadian word *âpum*, later *âpu* (often written *a-bi*, that is *a-pi*) meaning commonly a "forest or thicket of reeds (cane-brake)", a singularly fitting description of the eastern Damascene, a region called by the Arabs *El Merj*, "the meadow land", which is replete with reed-filled lakes and marshes, extending for a greater distance than do perhaps any similar marshes in Western Asia, exclusive of Babylonia and Susiana.[58]

At this early period the Damascene already appears as an important political entity, and the names of several princes or kings of the region occur in the Brussels texts and the Mari documents. The first published name *A-a-ia-a-bu-um*,[59] which appears as *'ybm* in the Berlin execration texts, was correctly equated with biblical Job, *'Iyyob*, by Albright in 1928.[60] The second *Zu-ú-zu* may be explained as *Sus*, "swallow".[61] The third, vocalized *Aḥu-Kabkab*, means " The God of the Morning Star is Brother".[62] Thus the horizons of the execration texts and the Mari documents, overlapping in the region of Damascus in the east and Byblus in the west, are adding new data to our knowledge of this region in the pre-Patriarchal and the Patriarchal Periods.

III. DAMASCUS IN THE PATRIARCHAL AGE

It is possible that the Patriarchal Age of Hebrew history is to be located somewhere in the latter half of the Middle Bronze Age in Palestine and during the late Middle Empire and the Hyksos period in Egypt, that is between 1750 and 1500 B.C.[63] This uncertainty, of course, would vanish if the date of Abraham's migration from Mesopotamia or some other event in the life of the patriarch could be determined by some precise link with extra-biblical history. According to the Hebrew Bible Abraham left Mesopotamia on his journey to Palestine some 645 years before Israel left Egypt, that is, in the late twentieth century B.C., reckoning from the most likely date of the Exodus. If some connection is assumed between Israel's entrance into

Egypt and the Hyksos infiltration, and three or four generations are added, a date between 1900 and 1750 is arrived at for Abraham's migration.[64]

The royal archives of Mari during the reign of the last native king, Zimri-Lim (c. 1730–1700 B.C.) and unearthed in 1936 by André Parrot, greatly illuminate the Patriarchal Period and strikingly confirm Hebrew tradition, according to which their ancestors migrated to Palestine from Harran in northwestern Mesopotamia. Contemporary cuneiform sources show that Harran itself was a prosperous city in the nineteenth and eighteenth centuries B.C. At the time of Hammurabi (1728–1686) it was under Amorite suzerainty. The Mari tablets also make frequent allusion to Nakhur, biblical Nahor, specified as Rebekah's parents' home in Genesis xxiv, 10, and also under Amorite control in the eighteenth century B.C. Besides the location of the Patriarchal cities Harran and Nahor in northwestern Mesopotamia, names of Abraham's forefathers occur which correspond to the names of towns near Harran: Serug (Assyrian Sarugi, Syriac Serug), Nahor, and Terah (Til Turakhi, " Mound of Terah", in Assyrian times).[65]

Another example of a striking parallel in proper names is "Jacob", which stands for Ya'qub-'el, "May El Protect", which was found in the recently published documents from Chagar Bazar in northern Mesopotamia (early eighteenth century B.C.) as Ya-ah-qu-ub-el. The publication of the economic tablets from Mari promises to bring to light many socio-legal similarities to the narratives of Genesis.[66]

A wealth of other information is now available in addition to the parallels involving personal names and geographical links between the Hebrew Patriarchs and their traditional home in Padan-Aram, "The Plain of Aram", showing that the ancestors of the Hebrews were not only actual historical figures,[67] but that they really emigrated from northern Mesopotamia, where they were subject to mixed Accadian, Amorite, and Hurrian influence. The publication of the Nuzi documents of the fifteenth century B.C. has also revealed many striking parallels between Nuzian social and legal practice and the customary law reflected in the Patriarchal accounts of Genesis,[68] evidencing the fact that the latter fit better into the framework of Nuzian social and legal practice than they do into later Israelite history, or into that of the Babylonian laws and economic documents of the nineteenth century, or the similar Assyrian material of the twelfth century B.C.[69]

A possible time for Abraham's removal into Palestine was toward the end of the seventeenth century B.C. when Egyptian control in Syria was practically nil because of the internal disorders due to the Hyksos invasion, but it may well have occurred earlier. The regions where Abraham sojourned, especially the Negeb, were undoubtedly thinly populated, and offered opportunity for strangers to settle. It is interesting that the Abrahamic migration, which is but the single wave historically reflecting the movement of a great stream of humanity, should have flowed toward southern Palestine rather than toward the more alluring region of Damascus or Hamath. The reasons, besides those of a providential nature assigned to the patriarch's movements by the Hebrew Bible, must be sought in the growing strength of the Amorite states of Coelesyria, as well as the Hittite advance.

The dominant power of the Amorite Kingdom of Kadesh on the Orontes and the strong Syrian states under its leadership at the time of the first Asiatic campaign of Thutmose III (c. 1468) presupposes at least a century and a half of growth and expansion during which the Amorite states of central Syria were attaining to the position of vigour which enabled them to present a solid front against invasion and manifest great strength at the time of the Egyptian threat to their autonomy. There is reason to suppose that during the course of this period Damascus and the Haurân, as well as the strong cities in the plain of Esdraelon,[70] came under the control of Kadesh. During the same period there was a concomitant development of Amorite power east of the Jordan which by the time of the Mosaic age and the Exodus had grown into formidable kingdoms—those of Og of Bashan and Sihon of Heshbon. During the acme of its career Bashan must have exerted strong influence upon Damascus from the south and east, if not intermittently direct control, for Og is said to have ruled in Mount Hermon less than twenty miles distant.[71]

Already as early as the time of Jacob the Amorite states of central Syria must have attained a considerable degree of power. This was ostensibly a factor in Jacob's removal from Gilead, and his migration to the region west of the Jordan. The cessation of all connection of the Hebrews with Aram subsequent to Jacob's separation from Laban and his Aramaean kin in Mesopotamia where he had lived for two decades, suggests that at that time there arose in the region of Gilead a power which prevented Hebrew settlement there, and thereafter proved a separating barrier prohibiting further intercourse. It was natural under these conditions for the Hebrews to lose their Aramaean character and to become markedly Canaanite in language, custom, and culture. The preservation of the tradition of the old blood relationship and the belief in later times of a common descent from a " fugitive Aramaean ", *'Arammi 'ōbhēdh*,[72] as Jacob is called, are all the more remarkable in the light of this break in relationship with their eastern relatives, who are always referred to as " Aramaean " in Genesis.

The ethnic and linguistic background of the Patriarchal Period, while as yet characterized by great obscurity, bids fair to be brightly illuminated when the mass of contemporary documents is studied and published. The Mari tablets seem to reflect definite traces of a West Semitic dialect current in northwestern Mesopotamia in the early second millennium B.C. from which the Aramaic language subsequently sprang, to become, in due course of time, the *lingua franca* of all Western Asia. Presumably this dialect was the common speech current in Harran when the patriarchs arrived from Babylonia, and was adopted by them, to be carried with them into Palestine. There, however, it was gradually adapted to local Canaanite dialect, so that the resultant language was not identical with the standard speech of sedentary Canaanites, but closely akin.

Ethnically, as well as linguistically, the picture of Hebrew origins suggests a composite rather than a simple picture. The appearance of the non-Semitic name Arphaxad, as the grandfather of Eber, the ancestor of the Hebrews, in the standard genealogical lists is doubtless a reflection of the mixed genetic affiliations of the early Hebrews. Moreover, if the Hebrew migration into Palestine from Mesopotamia was roughly coeval with complex ethnic movements producing the Hyksos Age in Egypt, further evidence is furnished for a composite racial origin, embracing Hurrian as well as Semitic elements.[73]

The perennially vexing question of whether or not the origin of the Hebrews is to be connected with the *'Apiru (Khapiru)* who figure so curiously in the cuneiform records of the nineteenth and eighteenth centuries as well as in the Hurrian, Hittite, and Amarna documents of the fifteenth and fourteenth centuries, despite recent light from Ugarit, must still be considered to be undecided.[74] In 1939–40 Charles Virolleaud discovered from the Ras Shamra texts that the correct form of the name *Khabiri* is *Khapiri*, and that the name occurs in the plural as '*aprm* in Ugaritic.[75] This new reading, which had been maintained all along by Albright[76] since about 1930, who equated *Khapiru* with a Canaanite '*Apiru* (Egyptian '*A-pi-ir*, '*A-pi-ru*) is fully substantiated by the material from Ugarit. The new evidence at the same time disposes all such tempting etymologies as Dhorme's, who would connect the word with *ḥbr* or *ḫbr* " to bind " with the meaning of " ally " or " confederate ", or more recently " captive ".[77]

Since the publication of the Amarna letters, most scholars have equated the *Khapiru* (*Habiri*, etc.) with the Hebrews. The discovery that the true form of the name is '*Apiru*, although it does complicate the problem, does not, however, necessarily render identification with the Hebrews more uncertain and precarious than ever, as Kreeling maintains,[78] for '*Ibhrî* may indeed represent an earlier '*Iprî*, according to a phonetic development frequent in Hebrew at that period.[79] There are numerous examples in Hebrew and other Semitic tongues where stop-sounds become voiced (sonant) in conjunction with *resh*. Albright lists such instances as *drk-drg* (" to tread "), *skr-sgr* (" to stop up, shut "), *dpr-dbr* (" to drive ").[80]

In Syria and Mesopotamia the *Khapiru* figure as soldiers of fortune, mercenaries, raiders, captives, and slaves of heterogeneous racial origins. In Palestine they are presented in Canaanite letters of the early fourteenth century as raiders and rebels against Egyptian authority, at times in coalition with Canaanite princes. In the kingdom of Ugarit under Niqmad, a vassal of the Hittite king Shuppiluliuma, they appear, according to Goetze's illuminating analysis of the material,[81] as a distinct class of the population of Khalbi, living in a particular quarter of the city. As the list of towns and villages mentioned as controlled by Ugarit is written in Akkadian as well as in Ugaritic, Virolleaud was enabled to deduce four equations, three of which Goetze clearly demonstrates refer to parts of the city of Khalbi, so that the fourth entry " Khalbi of the Khapiru (*ḫlb* '*prm*) " likewise naturally denotes part of the town, the section where the *Khapiru*, a distinct class of the population, were living.[82]

Evidence is accumulating to suggest that the early Hebrews were in some way connected with the *'Apiru* (Khapiru). If Abraham had not been called a Hebrew, there would nevertheless be grounds for classifying him among this group. He was plainly a roving adventurer, appearing upon occasion at least, as in Genesis xiv, as a soldier of fortune. Hebrew *'Ibhrî* may well stand for an older *'Iprî*. The Septuagint renders the term in an appellative sense ὁ περάτης, " he who has crossed over, transient". In this particular *Khapiru* group there was in addition a growing ethnic consciousness of descent from a common Aramaic stock, coupled with the development of certain religious conceptions.[83] Abraham's warlike venture in Genesis xiv presents the patriarch in somewhat of the role of a soldier of fortune, which from the Amarna letters and other sources, is attested as a characteristic of some of the *Khapiru*. In this potentially valuable document, whose precise historical background is unhappily still lamentably obscure,[84] occurs the oldest biblical mention of the ancient city, unless we unnecessarily and unwarrantedly assume an anachronism, which fixes it as a place already in existence in the Patriarchal Age. Since already by the time of Thutmose III's conquests in Syria in the first half of the fifteenth century the city was prominent enough to be listed conspicuously among the conqueror's spoils, it stands to reason that a previous development of perhaps several centuries or more is not out of the question. Abraham is said to have pursued the defeated army of the invading kings to Hobah "on the left hand", that is to the north "of Damascus".[85] In addition Eliezer, Abraham's servant and heir, is said to have been a native of this city.[86] Although it may not as yet have been the chief city of the important district of Apum as it had become in Amarna days, it is not impossible that even at this early date it was a thriving settlement, already receiving the flow of trade which was to bring it future greatness. It is impossible to say whether it had yet become the royal residence and the capital city of Apum, which was to be its destiny at a later period. It probably was, since its location was so favourable, and the alternative sites for a capital were few.

CHAPTER II

DAMASCUS UNDER EGYPTIAN CONTROL

UNDER the powerful Eighteenth Dynasty and the empire built up under its might Egyptian supremacy gradually extended over Palestine and into Syria. Damascus, of course, with other Syrian states ultimately fell under the hegemony of the pharaohs. Conquest of this region by the armies of the Nile began immediately after the Hyksos were ousted by Amosis I about the middle of the sixteenth century B.C. Amosis' son, Amenophis I (1546–1525), apparently continued the push, and the next king, Thutmose I (1525–1503), invaded northern Syria.

This young pharaoh enjoyed brilliant success in the determined thrust of Egyptian power into Western Asia. It was not mere boasting when he declared that the southern limits of his empire stretched to the third cataract of the Nile, while the northern boundaries extended to the Euphrates. " Never had the like happened to other kings ".[1] This was undoubtedly the first time since the strong Twelfth Dynasty more than three centuries before that Damascus and the land of Upe again temporarily passed over into native Egyptian hands.[2] But Thutmose I was not the first monarch to learn that Syria-Palestine, although a rich prize, was at the same time, because of the geographical configuration of the country, very unfavourable for the amalgamation of its numerous petty city-kingdoms and small principalities into one great nation, as that process had taken place in the valleys of the Nile and the Euphrates. Consequently, it was easy for a conquest that seemed for the moment to be permanent in the long run to prove ephemeral. Syrian kinglets, under the spell of Egyptian prowess and pharaonic grandeur, might be induced by considerations of wisdom and expediency, to humble themselves by sending tribute to the Egyptian king. But scarcely had the invader withdrawn when they not only discontinued their gifts, but also made every possible preparation to ward off any similar incursion of Egyptian militarism.

13

I. THE EARLY PERIOD OF EGYPTIAN CONTROL

Neither Thutmose II nor the great queen Hatshepsut, with whom he ruled for a time, displayed much interest in foreign conquest. It was reserved for the next ruler, the energetic Thutmose III (1490–1436), to become the greatest of Egyptian conquerors, to extend the glory and prowess of Egyptian arms throughout all Western Asia, and to consolidate the Empire of the Nile. In seventeen campaigns involving almost twenty years of ceaseless warfare in Syria Thutmose brought the Egyptian empire to its greatest size and glory. The extent of his wars and conquests is indicated in his famous Annals, which constitute one of the most important historical inscriptions surviving from ancient Egypt, and which are recorded on the interior of the walls enclosing the corridor which surrounds the granite holy of holies of the great Karnak temple of Amun at Thebes. The range of his military exploits is further attested by two lists of vanquished Asiatic cities, preserved upon the pylons of the temple. Those belonging to the first campaign are preserved in triplicate on different pylons variously located in the temple structure. They are one hundred and nineteen in number, and comprise in general the territory extending from the northernmost limits of Palestine southward to an undetermined distance into central Palestine. The Negeb was already under Egyptian dominion, as Müller has shown.[3]

What is of importance for our study is that Damascus with its district is included in this catalogue. In the superscription which introduces the enumeration, the conquered places are characterized as a " list of the countries of Upper Retenu which his majesty shut up in the city of Megiddo ... on his first victorious campaign ".[4] The term "countries" points to the various city-states of the region, consisting of the chief walled town and the surrounding territory it controlled. By a comparison of references to the term it is evident that Upper Retenu at the beginning of the New Empire designated the more northerly hill country of Palestine and the more distant hinterland of Phoenicia, especially Coelesyria.[5]

Müller is doubtless correct in equating Lower Retenu with Naharên in its broader sense[6] as describing the flat lands on the Euphrates westward to the Mediterranean, excluding the strip of coast, and viewing the former expression as the older,[7] current in the Middle Empire but crowded out of the common speech in the New Empire by the more popular Semitic term and relegated to occasional poetic use, as in the case of Amenemḥeb.[8] There is no precise indication anywhere where Lower Retenu commences, and Thutmose's list comprehends only a part of Upper Retenu. If, however, at the time of the New Empire we consider Lower Retenu as embracing Northern Syria, including Naharen in its broader connotation, and Retenu without any modifier as equivalent to Syria in general, Thutmose's list would suggest that Upper Retenu also included central and northern Palestine[9] to the region of Damascus, while Lower Retenu probably comprised the territory north of Lebanon and Antilebanon. That the term without modifier is a general expression for Syria and comprehends territory stretching far to the north is suggested by Sethos I's use of the designation. He speaks of the vassals of the Hittites, who were at least located no farther south than Kadesh, which itself is north of the valley between Lebanon and Antilebanon, as " the great princes of the miserable Retenu, which his majesty carried away by his victory in the Hittite country ".[10]

There is a suggestion in the later conception of Retenu that the coastal territory was intentionally avoided, and the interior highlands of Syria were intended. The Annals constantly refer to the king as being " in Retenu " when he pressed more into the interior.[11] Likewise Syria, that is Coelesyria, stands in contrast to Phoenicia, and the former translates the hieroglyphic term which denotes "the east Retenu".[12] But the expression " east Retenu " is not a happy designation to differentiate eastern and western Syria, but suggests that Retenu as a whole lies in the east, for western Syria is mentioned already in the late erroneous *Kft* (*tt*) for Phoenicia ($\phi o\iota\nu\iota\kappa\eta$).[13] Accordingly, at the beginning of the New Empire Retenu was applied to the hill-country of northern Palestine and the hinterland of Syria, especially middle Syria.

In the Thutmose list Damascus alone occurs outside the actual confines of Palestine. The city appears as *Timasku*, thirteenth by order in the enumeration.[14] There can be little doubt that it was included because it was already a place of sufficient importance to be mentioned among the triumphs of a famous empire-builder whose conquests embraced many celebrated places.

Ancient records of the Asiatic campaigns of this royal strategist and his successes in Palestine and Syria shed much light on the social, political, and cultural history of this region during this whole general period. It is evident that the main goal of Egyptian conquest was the land of Syria with its prosperous cities and fertile plains, its rich mineral wealth and natural resources, and its strategic harbours and vital trade routes linking the land of the Nile with Asia Minor and the mighty empires on the Tigris and the Euphrates. Among the many city states which dotted this area Damascus must have appeared as no inconsiderable prize to the ambitious Thutmose III. Its strategic commercial position on main caravan routes running east and west, as well as north and south, making it a natural mart and factory of inland Syria, and its ideal location nestled in one of the most beautiful and fertile plains in the world, must have combined to make it an alluring trophy for Egyptian arms. Then, too, it was not too well protected by natural bulwarks and physical topography so that in this earlier period at least, long before it had reached the acme of its political and military power, it would be more exposed to the vicissitudes of fortune and subject to domination by one or another of the great empires of the ancient Orient than many other Syrian states. It is not surprising, therefore, to read of it in the "first victorious campaign", which was one of the most significant of Thutmose's many expeditions in Asia, and the most fully recorded. However, it must not be concluded from the superscription to the list of the one hundred and nineteen towns that Thutmose actually captured all of these places on his first campaign. This fact is not stated, and may not be inferred. All that is said is that these "countries" were shut up in the fortress of Megiddo, and that their children were carried away as hostages to Thebes on the pharaoh's "first victorious campaign".

Moreover, there is nothing in the account of Thutmose's first Asiatic expedition that would suggest his actual recapture of Damascus at that time. Probably continuously under Egyptian sway since the campaign of Thutmose I in Upper Retenu,[15] the city-state had joined the general revolt of Egypt's Syrian possessions from Sharuhen to the Euphrates. Likely represented by the local ruling dynast, it had joined the coalition of practically all Syria, headed by the king of Kadesh. According to the Gebal Barkal stela, the Syrian confederacy formed to resist Thutmose III's advance consisted of 330 chiefs, " with millions of men, hundreds of thousands of the foremost of all foreign lands ".[16] Although the figures are manifestly grossly exaggerated, the indication is plain that a formidable coalition attempted to block Egyptian advance in Syria. Worsted in a preliminary clash, the allies fled to Megiddo. Thutmose besieged the fortress for seven months before it surrendered. Then " that fallen one (the chief of Kadesh) together with the chiefs who were with him " sent vast quantities of war materials and rich spoil to the victorious pharaoh, at the same time pleading that their lives be spared. Thutmose took their oath of loyalty, and permitted them to return to their cities, carrying off their citizenry and their chattels as booty to Egypt.[17]

It is unfortunate that after the capture of Megiddo the record of Egyptian warfare in Syria degenerates into little more than a catalogue of spoils. There is a happy supplement, however, narrating the close of the campaign. A fortress was built in Lebanon, whither the king had marched after his victory at Megiddo. Among places listed as taken at this time are included Yanuamma in the Hûıeh Plain and Nugasa (cuneiform Nuk-hashshe) in the vicinity of Hamath, north of Damascus.[18] Although no further advance is mentioned, conquests and fortifications in such close proximity to Damascus, together with hostages carried away to Egypt as guarantees of submission, must have been effective reasons for the city's yielding to the Egyptian yoke, as well as for its prominent place in Thutmose III's first lists of Asiatic conquests.

However little the monuments of Thutmose's grandeur may have impressed the Thebans, these records, especially the long lists of his Asiatic triumphs recorded on the walls of the splendid temple of Karnak, are of incalculable value to the historian of the ancient Near East. They are also a priceless aid to geography. Many a name which had been known only through the Bible, such as our ancient city of Damascus, now makes its first appearance in these lists.[19]

The establishment of the Egyptian Empire in Western Asia was roughly synchronous with the rise of the strong non-Semitic kingdom of Mitanni, located within the great bend of the Euphrates, and having its centre in the Upper Khabur region.[20] It was inevitable that two such powerful states as Egypt and

Mitanni, both with ambitions in Syria, should eventually clash. There is evidence that Mitanni had done all in its power to encourage the rebellion of Kadesh and the Syrian states against Egypt, for Thutmose III was finally compelled to invade this formidable state and punish its king[21] before he could establish Egyptian suzerainty in Naharên.[22] The Mitannian kingdom soon saw that it would be highly advantageous to bolster Kadesh as a buffer state between itself and the menace of Egyptian militarism. But even so, eventual reckoning with an expanding Egypt was unavoidable, and from the Syrian campaigns of Thutmose III to the time of Thutmose IV (1423–1413) Egypt and Mitanni were almost constantly at war.

Before succumbing to the suzerainty of Thutmose III, it was inevitable that Damascus, together with the rest of the smaller and weaker city states of Syria, at the rise of the Egyptian threat in Western Asia would fall under the dominion, or at least under the strong influence of Mitanni, directly or indirectly through Mitannian pressure upon Kadesh. This is certain, for with the exception of Kadesh on the Orontes, the Syrian kingdoms of the hinterland in this period displayed little aptitude for government. This condition seems patently true of Damascus. Even later in Amarna days the city does not appear to have gained any great political significance.

By his thirty-third year (1457) Thutmose III had extended his conquests far enough in North Syria to be in a position to attack the suzerain power, Mitanni. Crossing the Euphrates, he smashed resistance on the eastern bank, thus putting a temporary end to Mitannian overlordship in northern Syria, and to some extent in Mesopotamia itself. In this thirty-eighth year (1452), after continuing his reduction of individual Syrian states, the victorious pharaoh received tribute from Alalakh, the new Egyptian domination there marking the end of Level V, according to Sidney Smith.[23] At Thutmose's death in his fifty-fourth regnal year, all Syria was virtually under Egyptian control, but general revolt in the North greeted his successor Amenophis II, who quelled this uprising in his second and third years. Heretofore, in the absence of the record of any further Syrian campaigns during the reign of the new pharaoh, one might have supposed that perhaps Amenophis II had been ousted from north or even central Syria. That this was not the case is proved by the stela of this monarch discovered some years ago in the ruins of Memphis.[24] The new inscription is a report of two campaigns of the pharaoh in Asia—one in central and north Syria in his eighth year, and the other in Palestine in the ninth year of his reign. In his first campaign Amenophis II went as far as the land of Nîya, almost due east of Aleppo, and the country of Zalkhi in the region of Ugarit. On his return to Egypt he passed Kadesh on the Orontes, and hunted in the forest of R;b'w, probably Lab'u of Tiglathpileser II, biblical Labo Hamath (now Labweh on the Orontes). The list of the captives taken from Syria at this time sheds remarkable light on the ethnic complexion of South-western Asia during this period.

Four " ethnic " groups are mentioned in the stela. *Thuru* (cuneiform *Khurru*, Ugaritic and Hebrew, *Ḥôrî*), a name describing the inhabitants of the Egyptian province *Khuru*, that is, Syria and Palestine. *Shûsu*, the nomads, *Nugasu*, the inhabitants of Nukhashshe in northern Syria, and the *'Apiru*. Besides these groups appear the *maryannu* (*maryana*)[25] " chariot warriors " of the Syrian aristocracy and the *Kyn'nw* (*Kina'nu*), the moneyed class of merchants and tradesmen of the coastal commercial centres of Syria and Palestine, corresponding to the *Kena'anîm* " merchants, traders ", particularly " Phoenician traders " of the biblical sources. Especially in Mitanni, but also in Alalakh and elsewhere, the *maryannu* formed a very definite social class, as is now becoming increasingly evident. They apparently constituted a patrician stratum in society, men of rank and of some wealth who could afford a chariot and two horses at least. In the Mitannian state, as likely elsewhere, they could be called upon for service for the king. The term seems to be derived from Vedic *marya*, denoting a " youth " or " warrior " (plural *maryas*). The form is perhaps based on the accusative plural, with the Hurrian suffix *ni*.

The *Kyn'nw*, a caste of traders, comprising heads and members of trading companies in the Late Bronze Age, became a class of great importance, especially in Phoenician coastal towns, which became the centre of a highly developed purple industry. Red purple, **kina* (*kna'*), became merchandise *par excellence* of the Canaanites, and " Canaan " (Hebrew *Kn'n*, Egyptian *p', Kn'n*), as early perhaps as the fifteenth century B.C., came to be applied to the Egyptian province in Syria generally, and to the Phoenician coast in particular. The inscription of

Amenophis II is thus of special importance in that it recognizes the *Kyn'nw* as a particular class of people in Syria. But it must be remembered that *p', Kn'n* as the designation of the country did not come into use in Egyptian until the last quarter of the fourteenth century.

Whether in the reign of Amenophis II or later, Aleppo made an alliance with the Hittites, and, with the neighbouring states, acknowledged the suzerainty of Khanigalbat.[26] With the resurgence of Mitannian power under Saushshatar Syria again reverted to Mitannian sway. It is very probable in view of the fact that Saushshatar's empire reached such formidable proportions eastward, where he plundered the city of Asshur and extended his dominion east of the Tigris as far as Arrapkha, that Mitanni's sphere of influence also extended westward, possibly as far as central or even southern Syria, and it is not unlikely that Damascus, during the period between Thutmose III's death and Thutmose IV's Syrian expedition, which reached Naharên, oscillated between Egyptian and Mitannian control. It is a mistake to consider Egypt's Asiatic boundaries in any sense intact for this era any more than for the period following the extended conquests of Thutmose I and the rise of Thutmose III, who evidently had to reconquer practically all of southwestern Asia, which had belonged to his predecessor. The chequered history of Palestine-Syria shows how shifting and insecure the boundaries of Empire often were within its borders, whether those of the great powers on the Nile, the Halys, or the Euphrates.

Thutmose IV's Syrian expedition must have resulted in no very great lasting success—a circumstance which made him willing to come to terms with Mitanni. On the other hand, signs that the Hittites were awaking from their sleep of two centuries and exerting pressure on Mitanni from the northwest, furnished sufficient reason for Artatama I, son and successor of Saushshatar, to desire an agreement with Egypt, which we may conjecture was liberal in so far as the latter was concerned. Accordingly, a peaceful settlement of differences was arranged, and a policy of intermarriage was inaugurated. For three successive reigns Mitannian princesses married pharaohs,[27] during which time Damascus was under Egyptian administration, which, however, as the Amarna letters reveal, was not firm or efficient enough, at least during the latter years of Amenophis III and during the reign of Amenophis IV, to guarantee the district of Upe an interval of quiet and stability, undisturbed by lawless adventurers.

At this period of Mitannian friendship the pharaoh's Asiatic possessions may be said to extend from Sillu, on the Isthmus of Suez, through the Sinaitic peninsula, the Negeb, and all Canaan, as far as Upe in the land of Damascus, generally called Khurru by the Egyptians,[28] and evidently northward to Qatna, Nukhashshe, Nîya, Zinzar and Tunanat in Syria proper. Since the last-named Syrian states, with Damascus, are said to have remained loyal to Egypt in the general uprisings in Asia in the early part of Amenophis IV's reign,[29] they must have formed a part of the Egyptian Asiatic Empire during the period of Mitannian friendship.

The Amarna correspondence introduces us to an insurrection against Egypt in the general region of Upe and gives us an intimate view of the political configuration of Damascus and the surrounding city-states at the time.[30] One of the pharaoh's Syrian vassals, king Akizzi of Qatna[31] about 1375–1370 B.C.,[32] writes to Amenophis IV vividly describing the revolt as endangering his own allegedly loyal realm and calling for assistance against Aitugama, the Syrian prince of Kadesh, who, in coalition with the king of the Hittites, was doing everything possible to incite an insurrection against the pharaoh in the land of Upe.[33] The defection was so dangerous to the pharaoh's interests in central and southern Syria, that, unless aid was dispatched at once, the district of Upe, and of course its chief city Damascus, as well as the realm of Qatna, would be lost to Egypt. Akizzi, whose realm bordered on the north of Damascus, if not actually included in the district of Upe, pays high tribute to the city's evident submissiveness to Egyptian rule, for he uses its fidelity as a standard of comparison for that of his own realm: " O Sire, as Damascus (al Ti-ma-aš-gi)[34] in the land of Upe (i-na mat Upe) is faithful to the pharaoh, so Qatna (al Qatna) is likewise loyal".[35] Perhaps throughout the years since the death of Thutmose III, like its neighbour Qatna, it had remained consistently under Egyptian suzerainty, even in time of Syrian revolt, such as that which spread throughout the Asiatic domain upon the death of the great Thutmose and the succession of his son Amenophis II. The situation of the city on the great commercial and military highways of the ancient world exposing it more readily to the armies of the Empire on the Nile than other less accessible places, might well furnish ample reason for hesitation in offending the pharaoh.

The alleged traitor, Aitugama,[36] emboldened by his alliance with the vanguard of the rising Hittite power from Asia Minor, is represented as trying to lure Akizzi away from his allegiance to the pharaoh, but in vain. In consequence of his refusal to join the coalition against Egypt, both Akizzi's life and realm were placed in the greatest peril, as well as the whole neighbouring country of Upe, where Aitugama was doing all in his power to bring the area under his sway. Already he had plundered the house of Biriawaza, the pharaoh's viceroy in Upe,[37] and, aided by other recalcitrant vassal kings, was burning and laying waste the countryside.[38] This is especially ominous news for the pharaoh, since it does not represent an attack against some merely local vassal king, but is apparently aimed directly at the Egyptian administration in the whole district. In this period it is evident that Damascus was the chief city in the country or province of Upe and was the headquarters of the Egyptian administration[39] rather than Hamath,[40] which was likely not in the land of Upe.[41] The sacking of " the house of Biriawaza ", by which expression the imperial embassy seems to be meant, was, therefore, a special insult and outrage against Egyptian suzerainty in the district. Akizzi, accordingly, makes the most of the incident in his desperate plea for aid, and to stir up the lethargic pharaoh, Amenophis IV, to action. The course of events during this period demonstrates how precarious the Egyptian position was with the Syrian dynasts incited to rebellion by their own ambition and goaded on by Hittite intrigue. Upe was undoubtedly regarded as a rich prize for Akizzi makes much of the extreme danger of its being lost to the Egyptian crown in his almost frantic appeal for troops. If Aitugama's allies, the kings of Lapana and Rukhizzi,[42] get a foothold in Upe, and Biridashwa,[43] perhaps the vassal of the Hittite king, establishes himself in Amki or Hollow Syria, such a strong intrenchment of hostile forces would be fatal to Egyptian hegemony in the whole area. Concerted effort was focused upon the district because it was evidently the centre of Egyptian influence in south-central Syria, for the disaffected dynasts were unrelenting in their demands that Aitugama come and take possession of all Upe.[44]

Intrigue and local rebellions were not confined to the district of Upe or to the reign of Amenophis IV. Under Amenophis III Abdi-Ashirta of Amurru had been a powerful antagonist, and at his death, his place had been taken by his sons. The earlier letters of Rib-Adda of Byblus belong to this period. The rise of Abdi-Ashirta's son, Aziru, to power in Amurru, and his entire career, including his final victory over Rib-Adda, belong to the second period covered by the Amarna letters, extending to the very end of the reign of Amenophis IV.[45] The later correspondence of Rib-Adda, as well as that of Abimilki of Tyre, is to be dated during these years.[46]

Rib-Adda's voluminous correspondence with the Egyptian chancellery in particular throws much light on the amazing amount of intrigue carried on at this time and the consequent difficulty in differentiating friend from foe. Too often the claims of the disloyal princes were so skilfully made to the resident deputies and transmitted to the pharaoh that in many instances it was not clearly known who were the staunch vassals and who were the secretly rebellious. Thus, for instance, the alleged traitor Aitugama wrote to the pharaoh accusing Biriawaza of laying waste the pharaoh's lands and of delivering over the territory of Kadesh and Damascus to the Khapiru,[47] while in the meantime the notorious insurgent, Aziru, employed the Khapiru against the faithful Rib-Adda of Byblus.[48]

To be sure Biriawaza employed the Khapiru as mercenaries in Upe and Damascus[49] but he apparently did so to enforce the Egyptian regime there. It seems Aziru cleverly misrepresented the operation of the pharaoh's loyal official in favour of those who laid waste the country to cloak their own treachery to the crown. It appears that Biriawaza was hard-pressed to defend the Egyptian administration in Upe, and success in the contest shifted, for in one of his letters to Egypt Rib-Adda reported that Aziru was " in the city of Damascus with his brothers ", ostensibly meaning he had conquered it.[50] Egypt's vassal at the same time pleads earnestly for troops to be sent to capture Aziru that the king's land (*mât šarri*) might become peaceful.[51] Evidently Rib-Adda of Byblus, like Akizzi of Qatna, also regarded Damascus and the land of Upe as a very important part of the royal Egyptian domain in Syria.

The composite picture of the land of Upe furnished by the

Amarna letters is fairly comprehensive in general outline, but
not too clear in detail. That the term embraces the territory
around Damascus, which was the chief city of the district, is
certain. But the precise limits of the region are obscure.
Although Qatna must have formed the boundary on the north,
and such city-states as Lapana, Rukhizzi, Amki and Takhsi
appear in various passages in closest connection with the land
of Upe, it cannot be said with certainty that any of them
formed an actual part of the territory. The region appears
evidently more as a geographical than as a political entity. If
there was a " king " of Upe, as seems certain from the Boghazköy texts,[52] he is not mentioned in the Amarna letters. The
territory, embracing a natural geographical unit, was governed
therefore as a whole, under a district administration created or
sanctioned by the pharaoh's regime, as in the case of
Nukhashshe in the north, Amurru in the north-west, and
Canaan in the south.[53]

The representative of the Egyptian administration in this
section, Biriawaza, significantly bears an Indo-Iranian name.[54]
Names of this sort, although relatively few, are widespread in
the Near East during this period. The rulers of the Hurrian
state of Mitanni bore these Indo-European names, and in
Mitanni and elsewhere Indo-Iranians had associated themselves with Hurrians as a kind of aristocracy, it would appear,
and over the latter they presumably formed the ruling class.[55]
Inasmuch as the closest ties had been established between the
royal houses of Egypt and Mitanni since the reign of Thutmose
IV, who had married a Mitannian princess, and inasmuch as
this intimate kinship continued throughout the long reign of
Amenophis III and into the reign of Ikhnaton, it is not unreasonable to conclude that Biriawaza was a Mitannian prince
or noble appointed by the pharaoh as his official representative
in the imperial government in Upe.

If this conclusion is correct, the proximity of Upe to a
powerful northern ally with such close affinities with the
Egyptian sovereigns was doubtless a prime reason for such a
peculiar policy in provincial administration. That such an
arrangement did actually exist seems indicated by the contents
of the letters of Biriawaza to the pharaoh.[56] The former
obviously sustains a very important relation to the royal family
of Mitanni, indicated not only by his own name, but by the

emphasis he lays upon his genealogy by the mention of his father, Shutarna (a good Mitannian royal name), as well as that of his grandfather, which is mutilated and unreadable.[57] Accordingly, he is scarcely merely a chieftain, for in that case such prominence given to his lineage would be highly improper and unusual.[58] His close connections with the reigning family of Mitanni are evidently meant, and his promise of protection to the caravans, which the pharaoh had sent to Naḥrima (Mitanni), point to the same conclusion.[59] If the restoration of the damaged passage,[60] in which he is styled " son " of the pharaoh is correct, further corroboration is furnished that Biriawaza was a Mitannian prince or noble linkèd distantly perhaps by marriage to the Egyptian royal family—although such a close relationship as a son-in-law of the pharaoh is not possible.[61] A blood relationship to both the ruling houses of Egypt and Mitanni might explain king Akizzi's humble and zealous protestations of loyalty to Biriawaza as the pharaoh's high official representative placed over him and his realm of Qatna.[62]

II. The Interlude of Non-Egyptian Control

Egyptian control of Damascus, which during the Amarna period was administered under circumstances of close diplomatic and blood relationships between the reigning houses of Egypt and Mitanni, was to suffer a temporary disruption with the rise of Hittite power in Syria. Tushratta, who had succeeded his father Shutarna II to the throne of Mitanni, maintained the tradition of intimate diplomatic relations with Egypt established by his grandfather Artatama I,[63] giving his daughter Tatu-Khepa in marriage to Amenophis III,[64] and, after his decease, to Amenophis IV.[65] Collision with advancing Hittite power, which began to make itself felt during his reign, resulted in initial victory for Mitanni,[66] and in one of his earliest letters to Amenophis III, Tushratta mentions sending his royal Egyptian colleague gifts of booty taken from the Hittites.[67]

With Hittite power on the increase Shuppiluliuma (c. 1380–1346), intent upon conquest, soon found excuse to invade northern and central Syria. As the date of his second Syrian campaign, which is the one described in the treaty with Matti-waza, can now be fixed with a high degree of probability in the latter part of the reign of Amenophis IV, instead of before his accession,[68] deterioration in the Egyptian position in Asia was doubtless a contributory cause for Hittite advance. However, in the opening lines of the contract with Mattiwaza[69] Shuppiluliuma's treaty with Artatama II, "king of Khurri", which provoked Tushratta, "king of Mitanni", to war against the Hittites, is presented as the reason for the outbreak of hostilities.

Taking advantage of a pretext for aggression, Shuppiluliuma crossed the Euphrates and proceeded victoriously southward to Mitanni proper, where he sacked Shuta and Washshukkanni, Mitannian cities.[71] Then he turned back, recrossed the Euphrates into Northern Syria, conquering Khalpe, the land of Aleppo, and Mukish, the territory of ancient Alalakh (modern Tell 'Aṭshanah)[72] lying east of one of the great bends in the Orontes just before it turns westward to the sea, and Nîya, located south-west of Alalakh on the Orontes River, probably north-west of Hamath.[74] Qatna, on the threshold of the land of Damascus, surrendered. On their way to by-pass Kinza (Kadesh) some thirty-five miles south-west of Katna, and in order to make a quick drive into the Damascene plain, the Hittites attacked this city-state and conquered its territory before advancing to the land of Apina, which is clearly to be identified with Upe (Ape) of the Amarna letters,[75] and is not to be located with R. Dussaud on the middle Orontes.[76]

Ariwana, king of the land of Apina (*šâr mât al A-pi-na*), who may have been Biriawaza's successor, together with *U-a-am-ba-du-ra*, *(A)k-pa-ru* and *Ar-ta-ya*,[77] his "great men", advanced against the Hittite, but, according to the Hittite version, were defeated and their land despoiled.[78] The expedition was doubtless more in the nature of a razzia, and Shuppiluliuma's forces apparently withdrew at least from the Damascene plain, after despoiling the country, as the account specifically narrates,[79] for permanent Hittite control was not established so far south. However, the situation was different farther north, for by way of summary, the Hittite monarch states that in one year he despoiled all the lands between Lebanon and the Euphrates and incorporated them into his state.

The years immediately preceding this Hittite campaign into Syria must have witnessed a rapid decline in Egypt's position in the territory of Upe, a condition already apparent in the middle Amarna period, and there is reason to believe that the Mitannian sphere of influence in the later years of Tushratta to a large degree had extended over north and central Syria as far south as the land of Damascus. This fact appears all the more certain in the light of the notices in the Mattiwaza Treaty which represent the military activities of Shuppiluliuma's second Syrian campaign as directed against the lands belonging to the kingdom of Tushratta or standing under its political influence.[80] In two places[81] the Hittite king refers to the fact that he invaded these lands in war against Tushratta, who elsewhere,[82] we are told, provoked the Hittite advance by his attack on Sarrupshi of Nukhashshe, a vassal of Shuppiluliuma. If the land of Upe had not come within the sphere of Mitannian influence, it would be difficult to understand Shuppiluliuma's invasion of the territory in a campaign which was obviously of a punitive nature. Then, too, the Hittites may have considered Damascus *de jure* Mitannian, disregarding Egyptian claims.

The rise of Hittite power under Shuppiluliuma completely eliminated Mitanni as a political factor in Syria. Although Artatama II seized what he could after Tushratta's unsuccessful Hittite war and the latter's murder by an unnamed son of his,[83] large concessions had to be made to Alshe, a northern kingdom, and to Assyria, now under the rule of the powerful Asshur-uballit I. In Shuppiluliuma's reorganization of his Syrian conquests, a series of small vassal kingdoms were established in the tradition of the conquered states. At Aleppo, for instance, he installed one of his own sons, the priest Telebinus, but Hittite control did not extend farther south than Kadesh and Amurru, which Shuppiluliuma mentions as the boundaries of his advance.[84]

At this time Damascus and the land of Upe must have reverted once more to the sphere of Egyptian influence. An essential part of the reorganization was the support given to Mattiwaza, the son of Tushratta, who had appealed to Shuppiluliuma for help. To the latter's son, Biyassilis, king of Carchemish, was allotted the task of reconquering Mitanni and reinstating Mattiwaza as king, which was accomplished.[85] However, the Khurri kingdoms of Mesopotamia never recovered, and were gradually incorporated into the spreading domains of Assyria, while Shuppiluliuma retained Syria, delimited by the Euphrates on the east and Lebanon on the south,[86] and Biyassilis added lands lying to the south along the Euphrates to his realm of Carchemish. Mattiwaza, with whom the history of Mitanni comes to an end, evidently had his territory restricted to lands in Mesopotamia.[87]

III. THE FINAL PHASE OF EGYPTIAN CONTROL

Following the first inroads of the Hittites into Syria, together with incursions of the Khapiru and the desert Akhlâmu during the Amarna period, the Egyptian outposts in Asia gradually had to give way, and with the passing of Mitanni from the stage of history, Damascus during the next century and a half lay upon the vacillating frontier between two great powers—the Hittite and the Egyptian. Shortly after this Kadesh on the Orontes became the centre of a revived Amorite state in central Syria, which the Hittite documents show was a continuation of the dynasty of Abdi-Ashirta and Aziru.[88] It naturally wavered between allegiance to the Hittites, entrenched in north-central Syria, and the Egyptians—seeking the friendship and protection of whichever one appeared the stronger at the time. Damascus must have been shut up to a similar policy of political expediency, if indeed it was independent, and not actually under Amorite control itself. The Amorite states east of the Jordan must have enjoyed reinvigoration through this concentration of Amorite power.[89]

The disintegration of the Asiatic Empire of Egypt, accelerated under Akhnaten, was not measurably arrested during the remaining years of the Eighteenth Dynasty, nor during the Nineteenth until the time of Sethos I (1319–1301), who first began in earnest to reconquer the lost Syrian domains. First Palestine had to be secured, and the semi-nomads, who were a continual threat to the eastern frontier, had to be routed. Having accomplished this, Sethos' next exploit was to vanquish the insubordinate princes of the Galilean cities, capturing Bethshan, which dominated the eastern entrance to the Plain of Esdraelon. Next he stormed Kadesh on the Orontes where Pézard found a stele of the pharaoh.[90] The pharaoh's subsequent venture to dislodge the Hittites from Syria, marking the first clash of the Egyptians with the northern invaders known to us, resulted in a peace, which, although it seemed for the moment to have checked the Hittite advance, served only to afford the Hittite king, Mutwatallis, an opportunity to bend every effort to make his position in Syria impregnable. Operations east of the Jordan were undertaken by Sethos, who erected a stela of victory in Hauran at Tell esh-Shihâb.[91] It is not certain that he did not advance as far as Damascus and retake the country of Upe. In fact it is possible that he marched as far north as Naharên, as he claims in his lists, for the entire upper row of his reliefs on the North Wall of the Great Hall of Karnak, or about one third of them, is lost. As the capture of Kadesh shows, this topmost series dealt with his northernmost advance inland. It is, accordingly, very likely that it contained the full attestation of the northern campaign claimed in the record.[92] But since the Hittite power was virile and unbroken, the conquest of Damascus or the region farther north, if actual, could not be permanent. The limits of Sethos' suzerainty and stable boundary must be thought of as extending no farther north than an east-and-west line from the middle (or more probably the southern) Phoenician coast, eastward into Hauran.

By the time Sethos' son and successor, Ramesses II (1301–1234), was ready to undertake his ambitious plans to recover the great Asiatic empire of his eminent predecessors of the Eighteenth Dynasty, he was confronted by the formidably strengthened Hittite threat, powerfully reinforced by a great Syrian army securely entrenched in the fortified city of Kadesh on the Orontes. Mutwatallis had assembled a large force from " the entire Hittite land " and Naharên, as well as the strong Syrian and Anatolian princes of Carchemish, Kizzuwatna, Ugarit, Qede, Nukhashshe, Kadesh, and other towns, as well as levies from Arzawa.[93] When Ramesses set out upon his Asiatic war, pushing his Phoenician boundary northward to Beirût, and marching down the Orontes to clash with the Hittites at Kadesh, he was meeting the most powerful enemy Egypt had ever faced, and unwittingly inaugurating a conflict that was destined to last almost twenty years. The remarkable battle of Kadesh, despite the brilliant triumph painted by the fulsome Egyptian eulogist, was far from being decisive for Ramesses. On the contrary he was compelled to give up any dreams of quick conquest over his Hittite foe, and had to lead his battered forces back to Egypt. Mutwatallis, in fact, is said to have driven the disordered enemy as far as " the land Apa ", the region of Damascus.[94]

The second phase of Ramesses II's Asiatic war finds him battling to regain southern and northern Palestine, which had succumbed to a general rebellion, undoubtedly incited by the emboldened Hittites. Having reconquered the south, in the eighth year of his reign he had reached northern Palestine again, and retook the revolting cities of western Galilee. The only place named in the list which is not in the west Galilean region is a city "in the land of Amor (*'-m-w-r*'), Deper (*D-'pw-r'*)", which Breasted erroneously identified with the region of Tabor.[95] Müller locates the place on the upper Orontes near Kadesh.[96] The northern Transjordan region, Hauran, had evidently followed Palestine in revolt, but again (perhaps at this time) came under Ramesses' control. One of his officials erected a memorial relief of him there representing him in an act of worship.

The last phase of Ramesses II's Asiatic war is by far the most significant for the history of Damascus, for again, and doubtless for the last time, the city and the general region of the Antilebanon must have temporarily reverted to Egyptian hands. The successful suppression of the Palestinian revolt and successes in Hauran enabled Ramesses to make other attempts to push back the Hittites and Amorites. He took full advantage of these victories and pushed northward to Tunip and Naharên, certainly via the Antilebanon region, for it is extremely unlikely that long years of struggle against entrenched Hittite power in the Lebanon sector yielded him more than the upper Orontes valley.[97] A fragment of the Ramesseum displays him warring against the Hittites at Tunip in the land of Naharên. Evidently the pharaoh had previously taken the important city in the north, and there erected a statue of himself. Its subsequent revolt demonstrates that these northern districts had already been subjected to some degree to Egyptian control, doubtless as the result of arduous and protracted campaigning. The extreme difficulty of holding such dearly won conquests in the face of vigorous Hittite strength was doubtless a prime factor in the famous treaty of peace between Ramesses II and Hattusil, concluded in 1280 B.C., seventeen years after the beginning of the struggle, a cuneiform copy of which was found by Winckler at Boghazköy, the capital of the Hittite empire.[98]

Notwithstanding Ramesses' conquest of such northern cities as Tunip in Naharên, and his habit of referring to himself as the conqueror of the Hittites, he never really succeeded in breaking their power. Evidently he considered halting the southward drive of so formidable a foe ample reason for self-congratulation and a justification for regarding the consummation of the war as a personal triumph. In the actual treaty between the Hittites and the Egyptians no mention is made of a boundary adopted. However, it is possible that the boundary ran through Hauran, south of Damascus, as the monument at Sheikl Saʿad suggests. Quasi-independent Amorite states in all probability formed spheres of influence, now of the Hittites, now of the Egyptians, constituting the loose frontier of the major powers.

At the time of Tudhalija, the son of Murshilish, Istarmuwa of Amurru, held the region of Palmyra and Damascus, and the Hittite king, in view of the rising Assyrian power under Tukulti-Ninurta, found it convenient to conclude a treaty of peace with him.[99] A similar condition must have existed in the Amorite state on the Orontes, centred at Kadesh, which now enjoyed a large measure of autonomy under Hittite suzerainty.[100] There is evidence that its influence was quite extended.[101] In view of the lack of Hittite remains in the country south of Hamath, it is practically certain that the plain of Damascus was never occupied permanently by the Hittites themselves.

It may be that by the time of Ramesses III (1195–1164) Damascus had already come under Aramaean influence, but the evidence adduced for this by Müller is now open to serious question. He equates *Saramaski* of Ramesses III's records with *Timasḳu* of Thutmose III's Retenu list, and maintains that the latter's scribe merely modernized the standard Egyptian orthography by Aramaizing it through the insertion of an *r*.[102] But *Saramaski* has nothing to do with Dimasqu. Müller had the idea that the name had been transcribed from cuneiform (◁⫯⫯ equals *di* and *sa*). This, however, is baseless, and Edgerton and Wilson are correct in including *Srmsk* among the place names of Ramesses III's list still unidentified.[103]

The pre-Aramaic form of the name of Damascus remained for a long time in the popular usage, especially the Assyrian *Di-maš-ḳi*. For this reason the form *Dûmmeseq* occurs in the Massoretic text of II Kings xvi, 10, where an evident attempt has been made to correct the ר to ו to conform to the older Hebrew rendering. On the other hand *Darmeseq*, the Aramaic form, occurs frequently in the Bible. As Ramesses III's list is otherwise free from Aramaisms, and since his list purports to be " Amorite " cities taken in his Amorite war in Syria, further evidence is furnished against Müller's identification of *Saramaski* with Damascus. It is highly probable that Aramaeans were already penetrating the Antilibanus region, but it is extremely unlikely that they had yet exerted enough influence to Aramaize the city's name. Since we have concluded that Damascus is not mentioned in Ramesses III's list, no inference can be drawn as to whether the city at this time was under Amorite, Egyptian or Aramaean control.[104] Schiffer was correct, therefore, in warning that the passage cited by Müller as proof of Aramaean control of Damascus as early as the reign of Ramesses III is not free from objection.[105] Inasmuch as Damascus is not mentioned in his list, it is very unlikely that Ramesses III took the city or that his Amorite war had any permanent results. The Papyrus Harris, written later, and which gives a comprehensive view of all his exploits, says nothing of the Amorites, and makes no reference, despite other numerous petty details, to the conquest of a new province in Asia. This fact, together with the sparse number of allusions to his war in Amor, would allow the conjecture that his campaign had no lasting success and was rendered extremely precarious by the ceaseless influx of invaders from the North. Finally, in a great battle by land and sea, Ramesses III repulsed the advancing hordes and unified Palestine once more under Egyptian rule.[106] But the period of Egyptian sway in Syria-Palestine was drawing to a close.

The great onset of northern peoples[107] into Syria-Palestine, which had begun in the reign of Marniptah (1235–1227), destroyed the Hittite Empire, and greatly reduced Amorite power. It thus opened the way for the Aramaean invasion of Syria. The Biqa', the centre of Amorite power in Syria, especially suffered from the depredations of the invaders. The Egyptians describe the land as becoming as though it had never existed. The great fortresses and strongholds of Amorite power, like Kadesh and others, must have been pitilessly reduced. The rich plain of Damascus must have lain wide open to Aramaean occupation, if indeed it had not already fallen to them before the final downfall of Hittite and Amorite power in middle Syria. Doubtless even before the beginning of the great bar-

barian irruption, the Aramaeans had gained vital positions on the frontiers of the country from which they could at the opportune moment strike for the heart of the area. There is evidence that in the time of Marniptah the Aramaeans had already come within the cognizance of the Egyptian foreign office, for one of the imperial officials has left a record of the sending of messages to a city of the pharaoh " which lies in the territory of '*A-ar-mu* ". This looks like Aram, although it is clearly a scribal error for Amor ('*A-mu-ra*), which was what was intended. The reference may indicate, however, as Müller has pointed out, that the Aramaeans were not unfamiliar to the Egyptians at the time of Marniptah.[108]

Ramesses III's great battle by land and sea against the peoples from the north thrust them back, and enabled him to unify Palestine once more under Egyptian rule.[109] This triumph doubtless greatly weakened the invaders after they had in turn weakened the Hittites and the Amorites, and with the rapid decline of Egyptian prestige after Ramesses III, exposed central and southern Syria to Aramaic conquest. This general condition forms the background for the rise of the Aramaean states in central Syria. In the next three centuries Damascus with its strategic commercial and political situation in the fertile Ghutah of the Antilebanon was to take advantage of the absence of great world empires on the borders of Syria-Palestine to amass strength for the prominent role it was destined to play in ancient Near-eastern history during the period of the acme of its power. For the present, at least, it was free to pursue its own independent course of development under its Aramaean conquerors without having its political fortunes shift from one nation to another according to the caprice of the powerful empires on the Nile and the Euphrates, which in the past had dominated it.

IV. THE SOCIAL AND ECONOMIC CONDITIONS
UNDER EGYPTIAN CONTROL

Although Damascus did not attain to any great political importance until the ninth century B.C., there is every reason to suppose that because of its ideal location it had gained distinction as a commercial centre long before the period of Egyptian domination of Asia. From the earliest times to the present day a great thoroughfare has joined the Syrian city with the sea. During the course of centuries the precise route has varied according to the political complexion of the country. The sea-port of Damascus was sometimes Tripolis, sometimes Beirût, sometimes Tyre or Sidon, sometimes Accho. Accho alone is the natural port of Damascus. Leaving the mart of inner Syria and running to the south of Hermon, crossing the Jordan mid-way between the Waters of Merom and the Lake of Galilee, skirting Safed, this road comes by an easy way to Accho, avoiding the difficult and laborious routes over the double range of the Lebanons. By several branches it connected with the great South Road to Egypt through the Plain of Esdraelon, or ran through Samaria to Jerusalem, or down the Jordan Valley to Jericho.[110]

In the vicinity of Bethshan another great highway from Damascus came across Jordan, traversing level Hauran. It went over to the Mediterranean by Bethshan and Esdraelon, or up the wady Fejjas to Accho. Over these highways flowed the commerce and marched the armies of the ancient world. Although thus exposed to the encroachments of the powerful empires on the Nile and the Euphrates, which inevitably curbed its political significance, and naturally hindered the development of capacity for government, Damascus, like other cities of inner Syria, nevertheless possessed a high degree of civilization. The inhabitants of these city-states were skilled in the art of metal-working. They wrought weapons of a high quality[111] and manufactured chariots, which constituted an important industry. During the Hyksos domination of the Nile Valley when the horse and the chariot were introduced, they had taught the Egyptians much concerning the arts of war.[112] Their more vigorous climate required woollen clothing. The mountain shepherds of the Lebanon and Antilebanon would always have a supply of wool, so that Syrian craftsmen early attained skill in dyeing and weaving, producing textile fabrics of the most superb quality and artistic design.[113] Egyptian monuments indicate that the inhabitants of the Nile Valley as a rule wore white unpatterned garments, while the conquered " barbarians " of Palestine-Syria showed a preference for garments woven or embroidered with colourful patterns.[114]

With such a strategic commercial position on vital trade routes leading in every direction, it would be natural to conclude that the principal source of income to the people of

Damascus would be the constantly passing caravans carrying their wealth westward to the rich Phoenician cities of the coast, eastward to the empires on the Tigris and the Euphrates, northward to Asia Minor, and southward to Palestine and Egypt. But it was inevitable that a city so favourably situated in a veritable garden spot[115] and so richly endowed with natural resources, should trade on its own account. With Byblus, Arvad, Tyre, Sidon and Accho already bustling coastal emporia, there can be little doubt that one or the other of the last-named maritime centres of commerce served as the seaport of Damascus, and that even at this early date such commodities as " the wine of Helbon and white wool " from the Damascene region, products famous in Ezekiel's day, were being exchanged for the " handiworks " of Phoenician cities.[116] The Semites of Syria were already inveterate traders, and a brisk traffic was passing from town to town. The market place of Damascus was an animated scene of barter as it is today.

Trade meant wealth. This flourishing commerce must have made Damascus an opulent prize for pharaonic conquest. The substantial income of its inhabitants could sustain a handsome tribute to help maintain the magnificence of Thutmose III and his successors. There is ample evidence to indicate that Egyptian administration of Palestine-Syria was oppressive, seriously draining the resources of the country. The splendour of the Egyptian court and the large-scale building operations of such pharaohs of the golden age of the empire as Thutmose III, Amenhotep III and Akhnaten would necessarily require huge sums of money, and much compulsory labour for the crown (corvée). It was natural for the conqueror to make the conquered pay. The Egyptian bureaucracy, moreover, became notoriously corrupt, as numerous documentary allusions testify, so that troops dispatched to support the Egyptian commissioners, called " inspectors " (râbiṣu in Accadian), who collected the tribute, and looked after such matters as the construction of roads, or the management of the royal grain fields of Jezreel, or the forest reserves of Lebanon, often failed to receive their wages. Whereupon they plundered the hapless provincials, who were doubtless already reduced to straits by the heavy imposts.[117] There was also a dangerous double administration of government which furnished further occasion for corruption and oppression, and boded ill for the populace under rapacious officials. In addition to the Egyptian commissioners or " inspectors " there were the local feudal princes, each of whom had the appellation " governor " (*khaziânu* in Accadian), who were supported by local detachments of patrician chariotry and plebeian footmen (khupshu). It was obviously an arrangement which lent itself to a two-fold temptation to oppression, for the local governors as well as the Egyptian administrators could abuse their power.

Archaeological evidence gleaned from excavations of many Late-Bronze sites of Palestine suggests that Egyptian administration of the Empire in Asia was very oppressive. Not only were very few new towns established in this area, but a progressive thinning out and impoverishment of the population point to an economic stress retarding commercial growth and prosperity. The explorations of Nelson Glueck in Transjordan have noted little if any advance in the frontier of sedentary occupation until the wane of Egyptian sway in Asia in the thirteenth century B.C. Increasing indigence of tombs points to a gradual impoverishment of the wealthier classes and a reduction in the general standards of living. This state of affairs is corroborated by the increasing inferiority of patrician houses, of fortifications, and of art objects.[118] Making due allowance for this decline of Canaanite civilization to inner weakness of the inhabitants of the land themselves, of which the Hebrew Bible takes note,[119] the destructive results of two or three centuries of unscrupulous and rapacious administration by Egyptian bureaucrats must not be ignored. That such a state of affairs existed is proved by the edict of Harmais (Haremhab), which makes numerous references to the dishonesty and corruption of Egyptian officialdom and soldiery about the middle of the fourteenth century B.C.

There is no reason to conclude that this sad situation was confined to one part of the Asiatic Empire and not to another. Lower and Upper Syria as well as Palestine felt the weight of Egyptian tribute, and although their wealth in men and money flowed into the Nile Valley and made possible the great and splendid buildings of the Eighteenth Dynasty, it must not be supposed that Egyptian rule over conquered territories was efficient, or that every part of Syria was effectively subdued. On the contrary revolts were continually breaking out because of bureaucratic oppression and official dishonesty, affording excuse for further plunder to supply the pharaoh and his army. As time went on repeated uprisings brought more serious reprisals, and fortresses were constructed in various parts of the country to exercise a more efficient control over the recalcitrants, as for example, the Egyptian garrison at Bethshan, first established *circa* 1450 B.C., according to recent excavations there.

Despite bureaucratic bungling and indications of a burdensome economic drain on the country, Palestine-Syria under the Egyptian regime displayed remarkable vitality and was capable of continued exploitation by its foreign conquerors. Western Asia was rewarded with a stability of government and a widespread public security which had hitherto never been enjoyed. The roads were comparatively free from brigands, and caravans moved continuously. In a time of political decline as in the days of Amenophis IV the caravans of Burnaburiash of Babylon, for instance, were waylaid and despoiled within the limits of the pharaoh's dominion,[120] but such occurrences were not common, especially in the heyday of Egyptian sway under more puissant and energetic rulers. Trade inevitably developed as never before. The freight of the world via land and sea flowed in a ceaseless stream into the land of the Nile. Damascus was alive with a steady traffic passing through the heart of the city. Caravans bearing rich stuffs from Syria and precious stones and goods from the East flowed westward to the Phoenician coast and south-westward to exchange their products for the wares of Egypt.[121]

CHAPTER III

DAMASCUS AS A CENTRE OF ARAMAEAN POWER

IT is possible that the Aramaeans had begun to filter into northern and central Syria before the wane of Hittite and Amorite power in this region.[1] Inasmuch as they were nomadic or semi-nomadic tribes roving on the fringes of the desert skirting the fertile settled areas, their origins and movements are necessarily obscure. However, with the collapse of Hittite-Amorite rule under the relentless impact of the invasion of the sea peoples, which had begun in the reign of Marniptah (1234–1228), it is easy to see how the rich settled areas, devastated and plundered as they were by the invaders, were left open to anyone who would come in and occupy them. That these nomadic Semitic tribesmen in large numbers abandoned their migratory existence and seized the opportunity to settle down in the best sites in Syria, the history of the next several centuries abundantly attests. The region open to them was not only fertile, but healthful. The Antilibanus region has always been a great reservoir of man power, continually replenishing a vigorous population to furnish a constant supply for the so-called " Libanese diaspora ". It was natural for Damascus in the course of time to become one of the greatest centres of Aramaic power and influence, as Harran in Mesopotamia had been in an earlier period.[2]

I. DAMASCUS AND THE ARAMAEAN EXPANSION IN THE WEST

To trace the rise and the expansion of the Aramaeans in the West we must go back to the nomadic *Sutû*[3] and *Akhlâmu*,[4] their predecessors in the earlier period. These Bedawin tribes, spreading north from the Syro-Arabian desert during the fourteenth century and later, offered a serious threat to the inhabited regions of the Fertile Crescent from Amurrû to Babylon. In the twelfth century the Akhlâmu begin to be more precisely designated as *Aramaic Akhlâmu* in the records of

Tiglathpileser I, who in the year 1112 B.C. repulsed an invasion attempted by them in the region at the mouth of the Khabur river.[5] Inasmuch as frequent later references are specifically to *Aramaic Akhlâmu*, and not merely *Akhlâmu* as in the earlier cuneiform records, M. Streck[6] and S. Schiffer[7] concluded that by the latter term the Aramaeans are to be understood. However, the validity of this conclusion, which would place the appearance of the Aramaeans in Mesopotamia several centuries earlier, is denied by E. Forrer,[8] who sees in the more precise terminology of the Assyrian sources an indication that the *Akhlâmu* without the qualification were not Aramaeans at all. On the other hand, since we know that Aramaeans were settled in the Khabur district of Upper Mesopotamia from early Patriarchal times, it seems questionable whether Forrer's deduction can be insisted upon. Indeed it is now doubtful whether we are to attribute the first cuneiform occurrence of the name *Aram* to the middle Assyrian era. It is possible to see its occurrence in an ancient clay tablet of Naram-Sin, the grandson of Sargon the Great, dating from the old Accadian period (*c.* 2360–*c.* 2180). The inscription reads " Naram-Sin, king of the four regions—when he warred against Harshamadki, Lord of *A-ra-am* and of *Am*: in *Ti-ba-ar*, the mountain, he overcame him."[9] Dhorme concludes that there is nothing in this reference to prohibit identifying Aram here mentioned with the later Aram Naharaim.[10] Other such pre-Amarna references to Aram would square remarkably well with the Patriarchal narratives of the Bible which give a vivid account of Aramaean peasant life in the tales of Jacob's sojourn in Aram Naharaim. Inasmuch as the Patriarchal accounts have in recent years been demonstrated to give an accurate account of these early times, the vast quantity of relevant documentary material which is yet to be analysed and published, may reasonably be expected to go a long way toward solving the complex ethnic and linguistic background of the Patriarchs, which is hardly yet ripe for solution.[11]

At any rate, whether we view the Aramaeans as making their historical debut in the twelfth century B.C. or earlier, the old theory of an accelerated mass irruption of the Aramaean Bedawin from the Syro-Arabian desert, dated sometimes as early as the Hyksos invasion, must be abandoned. Prior to the effective domestication of the camel in the twelfth century B.C.

and the consequent use of the animal as a social force, migrations in desert lands on a large scale were out of the question.[12] The process of Aramaean expansion, therefore, was gradual. A slow accumulation of desert wanderers on the fringes of the town, which perhaps had been forming for centuries, would naturally crystallize in such movements as are historically reflected in the *Sutû* and the *Akhlâmu*. In the twelfth century B.C. the situation in Syria, as a result of the invasion of the sea-peoples, offered an unparalleled opportunity for the Aramaean Bedawin to move in and possess choice spots. Numerous historiçal examples illustrate how the forces of the desert almost involuntarily surge in upon the settled areas at the least sign of yielding on the part of the sedentary populations.

On the other hand, it must not be forgotten that considerable time was required for the Aramaeans who first settled in central and southern Syria to adjust themselves to their new environment and to avail themselves of the rich resources of the country to build up organized states. Accordingly, not for about a century and a half until the time of Saul (*c.* 1025) do we hear of a clash between Israel's growing power under the newly established Hebrew kingdom and the expanding military might of the south Syrian principalities. The case was different with the Aramaeans of Mesopotamia. Having been settled in the country for a considerable period, and relieved for the time of any threat from the East in the temporary wane of Assyrian prestige, they possessed sufficient vitality toward the beginning of the period of the Judges to undertake a predatory incursion into Palestine and dominate the amphictyonic Israelite tribes for some eight years.

This vague reminiscence of a first warlike collision between Aram[13] and Israel, preserved in Judges iii, 7-11, bristles with difficulties. Othniel, the first judge, fits well into the historical picture of the period, but a certain Cushan Rishathaim, called " the king of Aram Naharaim," who is said to have enslaved the Israelite tribes for eight years until they were delivered by Othniel, is historically very obscure.[14] Some scholars have maintained a reference to an invasion from Edom rather than Aram Naharaim.[15] But this is historically unnecessary, despite the fact that no extra-biblical evidence for an independent imperial power in Syria in the early twelfth century has yet been found.[16] Nevertheless, with the hegemony of Ramesses III in

Syria-Palestine broken by the invasion of the sea peoples and Assyrian pressure upon the Aramaeans curtailed after the death of Tukulti-Ninurta (c. 1260), the situation in Western Asia about 1185 B.C. presents no difficulties that would render an attack by a semi-nomadic Aramaean chieftain upon the disorganized lands to the south historically impossible. There is no reason, either, to suppose that the term *melek* must designate more than a powerful chieftain of a certain region, or must necessarily comprehend the idea of a well-organized state.

A study of the meaning and historical implications of the name *Aram Naharaim* has led R. T. O'Callaghan[17] to conclude that the term was a territorial designation rather than an Aramaean state. In interpreting the sources he has correctly given the broader connotation to the expression as not only including Mesopotamia proper, but as also embracing northern and perhaps even central Syria.[18] The fact that the term was to be equated with Egyptian Naharên was already emphasized by W. Max Müller,[19] so that Cushan Rishathaim's territory may have been much nearer Israel than has been commonly supposed, perhaps in north central Syria. In any event the invasion is not *a priori* to be dismissed as impossible, even if originating in Mesopotamia proper.

During the period of the Judges we may picture the Aramaeans as assiduously establishing themselves in their new home, and developing the rich resources of central and southern Syria. They must have been too much taken up with stabilizing their own interests to be much concerned about their neighbours, for the territory on the northern limits of Palestine in the region of Laish at this time lay exposed to conquest by the Israelite tribe of Dan without suffering molestation from the powerful Phoenician cities on the coast, notably Sidon, or from the near-by Aramaeans.[20]

The Danite scouts dispatched to spy out this region found it rich in every natural resource, large in extent, and the inhabitants dwelling in unmolested security, enjoying complete independence from neighbouring Phoenician and Aramaean kingdoms. The reason assigned for their freedom from Sidonian interference was the distance. "They were far from the Sidonians".[21] Their safety from growing Aramaean influence, on the other hand, was apparently due to the fact that the Aramaean tribes were too busy consolidating their own positions and developing the rich and extensive territories they were occupying to think for the moment of further conquests. This state of affairs in northern Palestine and southern Syria, which left Laish open to Danite settlement, is reflected in the general historical scene presented in Judges xviii, and is rendered more certain, if following Kittel and others אָדָם is emended to אֲרָם in verses 7 and 28 . . . "And had no dealings with Aram ".[22]

II. DAMASCUS AND THE SOUTH SYRIAN STATES

The Bible notes that Laish was situated "in the valley of Beth Rehob ",[23] thus locating the latter in the Upper Jordan Valley, possibly in a southerly direction from Laish-Dan, but much more likely north of it in the lower Biqaʻ, since Rehob, mentioned as lying in the vicinity of Hamath,[24] is certainly to be considered in the same state. The whole of Coelesyria must then be considered as the territory of Beth Rehob, thus the heir of ancient Amurrû. This is the Beth Rehob most naturally referred to in II Samuel x, 6–8 (cf. I Samuel xiv, 47 LXX) as being closely allied with Zobah and Beth Maacah. In this case Zobah would be situated to the north, a location which agrees with the conclusions of the latest studies,[25] and Maacah would lie to the south, with Beth Rehob between. Although it is correct to insist on the close relationship of Zobah and Beth Rehob in Coelesyria, Meyer goes too far in maintaining that the two Aramaean states were actually identical because Hadadezer, king of Zobah, is said to be the "son of Rehob", thereby signifying him as the founder of the dynasty.[26] But "son" employed with a genitive of place, as is common with the Semites, frequently denotes simply a native of that place.[27]

Similarly Ba'sa, prince of Ammon and a leader of the Ammonites in the battle of Qarqar in 853, is referred to as a "son of Rehob". Winckler[28] and later Kraeling[29] misconstrued this notice with the result that they erroneously located Beth Rehob just north of Ammon, fixing its capital at the ruins of Riḥâb, east of Gerasa. However, besides drawing an unwarranted conclusion from the common Semitic idiom Ben Rehob and ignoring the reference to Rehob in Numbers xiii, 21 and Judges xviii, 28, located, as we have noted, in the vicinity of Laish-Dan, this identification has been further discredited by the absence of Iron Age pottery at Riḥâb.

If Beth Rehob thus occupied the region of the Biqa' north of Laish-Dan, the location which squares best with the biblical notices, it would be natural to fix the location of Zobah in the lower Antilibanus region, north of, and very likely including Damascus, until Rezon at a later period renounced allegiance to Zobah and established an independent Damascene kingdom, which shortly thereafter rose to the position of the leading Aramaean state. It thus appears that Friedrich Delitzsch,[30] who long ago maintained that Zobah was a place on the fringe of the desert between Damascus and Aleppo in the region of Ḥums and the Antilibanus, was substantially correct as against the contentions of H. Winckler and H. Guthe,[31] who placed it in the land of Haurân (biblical Bashan) south of Damascus, or S. Schiffer and E. Kraeling, who narrowly fix it in Hollow Syria.[32] Latest studies on the subject involving an analysis of Assyrian provincial organizations, which were erected on older foundations, have proved conclusively that Delitzsch's original position is correct, and that Zobah, Assyrian Ṣubatu,[33] was situated north of Damascus, not south or west of it, and almost certainly embraced the country east of the Antilebanon range and south-east of Ḥums.[34] Ṣubatu in the seventh century B.C. has been shown by Forrer to have been a rendezvous of the Arabs, and hence must have extended to the edge of the desert.[35]

Zobah was the most powerful of the Aramaean states of Syria just before David's rise to power. The general situation in the Near-Eastern world, which was so propitious for the rise of David's empire, was no less opportune for Hadadezer. There is every reason to believe, moreover, that this important Aramaean king took full advantage of the favourable conditions for imperialistic expansion. His realm was extensive. At its zenith it stretched to the Euphrates river[36] and must have dominated Damascus, for the Aramaeans there are not said to have their own king as was the case at Hamath,[37] but must have been subordinate to Zobah, if not actually a part of that realm. At any rate, whether as an independent petty Aramaean principality or as an intrinsic part of Zobah, Damascus assisted Hadadezer when the latter was threatened by Israel's advance under David. As early as the reign of Saul, Zobah's power in Syria must have been formidable. It is easy to see how Hadadezer's influence would have extended into the country east of the Jordan so as to clash with the ambitions of Saul.[38] With the defeat of Hadadezer by David it is significant that Zobah vanishes from the stage of Hebrew history, its place presently to be taken by Damascus.

The Chronicler[39] lists Tibhath and Chun as the principal cities of Hadadezer's realm. The former is doubtless to be identified with Tubikhi and the latter with Kunu of the Egyptian list of Syrian towns conquered by the pharaohs of the New Empire. Both are certainly to be located in the region south of Ḥums and north of Damascus, since Kunu cannot be separated from Roman Conna (now Ras Ba'albek), and the Amarna Tubikhi is in the same general locality.[40] Betaḥ of the Massoretic text of II Samuel viii, 8 is a simple metathesis for Ṭebah, which is undoubtedly the correct reading, being a good Aramaic name[41] and confirmed by the Septuagint of I Chronicles xviii, 8 (recensio Luciana). The form Ṭibhath is a variant of Ṭebah.

The *Berothai* of II Samuel viii, 8, for which the Chronicler substitutes Chun, is to be taken as identical with the Berothah of Ezekiel xlvii, 16, a variant of the same name. Ezekiel locates this city on the ideal northern frontier of Israel between Damascus and Hamath, and incidentally furnishes an added detail confirming our location for Zobah, north of Damascus. Both of Hadadezer's principal cities, Ṭebah and Berothai, were noted for their wealth in copper, and Halévy, followed by Schiffer, plausibly maintains that Zobah is an abbreviated form of צְהוֹבָה meaning "bronze", and is an appellative denoting "the copper country".[42]

The Chronicler's reference to Hamath-Zobah as existing in Solomon's time is very perplexing.[43] The name may, of course, be a corruption, but on the other hand, may refer to Hamath on the Orontes. The distance so far north is hardly to be urged against this identification inasmuch as Hadadezer was well on the road to a Syrian empire when his ambitions clashed with those of David. His dominions, as we have noted from II Samuel viii, 3, stretched to the Euphrates river, and it was probably he who had wrested the Assyrian colonies, Pitru and Mutkinu, founded by Tiglathpileser I, from Asshur-rabi II (1012–972). Be that as it may, if this city was independent of Zobah before David's defeat of Hadadezer, which seems very unlikely in the light of evidence for Hadadezer's extension of power, it is difficult to explain how, by the time of Solomon, Hamath had become inseparably connected with Zobah. The fact that Hamath-Zobah is mentioned in close context with " Tadmor in the desert " and " store cities " constructed in " Hamath " (evidently the country) is a further suggestion that Hamath north of Damascus is intended. Julius Lewy, on the other hand, in an elaborate and learned theory, based, however, on tenuous assumptions, presupposes a second Hamath and identifies it with Hamath-Zobah, Greek Heliopolis (modern Ba'albek) in the lower Biqa'.[44]

Aramaean penetration as far as northern and north-eastern Palestine is attested by several other smaller states which had acquired considerable strength by the time of David's ascendency. Besides Beth Rehob, which we have placed in the Biqa' north of Laish-Dan, there were other smaller states as Maacah, Geshur, and Tob. Maacah evidently lay between Mt. Hermon on the north and Geshur on the south,[45] being probably bounded by the Jordan on the west. Although no certain indication of boundary is now possible, it is not unlikely that Maacah extended westward beyond the Jordan, for the city of Abel, which is commonly identified with *Abil el Qamh*, north-west of Dan, is also found as Abel Beth Maacah in I Kings xv, 20 and II Kings xv, 29. Inasmuch as the data give no conclusive evidence whether it was in or merely near Maacah, it may have been a colony founded by the inhabitants of Maacah, for all we know. Geshur, which occurs in close connection with Maacah,[46] is most probably to be located south of the latter, and east of the Jordan from the Lake of Ḥuleh to the southern extremity of the Lake of Galilee.[47] The Greek A and B texts of II Samuel xiii, 37 place Geshur actually " in the land of Maacah ", but these passages are perhaps too corrupt to be of decisive value. Geshur is known to have been an independent state at the time of David, for Talmai, the king, gave his daughter Maacah to David for a wife.

The location of Tob, too, is uncertain. In connection with the episode of Jephthah in Judges xi, 3 ff. the " land of Tob " seems to be identifiable with *eṭ-Ṭaiyibeh* above Gilead.[48] This may or may not be identical with the Tob of II Samiel x, 6–8, which may have been more in Golan itself, in closer association with Maacah. Abel, however, associates the two, and is perhaps correct.[49]

It is apparent that the Aramaean expansion in the west during the twelfth and eleventh centuries B.C. continued unabated throughout the period of the Judges, until the beginnings of the Hebrew monarchy. By that time the powerful Aramaean states of Zobah, Beth Rehob, Maacah, Geshur and Tob had grown up in Syria, and in north and east Palestine, forming a strong wall to thwart any sudden expansion on the part of the Israelite state. There was perhaps no great Aramaean pressure upon the Hebrews themselves, except in such districts as Bashan and Naphtali, which were overrun during this period. As long as they kept within the narrow confines of their own borders, had no strongly centralized government, and possessed no great national leader, there was little danger of any large-scale collision with the Aramaeans. But with the threat of an expanding Hebrew kingdom under a capable leader like David to challenge penetration of Syria-Palestine, the response of the Aramaeans to a call to check a common danger was immediate. The subjugation and incorporation of these peoples into the Israelite state was one of the prime factors in making possible the empire of David and Solomon.

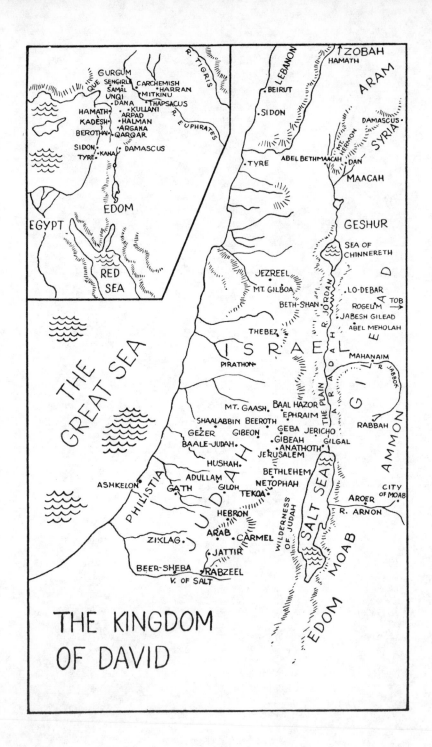

THE KINGDOM OF DAVID

CHAPTER IV

DAMASCUS UNDER HEBREW CONTROL

UNDER the expanding military prowess and capable leadership of David Damascus first comes into prominence in relationship to Israel. The Israelite king's accession to the throne over all Israel could scarcely have occurred at a more opportune time for expansion. That his army in comparatively few years was able to conquer all surrounding regions and raid such distant places as Damascus and the upper Euphrates country was due to the weakness of the great empires on the Nile and the Tigris-Euphrates in the tenth century B.C. Egypt had not recovered political strength since the middle of the Twentieth Dynasty, about 1150 B.C., when pharaonic power degenerated under pressure from the priests at Thebes, and was not to become a dominant state again until the reign of Shishak (c. 940–920). Assyrian power suffered a steady eclipse after the aggressive reign of Tiglathpileser I (1113–1074) and during the time of David's rule reached such a low ebb of influence under the feeble Asshur-rabi II (1012–971) that the Assyrian outposts along the upper Euphrates fell into the hands of the Aramaeans, as recent discoveries have shown.[1]

Solomon's contemporary, the impotent Tiglathpileser II (966–934), was helpless to improve Assyrian fortune, and not until after 875 did Assyria regain the upper Euphrates valley. The threat of a unified Hittite power had long since passed, although local Hittite dynasties in such cities as Carchemish and Hamath were only gradually superseded by Aramaeans.[2] The years of David's reign (c. 1000–950) thus offered unparalleled opportunity for Israelite conquest, since no major world power stood in the way of a free hand in Palestine-Syria. Fortified centres like Hamath and Damascus, and possible coalitions, such as the Edomites and the various Aramaean states, would present a formidable challenge to any conqueror, but it was a far different situation from facing an empire like the Egyptian, Assyrian or Hittite in the heyday of their power.

Although Hadadezer of the powerful kingdom of Zobah dominated north and central Syria, and seemed poised to take full advantage of the general propitious circumstances in South-western Asia to build up a great Aramaean state, David's inevitable clash with him and the consequent Israelite victory, left the stage clear for the drama of empire under David and Solomon.

I. DAMASCUS AND DAVID'S SYRIAN WARS

During the era of internal convulsion and attack from without which characterized the unstable period of the Judges, it was natural that a pronounced trend toward a strongly centralized government with a recognized leader at the helm should grow up in Israel. The cry was for a king such as the surrounding nations possessed to lead the people to victory against their foes. Saul, the first king of Israel, evidently enjoyed some military success.[3] However, concerning the political adminis-tration of his realm, which does not seem to have differed from older tribal organization, we know little. The accession of David to the throne brought about an ideal internal situation for the growth and expansion of the young monarchy which was to match the general favourable external conditions.

David's personal name is possibly unknown. We know him doubtless from his title, since *dawîdum*, denoting "leader", which is found centuries earlier in the records from Mari, seems identical with the name of the great king and poet of Israel. At any rate, whatever the correct etymology of David's name may be, the moment demanded " a leader " *par excellence*, and David supplied the need for such a leader.

The Aramaeans had not only penetrated northward toward Carchemish and beyond to Zendjirli in north Syria, but by David's time, as we have noted, had established strong kingdoms in central and southern Syria on the very borders of Palestine almost to the region of Gilead. David's wars, undertaken to establish Israelite supremacy over the surrounding neighbours, were in a very definite sense largely the continuation of earlier campaigns begun by Saul, who is said to have "fought against all his enemies roundabout, against Moab . . . and Edom, and the kings of Zobah . . .".[4] During many of Saul's wars David suffered banishment as a fugitive from the jealousy and rage of

Saul. It is singular that during this period David enjoyed the favour of neighbouring peoples. The king of Moab gave his parents protection while Saul hunted his life; Talmai, king of the Aramaean state of Geshur, gave him his daughter to wife; the Philistines, meanwhile, had shown him kindness, as well as the Ammonites. But when David was made king over Judah in Hebron, and somewhat later united all Israel under his sceptre, enabling him in the interim completely to defeat the Philistines, a notable change occurred. His neighbours, formerly amicable, now sensed a real threat to their autonomy with Israel united under such a strong leader, and suddenly became hostile. The basic cause of David's war with the Aramaeans must be laid to the fear and suspicion engendered by Israel's increasing power and prestige. The certainty of an ultimate reckoning with David alone could have induced the Ammonites so foolishly and rudely to rebuff David's obviously sincere overtures of friendship, and so basely to insult his embassage of good will.[5] Nothing but similar motives of apprehension and distrust could have impelled the various Aramaean peoples to ally themselves with the Ammonites in a war against David. They must have intuitively realized that the increasing strength of a consolidated Israelite state spelled the doom of any further penetration southward, if indeed it did not mean their actual expulsion from the rich and fertile sites they had occupied in northern Palestine and southern Syria.

Accordingly, without difficulty the Ammonites enlisted the aid of the Aramaeans of Zobah, Beth Rehob, Ishtob[6] and Maacah. Apparently only the small state of Geshur was absent from this general confederacy of Aramaean states. The intimate relation between David and the Geshurites is the evident reason for their non-participation in the anti-Israelite coalition.[7] The result of this swift stroke of Ammonite diplomacy was nothing less than a powerful alliance of adjacent kingdoms situated on the east and north-east, having as its avowed purpose to weaken, and, if possible, to destroy the formidable position being achieved by Israel under David, which would inevitably threaten their autonomy.[8]

David's first thrust against the powerful coalition under Joab's command hardly resulted in more than temporarily scattering it. The Aramaean forces were driven northward, and the Ammonite army was repulsed. The city of Rabbath Ammon, however, was not taken.[9] The initial collision with the expanding power of the Israelite army was sufficient to spur the Aramaeans on to a more thorough-going attempt to pool their common resources in a concerted effort to curb David's expansion toward the north and east. Hadadezer,[10] the king of the most powerful Aramaean state at the time, was the natural leader of the proposed campaign against David. Augmenting his forces by Aramaean contingents from across the Euphrates, 'eber han-nahar,[11] for which term the Chronicler employs the expression Aram Naharaim,[12] his general Shobach not only commanded the well-recruited army of Zobah, but also the armies of subordinate Syrian kings whom Hadadezer controlled, in addition to sizeable levies from Mesopotamia proper. Despite such a formidable concentration of military power, David mustered his army and unhesitatingly advanced to encounter the foe at Ḥelam.[13] That the Israelite king was able to inflict a crushing defeat on such a large concentration of Aramaean might at a considerable distance from his home base proves how well prepared he was. Archaeology gives evidence of this preparation. Both Tell Beit Mirsim and Beth Shemesh were found to be fortified with heavy chambered walls dating from the first half of the tenth century B.C., very likely belonging to the early period of David's political activity as king.[14] His administration over the united nation soon enabled him to prepare himself to cope successfully with any military situation that was likely to arise.

David's triumph over the Aramaeans at Ḥelam forced them to sue for peace and to abandon any further plans to ally themselves with the Ammonites against Israel. However, this does not seem to be the final crushing blow that permanently subjugated Zobah. Some time after the debacle at Ḥelam, Hadadezer apparently formed a third coalition in which Damascus was the chief ally. David again " smote Hadadezer king of Zobah near Hamath, when he (David?) went to extend his dominion as far as the river Euphrates ".[15] Worsted in the battle, the Aramaeans of Damascus come into prominence in offering Hadadezer aid to turn the tide of defeat. The interference of the Damascenes proved vain, and David slew 22,000 of the reinforcements they had sent against him. Moreover, he showed his resentment of the city's interference with his plans of conquest by garrisoning the town, subjecting it to Israel, and placing it under tribute. Large quantities of gold and bronze were also taken from Hadadezer's realm, giving evidence that David had conquered all of Zobah. The tribute of Thou, king of Hamath, sent by the hand of his own son, furnishes added proof of the thoroughness of David's conquests in the north. His realm now extended over all Palestine and Syria northward as far as Hums on the Orontes. To the south he controlled Moab and Edom to Ezion-geber on the Gulf of Akabah. What is most important for our study is that Damascus came under his control, and remained under Hebrew administration until Rezon, a local insurgent, revolted in the latter part of Solomon's reign.

II. DAMASCUS AND SOLOMON'S EMPIRE

The powerful kingdom which David bequeathed to his son Solomon with all the natural resources it contained, and the wealth which had already been amassed from it, presented the new Israelite Monarch with an unparalleled opportunity for a tremendous commercial and economic expansion. Having subjugated all neighbouring enemies in Syria-Palestine itself, and with Egypt and Assyria temporarily decadent, an era of peace and political security guaranteed Solomon supremacy in South-western Asia. The Aramaean states, notably Zobah, had tried but failed to get that place in the sun which had fallen to Israel's lot. The rise of Damascus, which had at first been thwarted by Hadadezer and later by David and Solomon, however, was assured in due time.

The remarkable economic prosperity of the Solomonic period, evidenced by an unprecedented revival in trade by land and sea, while doubtless bringing the cream of the wealth into the Israelite realm, nevertheless had great material benefit to the entire Near Eastern world. Damascus as one of the important commercial emporia from prehistoric times, and standing as it did on important lanes of trade between the East and the West, must have been one of the chief beneficiaries of the general prosperity, and quickly gathered strength for the important part it was destined to play at the zenith of its power for a century and a quarter after the disruption of the Hebrew monarchy.

The effective domestication of the Arabian camel not long

before the eleventh century B.C.[16] was a prime factor in the great efflorescence of caravan trade from the desert. Taxes from traders and tribute from Arabian emirs are mentioned as prolific sources of income for Solomon,[17] while Arabs appear in contemporary documents in the ninth century, and in the eighth Sabaeans are already seen emerging on the Assyrian horizon, indicating that caravan trade between the Fertile Crescent and South Arabia was already well developed. Meanwhile the Sabaeans had apparently extended their influence as far north as the central Hejaz.

This growth of desert commerce necessarily involved a long period of evolution, and probably is to be traced back to the Aramaeans' migrations of the twelfth century, which as we have observed, resulted in their occupation of nearly all Syria.[18] Domestication of the camel not only facilitated trade in the Syrian desert, where the animal was a decided improvement over the asses of earlier times, but actually gave birth to true caravan trade farther south, where too great distances between watering places had rendered desert traffic impossible. Solomon's domination of the frontier districts skirting the desert, including Zobah, Damascus, Hauran, Ammon, Moab and Edom, gave him a virtual monopoly on the entire caravan commerce between Arabia and the north, from the Red Sea to Palmyra.

This state of affairs in the United Monarchy led to the establishment of a dangerous precedent, later followed in the Dual Monarchy, of seeking to control Arabian trade which had its outlet in north-west Arabia. In the drama of politics during the next century and a quarter, Arabia played a significant role in the affairs of the Northern Kingdom, where almost incessant wars with Damascus for control of the Transjordanic trade routes continued until the latter state was repressed by the Assyrians in the eighth century. Similarly the Southern Kingdom sought to dominate Arabian commerce during the next two centuries after Solomon, for the lucrative trade channels out of the desert traversed the territories of Israel, whether to Gaza or to Damascus.[19] Loss of Transjordan would mean the forfeiture of the bulk of trade tolls.

Solomon undertook to make his state the chief middleman for the overland trade between Arabia and Egypt and the Hittite and Aramaean states of Syria and Asia Minor, as is

illustrated by the traffic in horses and chariots which he inaugurated. This ambitious plan, coupled with his inventive
policy of tapping Arabian trade from its sources by developing
a maritime route on the Red Sea, must have resulted in a
phenomenal increase in the volume of traffic as well as in the
variety of commodities in such marts as Gaza and Damascus.
A greatly augmented wealth was the inevitable result for these
and other important centres of exchange. That copper from
the mines of the Arabah was one of Solomon's main exports
and his merchants' principal stock in trade[20] is indicated by
Nelson Glueck's excavations at Tell-el-Kheleifeh, ancient
Ezion-geber, on the Gulf of Akabah. The discovery of a copper
refinery there, first built in the tenth century B.C. and rebuilt
at various later periods, practically certifies that the early Iron-
Age mines found by Glueck in the Arabah north of Ezion-geber
were operated, at least to a considerable extent, by Solomon.[21]
It is easy to see how Solomon, more than any of his precedessors
became famous for his wealth as " the first great copper king ",
and why the prosperous periods of the history of the United
Kingdom and later of Judah have a direct relationship to the
times during which they controlled the Arabah and a port on
the Red Sea.[22]

The Arabah with its mineral wealth and access to the trade
of Arabia and the commerce of the Red Sea was the chief cause
of the bitter warfare between Israel and Edom. Even at the
zenith of Israelite power Solomon found this rich prize
threatened when he had to contend with Hadad the Edomite,
who had returned from Egypt, whither he had escaped at the
time of David's conquest of Edom.[23]

If Arabia was for Palestine " not merely a back door but a
front portal ",[24] the Syrian desert was the same for Syria and
Damascus. As the natural mart and harbour of inland Syria,
it was inevitable that the Damascene state would seek the
hegemony and undertake to dominate the commercial highways
of Transjordan. The influx of new trade and wealth during the
Solomonic regime, despite Israelite monopolies, so strengthened
the city as to encourage such an attempt even during the latter
years of the undivided monarchy. Any signs of retrogression in
Solomon's power, such as the Edomite insurrection under
Hadad, must have reacted as a potent stimulus to such ambitions.

The rise of Damascus to its place of dominance in Syria in the next century and a quarter can be traced to this period when signs of decay first became noticeable in Solomon's kingdom. One of Hadadezer's supporters, a certain " Rezon, the son of Eliada", managed to escape when David shattered Aramaean power in Syria. In the downfall of the existing order in Syria he saw a possible opportunity to realize eventually his own desire for aggrandizement. Gathering a band of adventurers about him, augmented no doubt by larger Bedawin contingents from the desert, he bided his time to make a daring thrust at Damascus, a prize grown more opulent during the era of Solomonic prosperity. His capture of the city was like its seizure in Amarna days by Aziru,[25] although he took care not to destroy it, but to make it the centre of his opposition to the hated Israelite conquerors.

The establishment of an independent kingdom north of Palestine, of course, nullified any real control Israel might have exercised over Palmyra (Tadmar), Hamath, or Tiphsah (Thapsacus) at the height of Solomon's empire.[26] Solomon is said to have " built " Tadmar in the desert.[27] Since the nascent caravan trade in the Syrian desert, due to the effective domestication of the camel toward the close of the twelfth century B.C., this oasis had assumed considerable importance both from an economic and military standpoint, as Tiglathpileser I's occupation of it about 1100 B.C. indicates.[28] Solomon's building activities there were most likely principally of a military nature, fortifying it as a base from which the roving Aramaeans could be held in check.[29] Rezon's thrust at Damascus can only be explained on the basis that there was an increasing laxity in the Israelite administration, especially in the border states, resulting from a general decadence as wealth and leisure increased.

According to the late account of the Chronicler Solomon had attacked and prevailed against Hamath-Zobah,[30] and built store-towns in Hamath itself.[31] This datum would suggest that, although Hamath had tacitly submitted to David after the collapse of Aramaean power under Hadadezer,[32] it revolted under Solomon, who occupied it. On the other hand, whatever real sway Solomon might have exercised over it, Rezon's setting himself up as a chieftain in Damascus, must have nullified any direct control, if such had ever existed.[33] The same is true of

Tiphsah, marking the north-easternmost extremity of Solomon's domain.[34] Like Palmyra, this city on the right bank of the Euphrates just above the mouth of the Balikh tributary, possessed considerable commercial value as the converging point where the great caravan route east and west crossed the river by the fords nearby. Solomon, accordingly, found control of it necessary for trade monopoly.

The founding of an independent Aramaean state in Damascus thus placed Solomon's political and commercial interests in central and northern Syria in jeopardy. Hadad's uprising in Edom threatened access east to Arabia and south to the ports of the Red Sea. Solomon's enviable reputation for wealth and power, established at the acme of his kingdom, and the multitudinous matrimonial alliances, which had been a factor in maintaining peaceful and harmonious relations with his subjects and with his neighbours throughout his career, alone may have prevented complete collapse during the closing years of his reign, especially in the border states. But the forces of disintegration at work in the United Monarchy were to bring to a rapid close the crowning period of Israelite dominion. Even without the split-up of the monarchy, so soon to follow Solomon's decease, a drastic reduction in the spheres of Israelite sway was inevitable. It remained for the division of the kingdom to furnish the final and decisive blow to Israelite hegemony over Syria, and furnish Damascus with the long-awaited opportunity it had hitherto been denied, to rise to a position of ascendancy.

CHAPTER V

DAMASCUS AS A RIVAL OF ISRAEL

THE death of Solomon and the disruption of the Israelite Monarchy furnished Damascus with an unparalleled opportunity for the consolidation of its power and made possible its rapid rise to the position of the dominant Syrian state. Not only was the chief obstacle to Syrian expansion—a strong united Israelite state—no longer present but Israelite influence, already seriously weakened by division, suffered further diminution in the rivalries and oft-recurring wars between the Northern and Southern Kingdom, which drained these countries of vitality, and left them helpless to curb growing Aramaean might. In addition a multitude of problems was created which kept them so preoccupied with their own affairs that they had little time to devote to the formidable threat of a hostile and increasingly powerful Aramaean state forming so dangerously near at hand.

I. THE EARLY KINGS OF DAMASCUS

The succession of Syrian kings who lifted Damascus to the apogée of its power, and who were the inveterate foes of Israel for a century and a half, still offers some problems, although the recent discovery of the votive stele of Benhadad I had shed remarkable light on the whole question.[1] According to I Kings xv, 18 the order of succession is " Benhadad, the son of Tabrimmon,the son of Hezion, king of Aram, who dwelt in Damascus ". In Prof. Albright's rendering of the Benhadad stele the sequence is identical: " Bir-hadad,[2] son of Ṭab-Rammân, son of Ḥadyân,[3] King of Aram ".[4] The biblical list, confirmed by the Benhadad inscription, thus gives us the first dynasty of Syrian kings who ruled from Damascus, and Hezion[5] is the correct name of the first king. The name, moreover, is of more than passing interest since it is known to have been also borne by the father of the Aramaic king Kapara of Gozan (Tell Ḥalâf) who probably preceded his Syrian namesake by not more than a generation or two.[6]

56

Although the correct name of the first king of Damascus has been settled by the new extra-biblical evidence, the problem of the identity of Rezon, who seized Damascus during Solomon's administration and apparently ruled there, is still unsolved. Is Hezion identical with Rezon? If so, the form Rezon is secondary, and is to be regarded as a corruption of Hezion, probably having been confounded with Rezin, a later king of Damascus in the time of Tiglathpileser III.[7] If this proves to be incorrect, which seems to be unlikely, then Rezon, of course, must be considered as excluded from the dynastic list of I Kings xv, 18, which is improbable in view of the fact that he was clearly the founder of the powerful Damascene state.[8]

From the time of Rezon's revolt under Solomon to Benhadad I there is singularly scant light on affairs within the realm of Damascus itself.[9] In the rebellion against Israelite control, however, it is evident that Solomon suffered a permanent loss, and was unable to recover the city. Meanwhile, Rezon, while laying the foundations of the Syrian state, imparted to it that temper of hostility toward Israel, which was to become hereditary in the kings who followed, and which was to make it one of the most aggressive and dangerous of enemies. The Massoretic text of I Kings xi, 25 suggests that Rezon outlived the undivided Hebrew Monarchy, as he is said to have " reigned over Syria " and to have been " an adversary to Israel all the days of Solomon ". Until the recent discovery of the Benhadad inscription the name of Tabrimmon[10] was known only from the dynastic list of I Kings xv, 18 as the son of Hezion and the father of Benhadad I. Now, however, this, the first inscribed monument of importance bearing the names of kings of Damascus (Aram), not only confirms the name itself, but substantiates the accuracy of the line of succession as preserved in I Kings. Unfortunately, however, the document adds practically nothing to our knowledge of this Syrian ruler, either as to the length or character of his reign, or when he was succeeded by his son, the famous Benhadad I.

II. Benhadad I

By the time Benhadad entered into the succession Syria had grown so formidably in power that it was the strongest state in this region of Western Asia and ready to seize any opportunity to expand its domains. Such an occasion presented itself when the hard-pressed Asa, king of Judah (917–876), sent an urgent appeal to Syria for aid against Baasha, king of Israel (*c.* 900–*c.* 877), who, pushing his frontier southward to within five miles of Jerusalem, proceeded to fortify Ramah as a border fortress commanding the capital of Judah.

In desperation Asa sent what was left of the temple and royal treasure, plundered so recently by Shishak,[11] to Benhadad as a bribe to lure Syria into an alliance with himself against Israel. The situation offered Damascus the chance of a lifetime to extend its sway at the expense of both Israel and Judah, and Benhadad was not slow to seize the opportunity. Casting his alliance with Jeroboam and Baasha to the winds, Benhadad invaded northern Israel, capturing Iyon in the fertile Merğ 'Ayun west of Mount Hermon, Dan, Abel-beth-maacah, all Chinneroth (the rich plain on the western shore of the lake of Galilee) and all Naphtali, embracing such important cities as Kedesh, Hazor, Merom, and Zephath.

Asa obtained immediate relief, for Baasha had to retire to his capital city, Tirzah, and leave off building Ramah.[12] But the cost was more than Asa bargained for. He not only betrayed his own race and aroused a deep animosity that later resulted in an alliance of Israel and Damascus against Judah, but in laying himself under such heavy obligation to Syria, and in furnishing Benhadad such an unexampled opportunity for Aramaean aggrandizement, he placed both Hebrew kingdoms in a position, which for the time being at least, seemed semi-subservient to a mutual foe.

Continuously advancing in importance since its capture by Rezon in Solomon's reign, Damascus under Benhadad I's vigorous leadership became " Aram " *par excellence.* To be asked to intervene in Palestinian politics was sufficient proof of political prestige. The shrewd alliance with Judah was a diplomatic victory. The invasion of Israel was both a military and a commercial triumph. New rich territory was gained. But more important still the trade route to Accho on the Phoenician coast was guaranteed for the flow of caravan traffic from Damascus. Benhadad now held territory which extended to the sphere of Canaanite influence and which was eager for commerce from the East. The stage was thus set for Damascus' rise to a place of ascendancy, especially under virile leadership such as was furnished by Benhadad I.

Benhadad's invasion of Israel recounted in I Kings xv, 18 ff., must be placed about the year 879 B.C., that is a year or so before the death of Baasha (c. 877 B.C.). The time of this event is not fixed in Kings, but is dated by the Chronicler, who obviously followed a written source, in the thirty-sixth year of King Asa of Judah.[13] However, this synchronism, compared with the transmitted regnal years of the kings of Judah and Israel calculated according to antedating principles, would place the Syrian invasion nine years after Baasha's death.[14] This apparent discrepancy has been commonly attributed by most scholars to the " characteristic " carelessness of the Chronicler in assembling his data. But there is not only reason to believe that there were more extensive extant pre-exilic Jewish annalistic sources available about 400 B.C. than a century or two later, but there is also evidence, which has been increased of late, that the Chronicler used care and discrimination in collecting his facts.[15] It would be better, therefore, following Albright,[16] to solve the difficulty by reducing the reign of Rehoboam by at least eight or nine years, rather than using this synchronism as a " characteristic " illustration of the Chronicler's unreliability.[17] Such a reduction in Rehoboam's reign would order our chronology aright, and place Benhadad's invasion within the span of Baasha's reign, some time not long before his death in the vicinity of 879 B.C.

Before the discovery of the Melcarth Stela, scholars were almost universally accustomed to distinguish between Benhadad I, son of Tabrimmon, son of Hezion, the contemporary of Asa and Baasha mentioned in I Kings xv, 18 and Benhadad, the contemporary of Elijah and Elisha. Only occasionally did a biblical scholar, here and there, such as T. K. Cheyne,[18] recognize the possibility that the two might be identical. The majority, however, assumed that the so-called Benhadad I died some time during the early years of the Omride dynasty, and was succeeded by Benhadad II.[19] Even M. Maurice Dunand, director of Antiquities in Syria, who first published the Benhadad Stela (1941) in the Bulletin du Musée de Beyrouth,[20] despite his generally correct translation and interpretation of the text of the inscription, could arrive at no decisive conclusion in the matter, as he gave up the restoration of the mutilated but pivotal second line as an impossible job. Albright partially restored line two, and demonstrated by epigraphic criteria[21] that the script of the monument points to the reign of the Benhadad, who was Ahab's bitter enemy, whereas the patronymic certifies that this Benhadad was the same Syrian monarch who invaded Baasha's realm.[22]

Whereas the epigraphic evidence furnished by the Melcarth Stela strongly argues for the identity of Benhadad I and Benhadad II, hitherto, in the absence of such a sign-post pointing out the right direction, historical data have been commonly construed as presenting serious, if not insurmountable barriers against such an equation. Particularly, the traditional numbers of transmitted regnal years of Israelite kings from Baasha to Jehu, which would allot to Benhadad an abnormally long reign of at least a half century, were considered as fatal to the argument. Now, however, as the result of research in the field of Israelite chronology during the past quarter century by such scholars as Kugler, Lewy, Begrich, Mowinckel, Vogelstein, Thiele and Albright,[23] it is quite obvious that the numbers concerned, especially those involving the Northern Kingdom, must be considerably reduced.[24]

We have observed that a reduction of at least eight or nine years seems necessary in the case of Rehoboam of Judah.[25] A similar substantial reduction must be made in the total for the traditional figures of the kings of Israel from the death of Solomon to the accession of Jehu[26]—compensation most certainly to be effected in the numbers involving the Omride dynasty. Omri's reign must be dated about 876–869 B.C., and (following Albright) the traditional twelve years of his rule reduced to eight.[27]   Ahab's traditional twenty-two-year reign must be cut to twenty, and his rule fixed at about 869–850 B.C.[28] Four years or so may be lopped off the traditional twelve for Joram who held power from about 849–842 B.C.[29]   These revisions, with the rest of the transmitted figures remaining intact, would set our chronology in order, with the division of the Monarchy dated about 922 B.C., Benhadad's invasion of Israel in Asa's thirty-sixth year about 879 B.C. and his death about 843 B.C. Any abnormally long reign for Benhadad is thus obviated. Thirty-six years would be ample, although he may well have occupied the throne at Damascus for a full forty years like David, Solomon, and Asa.

A further argument of moment commonly urged against the identification of Benhadad I with Benhadad II is the word of the vanquished Syrian king to Ahab after the latter's victory at Aphek recorded in I Kings xx, 34: " The towns which my father took from thy father, I will restore; and thou shalt set up markets for thyself in Damascus, as my father did in Samaria." The reference can scarcely be to Ahab's father Omri, for available sources do not lend the least support to the theory that the latter suffered a defeat in a clash with Syria. The term " father ", especially when employed in connection with royalty, must frequently be construed as " predecessor " as is often the case in cuneiform and North-west Semitic texts.

Doubtless towns wrested from Israel by Hezion or Tabrimmon during the reign of Jeroboam I (c. 922–901 B.C.) or Nadab (c. 901–900) concerning which, however, we have no record,[30] are intended. This period, though extremely obscure with regard to events in Damascus, certainly witnessed a formidable rise and expansion of Syrian might. There is ample reason to conclude that the hard-pressed Jeroboam had to make important concessions to Syria at this time.[31]

Benhadad's use of the expression *Samaria* is to be understood as formulaic. The city was so strategically situated and enjoyed such growth and prosperity that at an early period its name was transferred to the Northern Kingdom of which it was the capital.[32] It is not unlikely that as early as two decades after its founding by Omri, *Samaria* had begun to be used as a popular designation of the whole country,[33] or at least as a concrete equivalent of " Israelite capital". The commercial privileges to which the Syrian king made reference may well have been established in Tirzah, Shechem, or some other Israelite towns.

CHAPTER VI

DAMASCUS IN CONFLICT WITH ISRAEL

THE general history of Syria in the first half of the ninth century B.C. and in the century and a half following is determined essentially by two primary factors the influence of which had already been established in an earlier time, but only then had begun to be fully worked out. First to be noted was the immigration of the Aramaeans, whose rapidly expanding power in Central and Southern Syria brought them in aggressive conflict with the earlier inhabitants for control of the land. Second, there was the rise of the newly awakened Assyrian Empire whose encroachments upon the West led to the most manifold and perplexing changes in the state of affairs in Syria. Now the Aramaeans are engaged in bitter warfare against the older residents of the country, now in alliance with them against the Assyrians; now Assyrians and Aramaeans are united; now one of the two assumes protection of the older people of the land against the other.

Out of this general situation arise the most diverse relations and conflicting problems, the solution of which often remains impossible because of the present fragmentary character of the sources, and the extensive gaps in our knowledge. Although it is not yet possible to construct a complete picture of this period, the chief lines of the historical development may be sketched.[1]

I. BENHADAD I AND OMRI

The reign of Omri (c. 876–869 B.C.) witnessed a constant and uninterrupted increase in Benhadad I's political, commercial, and military power. As Damascus controlled the rich caravan routes westward to Accho and the Phoenician coast since Benhadad's brilliant victory over Baasha some three or four years previously, the immense wealth which flowed into the city, enabled it to amass great strength for its important role as the dominant Syrian state. It was natural for Aramaean merchants to take advantage of this predominance to seek to monopolize Phoenician commerce and to capture the Israelite trade market. But Benhadad now faced a different situation in the founding of a new Israelite dynasty. Never before had the Syrian monarch been called upon to deal with such dangerous rivals as Omri and his son, Ahab, proved to be. The years of civil war, which according to I Kings xvi, 15, 21–23, were at least four in number, and which ushered in Omri's reign, were not able to obscure the political and military genius of the new Israelite ruler. Immediately he laid plans to offset the dangerous commercial expansion of Damascus, and undertook by astute diplomacy to establish close affiliation[2] with Phoenicia which was to culminate in the marriage of his son and successor, Ahab, to the daughter of Ethbaal, king of the Sidonians.[3] This important event in turn was to pave the way for a general religious syncretism in Israel in the years immediately following.[4]

In other directions Omri likewise showed vigour in dealing with foreign powers. The Mesha Stone[5] discloses that it was he who gained control of northern Moab, occupying its cities, and exacting a heavy annual tribute[6] which must have substantially enriched Israel. Domination of vital Transjordanic trade routes added other sources of revenue which helped make the extensive building operations at Samaria possible.

Moreover, as an accomplished military commander[7] Omri took definite steps to meet the constant threat of foreign invasion. Syria might swoop down on him at any moment, and a new terror appeared on the horizon in the westward march of an awakened Assyria. In view of the ever-darkening political situation, his own easy conquest of Tirzah[8] must have made him quite dissatisfied with his former capital as a location of sufficient strength. Hence with unusual foresight he selected the hill of Samaria, a site of superior strategic importance, capable of almost impregnable fortification, as his new royal residence and capital, and began building operations there.[9] From the first it became the stronghold of the Northern Kingdom, and more than once proved the sagacity of its founder's choice in withstanding prolonged sieges by the Syrians and later by the powerful Assyrians. That the Israelite state endured as long as it did in the face of the Aramaean and Assyrian advance was largely due to the strength of its capital. When

Samaria fell, the nation fell. Omri's fortification of Samaria was of prime importance in preserving Israel from political and military eclipse, and in assuring the nation a strong position as an aggressive competitor of Benhadad I in his bid for domination of Syria and Northern Palestine.

Besides the judicious and far-sighted measures adopted by Omri to cope with Benhadad's growing economic and political prestige, the Assyrian advance, although it brought with it a new source of anxiety to Israel, tended to act as a further restraint upon the Aramaeans. This is doubtless the reason why there is no evidence of a Syrian invasion of Israel during Omri's reign, or that the Israelite ruler was ever actually a tributary to Benhadad I.[10] However, whether merely by virtue of his foreign reputation as a ruler of energy and the founder of a new dynasty or in some more direct way, the initial contact between Israel and Assyria evidently occurred during Omri's day, for from now on Israel appears in cuneiform accounts as *Bît-Ḫumrî*, the official name of the capital city, called popularly by its earlier name *Shômerôn*. The name of the capital early began to be applied to the whole country, and its kings are styled *mâr-Humrî*, i.e., inhabitants of *Bît-Ḫumrî*, or Israelites.[12] Tiglathpileser III's reference to the land of Israel over a hundred years later by its official name, *Bît-Ḫumria*,[13] evidences the significance of Omri as a ruler in the history of Israel.

II. BENHADAD I AND AHAB

Ashurnasirpal II, by avoiding Damascus in his western campaign of conquest, left Benhadad's increasing power substantially unchecked. The real curb on growing Aramaean might, however, was not to come for the present from the formidable Assyrian but from the energetic son and successor of Omri, who was not slow to avail himself of any lull in Syrian hostilities, occasioned doubtless by the temporary threat of Assyria, to strengthen his kingdom within and without against the day of eventual dealing with Damascus. To this end Ahab (*c.* 869–850) assiduously continued the sagacious policies begun by his father.

Inheriting the keen military insight of Omri, Ahab continued developing Samaria as an imperial bastion and royal residence, besides building and fortifying many other places,

including Jericho.[14] Exhibiting keen diplomatic skill, he further
cultivated the " brotherly covenant "[15] with Tyre to assure the
free flow of Phoenician commerce into Israel and to ward off
the threat of monopolistic control by Aramaean tradesmen.
His marriage to Jezebel, the daughter of Ittoba'al, king of Tyre,
sealed such an agreement and the concomitant introduction of
the Tyrian cult of Baal into Israel further gave it the stamp of
permanency.

The new evidence furnished by the Melcarth Stele strongly
suggests that Benhadad I was not to be outwitted in his commercial transactions by the wily Ahab, but made a similar
diplomatic move to protect his lucrative Phoenician trade. In
the light of the Syrian's adoration of the chief Tyrian god
Melcarth,[16] the same deity whom Ahab introduced into Israel
and whose cult Jezebel so actively propagated during her
husband's reign, it is not difficult to suppose that another of
Ethbaal's children was married into the powerful dynasty of
Syria whose friendship was even more important to the Tyrians
than that of Ahab.[17] On his side Benhadad must have quickly
surmised that he could be out-manoeuvred by the clever Ahab
at the expense of his own flourishing traffic with the Sidonian-
Tyrian kingdom. Consequently there were reasons of sufficient
weight to induce him to show his devotion to the powerful god
of Tyre, whether contemplated as a deity adored by a relative
by marriage, or as a god brought within the sphere of his
worship by a treaty consummated between himself and a fellow
king that included no marriage at all.[18]

It is significant that in the introduction of the Tyrian cult
into Israel with all its appurtenances—temple, priestly and
prophetic personnel, with full cultic ritual—the new god is
never in our sources called Baal of Tyre or Melqart, but always
merely " Baal ",[19] offering added corroboration of the cosmic
character of the deity. Ahab's religious policy of fostering a
cultic syncretism to integrate his realm was singularly short-
sighted, and proved a disintegrating factor in contrast to his
effective foreign policy. The latter he carried forward with
some success, bringing to an end the long and bitter conflict
with Judah by a peaceful agreement, and cementing the alliance
with another royal union, giving his daughter Athaliah in
marriage to Jehoram, the crown prince of Judah.[20] This was
another diplomatic master stroke aimed at Syria, for not only

was a potential threat of war and invasion removed from the south, but a valuable ally was secured to enter the field in due time against Benhadad.

The long-threatened attack from Syria, against which both Omri and Ahab had been bolstering their realm internally and externally, finally came some five years or so before the end of Ahab's reign. Whether he sought to take advantage of the weakening effects of the famine in Israel,[21] or to force Ahab into an anti-Assyrian alliance, or to eliminate him as a potential ally of Assyria,[22] or merely to remove him as an increasingly dangerous threat to his own ambitions, Benhadad, at the head of a large coalition of vassal kings,[23] suddenly appeared before the gates of Samaria. Ahab's brilliant strategy in employing the levies of the district governors as a ruse to throw the Syrians off guard, followed by a quick attack of the regular troops, won the day. The besieging Aramaeans were completely routed, suffering great losses, and Benhadad, in spite of confidence in his numerical superiority, barely escaped with his life.

The return of the Syrians the next year (c. 854) to retrieve their humiliating defeat resulted in a worse disaster near Aphek.[24] Ahab, now ready for them, again displayed military competence in winning the battle. Vastly outnumbered, he encamped on the hills awaiting his opportunity to strike to advantage. On the seventh day his chance came, and attacking with sudden fury, a very great slaughter of the Aramaeans took place.[25] The survivors fled to the nearby town of Aphek, which was taken in the violent Israelite assault. Under the razed walls of the city 27,000 Aramaeans are said to have lain buried.[26] Benhadad was compelled to surrender, but was treated as a "brother", and allowed to go scot free after generously being privileged to state his own peace terms, which included restitution of cities which had been taken from Israel and commercial concessions in Damascus.

Ahab's lenient treatment of Benhadad shows that even in the hour of triumph over an inveterate enemy, and in the face of intense prophetic opposition, he did not abandon the essential principles of his consistent foreign policy. He determined, if possible, to make a friend of an implacable foe, calculating no doubt that a colleague won by kindness might be of greater service to his realm than a hostile nation, made still more inimical by having its king put to death. He realized, moreover, that the incorporation of Damascus into Israel was out of the question,[27] and that in prospect of the perilous Assyrian menace, merciful conduct toward a fellow monarch whose realm lay as a buffer state between himself and the rising danger, offered the possibility of a far-reaching coalition to stem a common threat.[28]

Whether as an actual provision of the treaty of Aphek,[29] or as a result of ominous warning afforded by Shalmaneser's advance in Upper Syria in the months immediately following the Israelite victory, the very next year (853) found Ahab and his hereditary foe allied together at Karkar to block the next Assyrian move southward. The formidable fighting machine built by Ashurnasirpal II, and now augmented and employed to such ruthless advantage by his son Shalmaneser III (858–824), had crossed the border of Ḥattina into the frontier of Hamath, easily capturing such cities as Adennu,[30] Parqâ,[31] and the royal town of Arganâ,[32] which was pillaged, and the royal palaces of King Irḫulenu of Hamath were set on fire. Continuing his victorious southward push through the Orontes Valley, Shalmaneser met no substantial resistance until he drew near the strategically important fort of Karkar, which guarded the approaches to the city of Hamath and all lower Syria. Here he collided with the powerful Syrian coalition under the leadership of Benhadad I of Damascus, who is called Hadadezer (Adadidri) in the Assyrian monuments.[33]

The necessity for such a coalition must have been a matter of serious consideration on the part of the Syrian principalities ever since the phenomenal advance of Ashurnasirpal II and Shalmaneser III toward the West. The realization that only such a combination of their forces could save them from a common disaster could be of no advantage unless strong leadership was available to head a confederacy. Hadadezer of Damascus was ostensibly the man for the undertaking. His long and successful reign, despite his defeat by Ahab, had naturally given him a certain pre-eminence of position throughout Syria before the attacks of the Assyrians began, so when the danger became acute, he was ready to assume leadership.

However, despite these considerations, it is not quite obvious, as Alfred Jepsen observes,[34] why the king who lived almost the farthest from the shooting was always looked upon as the real head of the coalition. Although it is true the common opposition to Assyrian encroachment held the states together, without Damascus necessarily having had any politico-legal precedence, Jepsen is correct in emphasizing that Hadadezer's personal influence upon the alliance ought not to be underrated, since not only did Shalmaneser III see in him the chief leader, but his death also spelled the doom of the federation.[35] Of course Hadadezer's personal leadership may only have been possible by virtue of the fact that he had a strong and well-organized state under him, capable of putting a powerful army in the field.[36] At any rate, it was doubtless he who conceived and carried through the idea of uniting the majority of the middle and south Syrian states into a great confederacy which was always powerful enough to throw back the Assyrians on the border of his territory and thus protect it.

The Bible is silent concerning the clash of the Syrian federation with the advancing Assyrian army, but the well-known Monolith Inscription of Shalmaneser, now in the British Museum, records the story of the famous battle. In spite of possible exaggeration in the statistics,[37] it furnishes striking evidence of the relative importance of Damascus and Israel among the Syrian states at the time, and by the mention of Ahab, *Aḫabbu Sir'elai*,[38] gives entirely independent confirmation of the fact that this king was on the throne of Israel just before the middle of the ninth century B.C.[39] As leader of the confederation and of the most powerful Syrian state, "Hadadezer of Aram" is appropriately listed first as contributing twelve hundred chariots and twenty thousand infantry. Irḫulenu of Hamath is mentioned second, but his mere seven hundred chariots and ten thousand infantry, as compared with Ahab's two thousand chariots ("the largest single contribution of this most aristocratic of services"[40]), and ten thousand infantry, would suggest that Israel's position as second, rather than as third, would be more fitting. Although other small states such as Irkanata, Shiana, Arvad, Ushana, in Phoenicia; Que, in Cilicia; Muṣri, probably in Cappodocia; and individuals like Baasha son of Ruḫubu, the Ammonite, and Gindibu, the Arabian, furnished lesser contingents, it is evident that Damascus and Israel were in the forefront as the important powers in Syria-Palestine at this time.[41]

The outcome of the battle was evidently not as decisive as the extravagant claims of the Monolith Inscription would indicate.[42] The initial clash at Karkar can be taken as an Assyrian victory, since Shalmaneser held the field, while the allies had to retreat southward to Gilzau. But at this juncture, where the retreat from Karkar would most naturally reach the Orontes, the Assyrians must have suffered a set-back, despite Shalmaneser's boasts that he dammed the river with the corpses of his enemies, for he failed to press on to Hamath, which he most certainly would have done had he considered himself in a position to do so. Nor was he able to report any further successes. More than that he did not again resume his attack on Hamath or Damascus until some half-dozen years later.[44]

The three-year period of peace between Syria and Israel[45] following immediately upon the Israelite victory at Aphek (c. 854) was terminated by Ahab's attempt to recover Ramoth in Gilead (c. 851). The temporary removal of the Assyrian menace by Shalmaneser's protracted avoidance of Syria in the years following the battle of Karkar caused the Syrian league, at least to some degree, to disintegrate. This fact, coupled with Benhadad I's inexcusable perfidy in failing to restore the Israelite towns which had been taken by Damascus, notably the strategic Ramoth in Gilead,[46] in accordance with the munificent terms of the pact at Aphek, so provoked Ahab that he resolved upon an attack. Supported by Jehoshaphat of Judah (c. 873–849), Ahab's military and diplomatic career was abruptly brought to an end by death on the field of battle in the ensuing clash with the Aramaeans. Benhadad's ruthless command to the captains of his chariotry to fight with no one but the " king of Israel "[47] demonstrates what a dangerous evaluation the Syrian monarch placed upon Ahab's capacity for leadership.

III. BENHADAD I AND JORAM

According to available documents Ahab was the last ruler of the Omride dynasty to be listed in the Assyrian records as a foe of Shalmaneser. During the brief reign of his weak and sickly son Ahaziah (c. 850–849), the Assyrian danger was still temporarily in abeyance. Furthermore, after Ahab's death, Israel was kept occupied with revolt in Moab.[48] With the accession of Ahaziah's brother Joram (c. 849–842) unsuccessful attempts to quell a full-scale Moabite revolt monopolized the new Israelite ruler's time, so that, although in 848 B.C., in the eleventh year of his reign, Shalmaneser III made another thrust into Syria, and was met by a confederation of " twelve kings of the seaboard " again headed by Adadidri (Benahadad I)[49] of Damascus, and Irḫulenu of Hamath, no actual mention is made of Israel's participation in the coalition.[50]

The same thing is true of the notable campaign in his fourteenth regnal year (845), when he made a supreme effort in the West, as the Bull Inscription records. Levying a huge host of 120,000 troops from his wide-extending domains, " a maximum for the size of Assyrian armies and an indication of the gravity of the situation ",[51] Shalmaneser once more marched toward central Syria to hurl this huge force against a new Syrian combination, this time in an all-out effort to crush resistance to his vaulting ambitions. Adadidri (Benhadad I) is once more mentioned at the head of an alliance augmented to meet the new peril. He is assisted by " Irḫulenu of Hamath, with twelve kings of the seacoast, upper and lower ", who called out their troops without number, and marched to meet the Assyrian.[52] Although Shalmaneser insists he defeated the coalition, confiscating chariots, cavalry and equipment, and compelling the foe to flee for life, the total absence of concrete evidence of gains or advances, makes his claims very dubious, especially since during the next three years he was occupied with operations in Nairi, Namri, and the Amanus.[53]

It is possible of course that Israel was included in the Syrian federations of 849, 848, and 845,[54] but as the Assyrian records do not enumerate the allied enemy troops in detail, nor actually name Israel as had been done for the year 853 in the Monolith Inscription, there is no way of knowing. To assume Israel's participation in the later coalitions is perhaps warranted, but must be held with reserve and ever open to question. However, to proceed farther and to insist on a stringent alliance, rigidly binding, and indefectibly observed without a break, especially by Israel and Damascus from 853 to 845, as Jepsen does,[55] thereby creating greater and more irreconcilable discrepancies between the Syrian records and the biblical representations, is totally unwarranted. Inasmuch as I Kings xxii represents Ahab as struggling with Damascus after 853, and II Kings vi and vii also picture the reign of Joram as characterized by Aramaean wars,[56] Jepsen must proceed radically to substantiate his hypothesis which views these passages as misplaced in the time of Ahab and Joram, and maintains that in so far as they reflect generally recognizable historical events, belong later to the time of Joahaz and Joash in the dynasty of Jehu.[57] Accordingly, his conclusion that we are directed to the Assyrian records alone for the history of Damascus and its relations to Israel at the time of the dynasty of Omri is inescapable.

But the difficulties which obtain from a comparison of the Assyrian with the biblical tradition, while scarcely admitting of so simple a solution as the complete elimination of the latter, have of late been so substantially reduced by archaeological evidence that such an extreme procedure is now no longer justified. Presuppositions with regard to the supposed inflexibility of the Syrian coalitions for 849, 848, and 845, especially when Israelite participation yet remains to be proved, can hardly be of sufficient weight to furnish the basis for such radical criticism.[57] One of the principal difficulties giving rise to such an approach is the Benahadad-Adadidri problem. But as this heretofore vexing question has been cleared up by the new evidence supplied by the recently discovered Aramaic stele of Benhadad I, the main reason for relegating the data in I Kings xxii and II Kings vi and vii to the period of the Jehu dynasty, rather than to Ahab and Joram, as tradition represents them, is obviated.[58]

The other historical difficulties adduced as allegedly necessitating such a critical attitude for the most part offer singularly weak support to such a revolutionary hypothesis. This is especially true with regard to the traditional circumstances of Ahab's death and the occasion of his last struggle against the Syrians at Ramoth-gilead, as given in I Kings xxii. This chapter, according to Hölscher,[59] in its present form is assumed to stem from the Judaean prophetic circle shortly before the exile, and to be essentially an account of a similar battle from the later era of Joash, adapted with legendary motifs by a Judaean author to the time of Ahab to represent the latter's death as occurring at the hands of the Syrians. According to Hölscher,[60] the notice of Ahab's decease in I Kings xxii, 40 implies that the king died a natural death, and is at variance with the tradition of the rest of the chapter, which presents him as dying in battle at the hands of the Aramaeans. Despite the fact that Hölscher's observation[61] is evidently sound, and Ahab is apparently the sole exception to an Israelite or Judahite king who did not die a natural death, and yet of whom it is said that "he slept with his fathers", it is seriously open to question whether any undue significance is to be attached to this expression, particularly if it gives rise to greater difficulties, or even demonstrable absurdities, as in this case. If it does actually indicate that the Chronicle from which the priestly redactor of Kings took this verse knew only of Ahab's decease from natural causes, and nothing at all of his death in battle with the Aramaeans, and if this latter tradition is an intentional invention of the Judaean author of I Kings xxii, as Jepsen assumes, then we must further resort to the highly improbable and artificial assumption that the author must have followed the tradition of a battle similar to the one he describes, so as not to make his account too incredible.[62] This involves, besides the needless conjecture regarding the essential integrity of the author, and, indeed that of the whole pre-exilic prophetic circle in Judah, the additional surmise that such a tradition is found in the present form of I Kings xx.[63]

Verses 1–34 of this chapter are supposed to reflect events out of the reign of Joash (c. 801–768) when the actual victorious battle against the Aramaeans, presupposed as the basis of this alleged legend, is said to have taken place. The words of the conquered Syrian king in verse 34: " The cities which my father took from thy father, I will restore, and thou shalt make streets for thee in Damascus, as my father made in Samaria", are regarded as addressed to Joash,[64] instead of Ahab. Ahab's name is construed as a subsequent addition, together with verses 35–42.[65] The father-son relation and the circumstances of an Israelite king, who was at first hard-pressed, but who subsequently in several campaigns vanquished the Aramaeans and retrieved lost territories, in addition to other data concerning the Joahaz-Joash era are accepted as agreeing precisely with the picture presented in I Kings xx.[66]

However, closer scrutiny, unbiased in favour of a theory, discloses that the similarity between the events in I Kings xx and xxii, traditionally said to belong to Ahab's reign, and those of the Joash era is superficial. The events themselves, moreover, are found to be in contrast in very significant respects. While Ahab was in closest alliance with Jehoshaphat, king of Judah, and was assisted by him in a campaign against Syria,[57] one of the important notes in the very brief account of Joash is his open war against Amaziah of Judah.[68] Whereas the events of Ahab's reign are untouched by Elisha, and portrayed as occurring before the prophet's active career, at the time of Joash the prophet in his extreme age is presented as vitally connected with the Israelite king as an advisor in his victorious Syrian campaigns.[69] It is true, of course, that cities which his father had lost to Syria are mentioned as recovered by Joash, but there is a conspicuous absence of any reference to bazaars or trading concessions in Damascus, as in I Kings xx, 34. With regard to Benahadad's being taken prisoner by the Israelite king and placed at his mercy, which is a central feature of the Ahab narrative, there is not even the hint of a similar incident in Joash's wars with the Aramaeans.[70]

The small army of 7,000 men, which the Israelite king of I Kings xx, 15 was able to muster during the siege of Samaria,[71] is said to ill fit Ahab's time, and to be much more suitable to the reign of Joash, who had only the diminished remnants of a military force which Hazael had permitted his father Joahaz to keep.[72] However, this argument has slight force since it is almost certain this number did not include all Ahab's troops, but only the limited number then in the besieged city. Besides the size of the contingent does not appear in too bad a light when Ahab contributed only 10,000 foot soldiers in the great battle of Karkar.

The thirty-two kings represented as being in the combined armed forces of the Syrian king in his attack on Samaria were simply subordinate princes of the Damascene realm, as A. Alt correctly maintains.[73] To see in the setting aside of these kings for captains (governors)[74] a circumstance in the historical development of Aram about the year 800 B.C., when Benhadad, Hazael's son, is supposed to have abolished the independence of the subject kings, and to have replaced them by governors in a united Aramaean state, is highly problematical, and based on very slender evidence.[75] Placing the data of I Kings xx and xxii anywhere but in Ahab's reign raises more problems that it solves.

The other historical difficulty appearing in I Kings xxii, supposedly necessitating its being transferred to the time of Joash, is the traditional cause of the war with Syria; namely, that the Aramaeans had taken Ramoth-gilead.[76] Jepsen holds this to be scarcely possible, and apparently considers that there is no evidence to show that the city had, at this time, passed into Syrian hands.[77] Kraeling, however, is certainly correct when he maintains that Joram " asserted his independence by emphasizing his claims in Gilead (II Kings viii, 28). He attacked Ramoth, captured it, and then ' held the watch ' against Hazael, king of Aram (ix, 14) ",[78] Jepsen, on the other hand, insists that there is nothing to this effect in the narrative, and that it can only be said that Joram fought at Ramoth with Hazeal, and that the city itself was an Israelite possession. But how it is said to have become so, when Ahab did not conquer it, he says is not to be read into the text.[79] The problem, however, is largely imaginary, and of little importance. Kraeling manifestly has the natural and obviously correct interpretation of the facts as they appear from the record.

CHAPTER VII

DAMASCUS AS MASTER OF ISRAEL

BENHADAD I's long and energetic reign of some thirty-six or
perhaps even forty years,[1] which had lifted the kingdom of
Damascus to a position of pre-eminent power, came to an
inglorious end about 843 B.C. or slightly later.[2] By 841 Hazael,
an official of influence in the service of the Syrian court, had
already usurped the throne, as the Assyrian inscriptions reveal.[3]
An Asshur text describes this significant change in the dynasty
at Damascus, and strikingly confirms the biblical account.
" Adadidri forsook his land (i.e., died). Hazael, son of a
nobody, seized the throne "[4]. The Assyrian expression here
employed for " died," *šadâšu êmid*, means, as Weidner has
shown,[5] "to die an unnatural death", or in plain words, "to
be murdered ".

According to the more detailed biblical representations,
Benhadad, suffering from a serious illness, dispatches Hazael
to the Hebrew prophet Elisha to obtain an oracular reply to
the question whether his sickness would prove fatal or not.[6]
Elisha is represented as discerning that the king's malady itself
was curable, but that Hazael's personal ambition would result
in the murder of the king and the usurpation of the throne.
Whether Elisha's oracle hastened the death of Benhadad is its
reaction upon Hazael, as Meyer thinks,[7] or not, shortly thereafter, while alone in his sick chamber, Hazael smothers the
ailing king with the corner of a wet blanket to cover all traces of
murder, and then seized the throne of Damascus.[8]

Benhadad I's death and the inevitable confusion and uncertainty incident upon a shift in rulers at Damascus gave the
signal for Ahab's son, Joram, supported by his nephew, Ahaziah
of Judah, to make a quick thrust to recover Ramoth in Gilead.[9]
In 842, or perhaps in the early months of 841,[10] Joram captured
the strategic fortress " and held the watch " against Hazael,
king of Aram, doubtless before the latter could fully consolidate
his newly acquired position. However, Joram paid dearly for

his gains against Syria, and was compelled to retire to Jezreel
to recuperate from wounds received in the battle with Hazael.

I. HAZAEL AND JEHU

Hazael's contacts with the House of Omri were destined to be
short-lived. Not many months elapsed before he was confronted by a new dynasty of Israelite kings, headed by a usurper
like himself. Jehu (c. 842–815), who had served under Ahab,
had by the time of Joram become one of the commanders of
the army, and was among those who were left to defend Ramoth-
gilead when Joram had to retire to Jezreel. It was there he was
anointed king by a representative of the prophetic guild, and
with lightning speed inaugurated a thorough political and
religious revolution which was to eventuate in the extermination of the dynasty of Omri and the extirpation of the cult of
Baal Melqart from Israel.[11]

Whatever the final results for weal or woe this events would
have for Israel, the destruction of the powerful Omride line of
kings was bound to reduce the nation's foreign reputation, at
least temporarily.[12] Tyre of necessity was opposed to Jehu's
rule[13] and the close alliance with Judah, which the Omrides
had enjoyed by marriage, was ended. The new Israelite king,
in contrast to Omri and Ahab, seemed little concerned with
cementing good relations with his neighbours, especially Syria,
and when Shalmaneser again advanced against Damascus in
841, Jehu, who apparently was not compelled to render tribute
to the Assyrian, since such cities as Arvad, Simyra, and Ushana,
located much nearer the danger zone, did not find it necessary,
nevertheless, together with Tyre and Sidon, chose to submit
himself to the powerful intruder rather than join Hazael against
the foe. It was a decision of far-reaching consequences for
subsequent history, and bred an implacable hatred for Israel
which was later to spur Hazael on to commit terrible atrocities
when once he was relieved of the Assyrian menace and able
to wreak his vengeance on Israel.

Damascus must have acutely realized its extremely precarious position as Shalmaneser drew near in 841. The new
Aramaean leader indeed faced a formidable situation. With
the death of Benhadad I (Adadidri) the Syrian coalition had
fallen to pieces. It is not impossible that Hazael made desperate

overtures to the former allies of his predecessor to rally once more against a common peril. If such was the case, he was unsuccessful, for in 841, as well as in 837, Damascus stood alone against Shalmaneser.[15] Most of the middle Syrian states must have submitted to the Assyrian advance, especially Hamath, whose position as a sort of buffer state had protected Hazael's realm from the north.

The Assyrian army encountered Hazael entrenched at the mountain of Saniru "in front of the Lebanon", that is the Antilebanon range, at whose southern end Saniru or Hermon[16] is located.[17] Shalmaneser, according to a fragment of his Annals, overthrew Hazael, slaying 6,000 of his warriors,[18] capturing 1,121 of his chariots, 470 of his cavalry, together with his camp.[19] Whether the armies of Hazael, which the Assyrian says the Aramaean mustered "in great numbers", made his victory so costly that he was unable to lay seige to Damascus, is not known. At any rate the stronghold of Aramaean power remained intact, and the Assyrian had to content himself with laying waste the beautiful orchards and vineyards of the fertile Ghuta, and despoiling and devastating towns as far as Hauran. From this point he turned eastward to the coast, marching to Râs el-Kelb (Mount Ba'li-ra'si), a promontory at the Dog River above Beirût, where he erected a stele. At this time he received tribute from Tyre, Sidon, and from " Jehu of Beth-Omri " (Samaria).

The Israelite king seems to have presented himself in person at some designated place before the Assyrian emperor. The famous Black Obelisk, recording the military achievements of the first thirty-one years of Shalmaneser III's reign and containing reliefs depicting the payment of tribute from five different regions, actually pictures Jehu humbly prostrating himself before the Assyrian monarch, accompanied by Israelites bearing precious metal and other gifts.[20] The inscription reads: " Tribute of Iaua (Jehu) of Beth-Omri, mâr Ḫumrî. Silver, gold, a golden bowl, a golden beaker, golden goblets, pitchers of gold, lead, staves (?) for the king, javelins, I received from him ".[21]

For several more years Damascus was occupied with the peril of imminent attack from Assyria. In 837, in the twenty-first year of his reign, Shalmaneser III made a final effort to subdue Hazael. The Obelisk mentions his advance into central

Syria, the capture of four of Hazael's cities, and the collection of tribute from Tyre, Sidon, and Gebal (Byblus).[22] In contrast to Hazael, these coastal cities seemed prepared to pay any reasonable price to keep their trade routes free from interference. It was unquestionably Hazael's valorous and stubborn stand that frustrated Assyria's attempt to reduce Central Syria. His success in thwarting such a formidable danger practically single-handed not only evidenced his military prowess, but also proved his indomitable spirit and boded ill for those who like Israel had dared to conciliate the foe and had refused to aid him in his hour of desperate need. Although Jehu is not specifically named among the tributaries of 837, the die had been cast several years previously, and Hazael never forgave his southern neighbour. When Shalmaneser now had to abandon his Syrian campaigns to attend to more pressing problems in the North, Hazael at last found his long-awaited opportunity. As neither the Assyrian monarch nor his son Shamsi-Adad V (824–810) undertook a new campaign against Middle or Southern Syria, the Syrian king was left with free rein to resume his war with his southern neighbour, which, although it had had an inauspicious beginning, and had been interrupted for a protracted period by the Assyrian advance, could now be resumed with full success and with the same energy that enabled him to hold out single-handed against the Assyrians.

The biblical account of Jehu's regime, despite the fact that it is taken up almost exclusively with the usurper's religious and political revolution, significantly takes note of the fact that Hazael relentlessly harassed Israel, especially in the east-Jordanic country. By this time Jehu must have realized how badly he had gauged the international situation by placating Assyria. But this was not the worst feature of his regime. The new dynasty ostensibly lacked the vigour to evoke a unified response in the people who had been severely shaken by the events of the revolution, and to create a consolidated military power, as the Omrides had done. Consequently, Hazael was victorious in the entire region east of the Jordan. " All the land of Gilead . . . and Bashan "[24] and perhaps the highlands of Galilee, as Meyer[25] suggests, were lost to Israel, although it is very conjectural that Hazael actually conquered Jehu, or reduced him to a state of vassalage.

II. HAZAEL AND JOAHAZ

At Jehu's death in 815 a renewal of Hazael's relentless attacks on Israel soon reduced his son Joahaz (815–801)[26] to an extreme stage of abasement. Syrian armies overran the whole country and the Israelite king, whose realm had shrunk to such an extent as to comprise only the hill country of Ephraim,[27] became little more than a retainer of the Aramaeans. The brief data concerning the reign of Joahaz are contained in II Kings xiii, 1–9, 22, 25.[28] The Chronicler's note contained in verse 7, which is of special historical value in delineating the ignominious status of the Israelite king under his Aramaean overlords, reads like an extract from a treaty concluding a defeat. With an army of but 50 horsemen, 10 chariots, and 10,000 men (more likely only 1,000)[29] the Israelite realm sank to a new low level of prestige.

The rigid military curtailment imposed upon Israel not only allowed the Aramaeans to pass at will through the country, but the example of Hazael's ruthless despoilment gave the signal for neighbouring states to make similar razzias, so that Israel was at the mercy of Philistines, Edomites, Ammonites and Tyrians, who further impoverished the land.[30] However, Syrian domination of the Northern Kingdom was doubtless gradual, and only completed toward the closing years of Joahaz's reign. As soon as he had succeeded in crushing Israelite power, Hazael was in a position to wage war against Israel's former enemies—the Philistines and Judah. The Philistine plain from the Mediterranean Sea to Aphek in Sharon (Râs el 'Ain), which, according to the tradition preserved in the Greek text of Lucian in II Kings xiii, 22 had belonged to Joahaz, passed over into Hazael's control,[31] and with it important Arabian and Egyptian trade monopolies.[32] These successes exposed the Philistine city of Gath, which lay west of Judah, to Hazael's arms. After capturing, and probably sacking the city,[33] nothing stood in the way of a campaign against Jerusalem. To avoid the miseries of a siege Joash ransacked the temple of its sacred treasures and gold, amassed since the days of Jehoshaphat, and with the available funds in the royal coffers, dispatched a substantial gift to Hazael, most likely accompanied by the assurance of an annual tribute, so that the Syrians did not attack the city.[34] Apparently because of a failure or refusal to pay the tribute, a small detachment of the Syrian army was sent against the city the following year, which, despite overwhelming odds, won a decisive victory. This time the " princes of the people " were despoiled, and their wealth confiscated by " the king of Damascus ".[35]

As far as the extension of his sway toward the south is concerned, Hazael appears as the greatest of the Aramaean conquerors, and well on the way toward the realization of a Syrian-Palestinian empire. The moot question as to whether he extended his dominion to any appreciable extent toward the north can hardly be settled one way or the other in the absence of express tradition. Kraeling is undoubtedly correct in concluding from available data that Hazael " wisely abstained from giving offense to Assyria by undue efforts in the north ".[36] Jepsen, on the other hand, undertakes to adduce reasons to support the theory that Hazael not only projected his conquests in Northern Syria in greater or less degree to the Taurus, but also by dint of force established a " confederated state " to take the place of the former Syrian confederacy of his predecessor.[37] His arguments, however, are for the most part singularly inconclusive. He maintains that the extension of Hazael's power toward the north is indicated by the fact that when the Assyrians under Adadnirari III in the years 805–802 advanced westward against the Syrian princes, who in the time of Shamsi-Adad V had rebelled and withheld their tribute, they had in any case to advance against Damascus, because there was the centre of resistance. There is no question concerning the ascendency of Damascus among the Aramaean states at this time, but there is scarcely any evidence in these data to suggest a " confederated state ". There is, in fact, a conspicuous lack of any indication of concerted action such as characterized a united Syria under Hadadezer. To be sure Damascus was not actually taken by Adadnirari III, but it was shown to be conquerable and placed under heavy tribute.[38] Significantly no mention occurs of any extraordinary battle or unusual resources of men or means thrown into the balance in defence of the city, as would be expected in the case of the capital of a " confederated state ", especially so, if, as Jepsen holds, Hazael had actually conquered the North Syrian princes, and thereby subjected them to compulsory military conscription.

The situation described in I Kings xx, 1, moreover, cannot

be employed to support the thesis of Hazael's North Syrian Empire.[39] Although the thirty-two kings joined with the Damascene ruler remind one of the state of affairs existing in the Zakir Stele, only by the most tenuous inferences[40] can the passage be placed in the Joahaz-Joash era, or the king Adadidri (Benhadad I) be identified with Hazael's son, Benhadad II. If the situation is considered as incongruous in Hadadezer's day, let it be remembered that available evidence exhibits this Aramaean ruler as much more successful in attaining real Syrian solidarity than Hazael with his programme of conquest.

The evidence from the Zakir Stele that the later Syrian kings extended their hegemony northward is more conclusive.[41] When Benhadad II went against Hazrak (biblical Hadrach), the kings of the North Syrian states levied their troops for him, as the inscription relates. Although the prestige of Damascus in North Syria is of course clearly discernible in this circumstance, it is quite unnecessary to assume with Jepsen[42] that the situation reflects a forced submission on the part of the Syrian princes to the Damascene king as the head of a confederated state, which, in turn, must be further assumed to have been built up, not by Benhadad II himself, but by his predecessor, Hazael. The state of affairs merely portrays another Syrian coalition after the Adadidri model, with participation on a more or less voluntary basis. Benhadad II seems to have displayed some of the diplomatic acumen of Hadadezer, which apparently Hazael lacked.

Although substantial evidence is accordingly lacking for extensive conquests in the north during Hazael's reign, comprising a unified Aramaean state in which there was compulsory military service, his rule nevertheless brought his country to the position of the chief power in all Syria, and embraced the period of the greatest territorial control. He seemingly relied upon conquest and coercion rather than upon diplomacy and statesmanship, and the reappearance of Assyria under Adadnirari III supplied the crucial test of his administration. The decisive shaking of his power in the last years of his reign demonstrates the essential failure of his policy. Conquest and coercion were found to be much less effective in producing real Syrian solidarity than persuasion and diplomacy. Whereas a unified Syria had met and checked Shalmaneser's career at the time of Hadadezer, Adadnirari III's march westward gives no evidence at all of such unity of action. Granting that Damascus escaped actual destruction, it apparently did so through its own resources, which, however, were insufficient to save it from the exactions of an oppressive tribute. Even the countries which Hazael is known to have taken, such as *Bit-Humri* (Israel) and Palastu (the land of the Philistines), revolted in the crisis, and sent tribute to Assyria.[43]

Notwithstanding his failure to achieve an intrinsic solidarity among the Syrian states, which alone could have successfully repelled Assyrian aggression in the West, Hazael remains as one of the most significant of the Aramaean kings of Damascus, who unquestionably made a lasting impression upon his time. Israel especially had ample reason to remember him as the most terrible of Aramaean oppressors, who reduced them to a pitiable state of weakness and " threshed Gilead with threshing instruments of iron". The prophet's announcement that Yahweh would " send a fire into the house of Hazael ", that would " devour the palaces of Benhadad " must have been welcomed with unmitigated joy.[44]

The precise date of Hazael's death is enshrouded in considerable obscurity. According to II Kings xiii, 22 the Aramaean strongly pressed Joahaz " all the days of Joahaz ".[45] Taken in a strict sense this notice would place Hazael's decease after the death of Joahaz (*c.* 815–801). Accordingly, after a long reign of at least forty years (like David, Solomon, Asa, and Uzziah in Judah, and like Jeroboam II in Israel), Hazael died in the year 801, or slightly later. Jepsen is correct in maintaining that this hypothesis rests upon concrete data which scarcely permit of another meaning, and is to be accepted until proof to the contrary is adduced.[46] The fact that Adadnirari III for the year 802 (and perhaps several years earlier) names *Mari'* as king of Damascus must be explained under the supposition that this term is a second name of Hazael, and is merely a popular title of the kings of Damascus.[47] Doubtless significant in this connection is the inscription found on one of the ivories from Arslan Tash in North Syria, which carries the name of Hazael. The fragment, obviously a dedication, is addressed to " our lord Hazael " למראן חזאל.[48] Other similar ivories were discovered at Nimrud, ancient Ninevah, and are securely dated by an Assyrian tablet of inventory, which lists them as booty from Damascus taken in the time of Hazael's successor.[49]

CHAPTER VIII

DAMASCUS AND THE
RESURGENCE OF ISRAEL'S POWER

BENHADAD II succeeded his father Hazael as king of Damascus at the latter's decease about 801 B.C.[1] Although the son of a usurper, and therefore not in the old dynastic succession, he nevertheless assumed the dynastic name at the death of his sire. In view of the gaps in our sources it is at present futile to attempt to solve the difficulties connected with the royal succession at this particular period. To state the precise relationship of Hazael and his son, Benhadad II, to the name *Mari'* of the contemporary Assyrian records is as yet impossible. All that can be said is, that if *Mari'* does not refer to Hazael, in which case we must reject the concrete data contained in II Kings xiii, 22, then the name is to be applied to Benhadad, for according to the evidence of II Kings xiii, 24 and the Zakir Stele there are no grounds whatever to insert another Damascene king, named *Mari'*, either before or after Benhadad II.

It thus remains to be seen that only new archaeological discoveries can solve the uncertainty. Just as the recent discovery of the Melcarth Stele has dissipated any remaining perplexity concerning the relationship of Benhadad I and Adadidri of the Assyrian monuments, so it may be confidently hoped that further royal inscriptions or other evidence bearing on the names of the kings of Damascus may be found to settle decisively the problem of the Assyrian appellation *Mari'*. It seems consonant with the evidence as it now stands[2] to construe the term as another name employed by Adadnirari III for Hazael, since it is difficult to place Hazael's decease earlier than 801 B.C.

I. BENHADAD II AND JOASH

Adadnirari III's conquests in Northern Syria (805–802), including his victorious campaign against Damascus, resulted in such a decisive weakening of Aramaean power during the last years of Hazael and on into the reign of his son Benhadad II that an extended period of recuperation and prosperity became possible for Israel. The task of restoring Israelite fortunes, which had fallen to such a low ebb, was reserved for Joash, the son of Joahaz, the twelfth king of Israel (c. 801–786), who " took again out of the hand of Benhadad the son of Hazael the cities which he had taken out of the hand of Joahaz his father by war. Three times did Joash smite him, and recovered the cities of Israel".[3] Although we do not possess concrete data regarding the precise extent of the territorial cessions of Joahaz, apart from the brief notice concerning the land of Philistia in the Greek Text of Lucian,[4] it can scarcely have been a matter of the Transjordanic country, as Jepsen[5] surmises, but must have also embraced the highlands of Galilee, as Meyer[6] suggests, if indeed not the general territory north-east and north-west of Samaria, exclusive of the hill country of Ephraim, to which Joahaz's realm must have been reduced in the days of his extreme abasement. Joash's territorial retrievement may accordingly be thought of as considerable.

Joash's war with Amaziah, significantly mentioned in the very sketchy notices in II Kings xiii,[7] and the data concerning his Aramaean successes are sufficient to indicate the outstanding events of his reign, which resulted in a resuscitated state and laid the foundation for a subsequent rule which raised Israel to the zenith of its power. The large contingent of Israelite troops hired by Amaziah from Joash's army[8] to prosecute his war against the Edomites, shows the latter had built up a powerful fighting force from the scattered remnants the Aramaeans had left Joahaz. Joash's brilliant victory at Beth-Shemesh[9] over Amaziah's forces, flushed with their recent triumph over the Edomites, furnishes additional evidence of the Israelite king's ability to restore the fortunes of his realm. His capture of Jerusalem and his destruction of a portion of the city wall, appropriating the treasures of the temple and the royal house, and carrying away hostages to Samaria to ensure the loyalty of the vanquished, not only greatly strengthened and enriched his kingdom, but made Judah practically a vassal.

II. BENHADAD II AND ZAKIR OF HAMATH

Benhadad II signally failed to protect the Syrian conquests his father had won in the South. Joash's vigorous restoration of the Israelite state set it well on the way toward regaining some of the power and prestige it had enjoyed under the Omrides, and effectually put an end to any Aramaean hopes of aggression toward the South. Benhadad II was clearly put on the defensive, in so far as Israel was concerned. Whether or not Joash succeeded in retrieving all alienated Israelite territories and in pushing Damascus back to its original borders, which is doubtful, Benhadad II's power still remained formidable despite its decisive weakening by Adadnirari III. There is nothing, however, in the fragmentary inscriptions of the Assyrian conqueror to indicate that he was able to curb Aramaean might permanently nor anything to suggest that Damascus continued to render tribute to him until his death in 782 B.C. Indeed, subsequent events show that his control over the city was ephemeral, consisting mainly in carrying away rich booty and in paying enormous tribute. The Aramaeans soon regained their customary place in Syrian leadership with the withdrawal of enemy troops.

Especially in Central and North Syria Damascene prestige displayed a remarkable vitality as is illustrated by the Zakir Stele. This important monument, discovered by Pognon in 1903, and published in 1907 in his *Inscriptions sémitiques de la Syrie, de la Mésopotamie et de la Région de Mossoul*, makes a very significant and astonishing reference in lines four and five to Benhadad II, that is, " Birhadad son of Hazael, king of Aram ", who is presented as heading a coalition of twelve to eighteen kings of North-Syrian states[10] against " Zakir king of Hamath and Lu'ash ". The operations of the confederation, in which only seven of the kings take part, as Zakir expressly mentions, are directed against Hazrek (biblical Hadrach[11]), the capital city of Lu'ash, a North Syrian principality south-west of Aleppo,[12] and north of Hamath, identified with the region appearing as Nuḫašše in the Amarna Letters.[13]

Besides the Aramaeans of Damascus under Benhadad II, who heads the list of the confederates as the leader of the coalition, Bargush occurs first as the king of Arpad, north of Aleppo;[14] next appear the king of Que, in Cilicia, the king of

'Umq on the lower courses of the Nahr 'Afrin and Kara Su, west of Aleppo; the king of Gurgum in the north Amanus mountains on the border between Syria, Cilicia, and Cappodocia; the king of Sam'al which lies in the plain of the upper course of the Kara Su between the Amanus and the Kura Mountains, and bounded on the south and the north by the above-mentioned states, 'Umq and Gurgum; and the king of Miliz, on the upper Euphrates, identified with Milid of the cuneiform texts.[15]

The real cause of the attack of the hostile coalition under Benhadad II appears, as was first correctly pointed out by Noth,[16] and later by Alt,[17] in the combination of Hazrek of Lu'ash with Hamath under Zakir's rule. This merger of two powerful and independent states in a "personal union", indicated by the double titulary of Zakir "king of Hamath and Lu'ash", and having a parallel in the Old Testament passages in which David and Solomon are designated as "kings of Israel and Judah",[18] was fraught with such peril to Damascus and the other North Syrian states that they were ready to resort to war in order to break it up.

Zakir plainly began his royal career as "King of Hamath", and the successor of the well-known Irḥulenu, who figures prominently in Shalmaneser III's records. His subsequent solemn enthronization over Lu'ash in the royal city of Hazrek[19] can mean only the addition of a new and independent kingdom to his royal domain. This ominous event called for the attack of the North-Syrian princes under the leadership of Benhadad II, king of Damascus, as is shown in the stele by its direct association with Zakir's accession to the throne of Lu ash in the capital Hazrek. Such a substantial increase in Hamath's prestige was sufficient to upset the balance of pow'er in Syria, and Benhadad II, who had reason to be made sensitive to declining Aramaean might by his losses to Israel in the South, was not slow to see in it a serious threat to the position of Damascus as still the leading power in all Syria.[21]

It is possible, of course, that the general political situation of the time was a prime factor in the Syrian coalition's move against Hazrek. The hypothesis[22] that Zakir was pro-Assyrian and that his extension of power jeopardized the other Syrian states especially Damascus in its consistently anti-Assyrian policy, is probable, but at best uncertain, for it is unhappily not known exactly what significance the campaigns of the Assyrians against Ḫatarikka (Hazrek), reported in the Eponym List for the years 772, 765 and 755, had.

In a very realistic fashion Zakir describes the siege of Hazrek and his victory over the hostile combination. The efforts of the attackers to undermine or scale the city walls were unsuccessful. The king piously attributes his success to Baalshamain (" Lord of Heaven "), who, in the light of the role the deity plays, is most probably to be thought of as the native god of Luʻash, and dutifully erects his stele in the sanctuary of Iluwer, a deity well-known from the Assyrian godlists, and identified by E. Ebeling with *i-lu-mi-ir* (god *mir*) equals (ilu) Adad.[23] Thus Zakir was able not only to preserve the dual kingdom for himself, but also evidently for his successors, for in the year 738 the city Ḫatarikka appears in the Annals of Tiglathpileser[24] as belonging to the territory of the kings of Hamath.

It is significant that Luʻash does not appear as such in the Assyrian records, but under the name Ḫatarikka, one of the cities of the kingdom of Hamath. The reason, as Alt[25] observes, is that it was really a state per se, being the chief place of an old political entity to which it gave its name. When the land of Luʻash became an Assyrian province in 738, in accordance with Assyrian custom, it received the name of its chief city Ḫatarikka,[26] just as Israel was called Bît-Ḫumri, i.e. Samaria. Accordingly, when the Eponym List indicates campaigns " against Ḫatarikka " for the years 772, 765, and 755 B.C., of course, the city alone is not meant, but the whole region of Luʻash of which it formed the capital.

The language and script of the Zakir Stele clearly point toward the period of Aramaean absorption of North Syria. The dialect is Aramaic with a dominantly Canaanite vocabulary. Zakir bears a good Aramaic name, while a generation previously the king of Hamath still bore a " Hittite " name Irḫulenu, demonstrating how in the interval the Aramaean element had come into the ascendency.[27] Alt explains the fact that the Zakir inscription is composed in Semitic and not in the Hittite script and the non-Semitic speech connected therewith, by concluding that the state of Ḫatarikka possessed a system of chirography independent of Hamath, where, he says, the hieroglyphic writing was ostensibly official, as the inscriptions from the city

and its immediate environs prove, and that Zakir respected this
state of affairs after the consummation of the personal union
with Hamath, he himself employing the language of his new
realm in his character as king of Lu'ash.[28]

After his victory over Benhadad II and the hostile coalition,
Zakir's energies, according to lines five to fifteen of the third
block of his inscription, were expended in strengthening the
defences of his kingdom, building cities, and erecting temples
for the gods that had aided him. In connection with his building
operations he mentions 'pš, long thought to be a common
noun, but which Dussaud[29] and Albright,[30] upon the disclosure
of the place where the stele was found at Pognon's death,
correctly construed as a place name, identical with modern
Âfis,[31] one of the cities which Zakir built, and in which he set
up his stele.

With such a powerful and victorious dual kingdom as
Hamath-Lu'ash to the north of him and a revived Israelite
state to the south, which had already won substantial victories
over his armies, retrieving important territories and growing
steadily stronger, Benhadad II faced a discouraging prospect
for the future of Damascene prestige in Syria, if indeed he did
not actually perish in the battle before Hazrek,[32] which is
possible, for with the prominent and very significant reference
to him in the Zakir Stele, he is lost to our sources. It is obvious,
therefore, that the date of the stele is of considerable importance
to our understanding the career of this Aramaean king. Unfortunately present available evidence will not permit a very
precise dating for the inscription. Noth[33] says it stems from
the beginning of the eighth century, and this is unquestionably
correct as far as a *terminus a quo* is concerned, for Benhadad
can scarcely have come to the throne before 801 B.C.[34] Possible
datings, however, may extend to about 773. Albright fixes
775 B.C. as an approximate date,[35] which might then place the
battle of Hazrek some five or ten years earlier, since Zakir
built Âfis, where he erected his stele, after his triumph over
Benahad II's coalition. If, however, the events of the relief
took place in the first decade of the eighth century, a possible
connection with the trouble in Manṣuate is not excluded. This
region north of Hamath (later an Assyrian province) and mentioned in close connection with Ḥatarikka,[36] according to the
Eponym List, was the scene of an Assyrian campaign for the

year 797.[37] If, on the other hand, the stele is connected with events of 773, when the Eponym List records an Assyrian expedition against Damascus, and of 772 when an expedition against Ḥatarikka is catalogued, it must be assumed that the coalition of Zakir's Relief was anti-Assyrian and that Damascus is thus indicated as the leader of the hostile federation. It must further be supposed that the campaign " against Ḥatarikka " was an Assyrian relief expedition of the new king, Ashurdan, enabling the pro-Assyrian Zakir to win his celebrated victory.[38] This hypothesis, although tempting in the exigency occasioned by the gaps in our sources, is at best very uncertain. It is questionable whether we are to get our cue from the Assyrian records, as the events recorded on our stele, while of moment to the history of Syria, had perhaps little actual bearing on affairs in Assyria.

It is accordingly impossible as yet to date the Zakir Stele precisely or to arrive at the exact time of Benhadad II's death. He doubtless survived Joash, who passed away about 786, and thus may even have lived some thirteen or fourteen years into the reign of Jeroboam II.[39]

III. BENHADAD II AND JEROBOAM II

The successes of Joash against Syria, resulting in the winning back of territories lost by his father Joahaz, were continued with uninterrupted achievement by his son Jeroboam II (c. 786–746), who not only recovered all Israelitish areas which had in the course of the years fallen into the hands of the Aramaeans, but engaged in offensive campaigns against Damascus and other surrounding countries with such favourable issue that his long reign marked the acme of the political and commercial expansion of the Northern Kingdom.

The Southern Kingdom, under the reign of Uzziah (Azariah, c. 783–742), a contemporary of Jeroboam II, who was on peaceful terms with him, and equally victorious in his respective sphere of rule, likewise enjoyed a similar prosperity. For precisely the same reasons both together were able to lift the fortunes of the dual monarchy to a record peak, and to control combined territories practically coterminous with the Davidic and Solomonic realm. The death of Adadnirari III, which occurred early in the reigns of Jeroboam II and Uzziah, initiated a period of approximately forty years of comparative weakness in Assyria and consequent inaction in the West under Shalmaneser IV, Ashurdan III, and Ashurnirari V. This situation in which Assyria struggled for its life against the powerful Vannic kingdom of Armenia, coupled with the initial gains of Israel over Benahadad II, made possible by the latter's reverses at the hands of Adadnirari III and in the war with Zakir of Hamath and Lu'ash, placed Jeroboam II and Uzziah in positions of decided advantage in extending the borders of their realms.

Precisely how much Israelite territory conquered by Damascus Joash had already retrieved it is impossible to say, as we do not know the exact losses suffered by Joahaz.[40] At any rate Jeroboam II early in his reign rounded out the Israelite border, recovering all areas that had previously belonged to the Northern Kingdom—Ijon, Abel-beth-maacah, Janoah, Kedesh, Hazor, Galilee and all the land of Naphtali—precisely the areas which had been captured from Israel by Benhadad I some one hundred years before,[41] including the cultic centre at Dan and its environs, now once more Israelitish, as Amos viii, 14 shows.

Nothing is specifically mentioned concerning the land east of Jordan in the skeletal notices dealing with Jeroboam II's reign, but Amos,[42] foreseeing a threatening invasion by a foreign power, shows in his pointed warning to the self-secure Israelites of his day " who rejoice in Lo-debar, that say, ' Have we not taken Qarnaim by our own strength?' " that these places in Transjordan, significantly Qarnaim,[43] located as it is at such a distance toward Bashan, were again Israelitish possessions, and that the national boundary was fully rounded out.

ANCIENT
BIBLICAL WORLD
8TH CENTURY B.C.

CHAPTER IX

DAMASCUS IN THE PERIOD OF DECLINE

JEROBOAM II was not content with merely restoring the normal boundaries of Israel. The wave of prosperity which had already begun to rise under Joash, and which mounted higher and higher in the early years of his own long reign, spurred him on in the face of unparalleled opportunities for expansion afforded by the generally propitious conditions in the near-eastern world at the time. He was thus enabled to enlarge his boundaries by a programme of conquest which apparently involved the extension of Israelite power throughout central and southern Syria.

I. DAMASCUS UNDER JEROBOAM II

Although our sources for Jeroboam II's reign, besides the prophecies of Amos and Hosea,[1] are unhappily very brief and confined to two short notices in the book of Kings, yet these are comprehensive and do not lack evidence to suggest that Israel actually prosecuted a successful war of retaliation against Damascus. The decisive blow struck by Assyria under Adadnirari III, and the losses sustained in the defeat suffered by the coalition in its attack on Zakir of Hamath, together with the further attack by Shalmaneser IV in 773, although it apparently had no great success, yet, added to the previous reverses, was sufficient permanently to cripple Damascus' power, which had been so formidable in Syria for a century and a half, and usher in an era of decline from which the proud Aramaean state, so often at the head in Syrian affairs, seemed unable to lift itself. When an extended period began under Ashurdan III (771–754), in which Assyrian weakness and pre-occupation gave a free hand to the Syrian states, Damascus was evidently too much weakened to assert itself. Jeroboam, enjoying great power, must have seized the occasion to make a bold attempt to conquer Israel's inveterate foe, even if II Kings xiv, 28 is not accepted as historical. Nothing is known of the actual steps in the campaign by which this was accomplished. The Massoretic text simply states the result that Jeroboam "recovered Damascus and Hamath . . . for Israel".[3] The decided tendency of critical opinion is to reject the historicity of this redactorial addition upon the assumption that the editor in his own way misconstrued the data in verse 25. But it is difficult to see how Jeroboam could have " restored the border of Israel from the entrance of Hamath unto the sea of the Arabah " without conquering Damascus and extending his sway at least to the southernmost extremities of Hamath. Furthermore, this position is open to question in view of the redactor's record for a high degree of accuracy in the use of his sources. It is unreasonable to suppose that in this matter he gave free reign to his imagination when in other instances he reports accurately what he read in the records at his disposal, and especially, when, in a number of cases, these data have been fully verified by archaeology.[4]

On the contrary he obviously envisages the re-establishment of an earlier condition that had existed in the period of Israel's greatest territorial control in the Davidic-Solomonic era. David had subjugated Zobah, had conquered and garrisoned Damascus, and exacted tribute from the Aramaeans.[5] Hamath had submitted to his suzerainty in central and southern Syria by sending presents,[6] and Solomon, according to the sources employed by the Chronicler, had to dispatch an expedition to retain control of "Hamath-Zobah", which was doubtless Israelite territory inherited from David[7] and most certainly comprised the southernmost extremities of Hamath, called "the approach to Hamath", and the territory of Zobah to the south, lying between it and the Damascene realm.[8] Thus the editor of Kings sees "the entrance of Hamath",[9] which since the days of the conquest had been recognized as the accepted northern boundary of the promised land,[10] restored by Jeroboam as Israel's northern territorial limits.

Elliger[11] and Jepsen[12] accordingly are justified in maintaining the essential historicity of II Kings xiv, 28. However, it seems unnecessary to do so under the latter's assumption that a purely tributary relationship between Jeroboam II and Damascus and Hamath is intended, and that these Syrian states were not actually included in Israel's restored boundaries specified in verse 25. That such a tributary relation between Jeroboam II and these Syrian states is certainly included and was at the time politically possible throughout[13] is not to be controverted. But it is open to serious question whether the reference, at least to Damascus, does not go farther and embrace the actual defeat and conquest of Aram and the restoration of the northern Davidic border in Syria.[14] Even in the case of Hamath it is very likely that Jeroboam II annexed the southernmost extremities of the country, together with Zobah proper, from " the entrance to Hamath " between Kadesh and Riblah in a south-easterly direction to Zedad and Hazar-enan,[15] comprising precisely the territory controlled by David and Solomon.

It is evident, therefore, that the redactor of Kings had an actual territorial relationship and not merely a tributary status in mind when he read in the annals accessible to him facts which justified him in saying Jeroboam "restored Damascus and Hamath . . . to Israel". But inasmuch as Israel's territorial control in the case of Hamath in the Davidic-Solomonic era was strictly limited, the earlier relationship, which is said to be resumed, must have involved principally the payment of tribute. Only once do we read of such an arrangement between Hamath and Israel when King Thou recognized the supremacy of David in central and southern Syria by sending gifts, which David viewed as tokens of Hamath's capitulation to Israel, since he devoted the tribute to Yahweh along with the wealth of " all the nations he sudbued ".[16]

If the redactor in his sources came across something of a similar mission of Hamath[17] to Jeroboam II, he would be justified in maintaining that a corresponding relation between Israel and Hamath, as it had existed in David's time, had now been re-established. At any rate there are no reasons of consequence to oppose the hypothesis that the notice of II Kings xiv, 28 recapitulates data from earlier sources according to which a former territorial and tributary arrangement, which had existed between Hamath, Damascus and Israel had now been reinstated. To consider this passage as a gloss of a later scribe is hardly tenable, for the question remains what glossator of a later period would have had an interest in Jeroboam and his glorification, especially when he is presented in an unfavourable light with respect to his loyalty to Yahwism.[18]

Fortunately, other sources exist to prove the extraordinary prosperity of Jeroboam's reign. Recent excavations at Samaria[19] have considerably cleared up the stratigraphy of Israelite times, and periods IV to VI have been assigned to the eighth century when the city was most prosperous. Jeroboam refortified the city with a double wall, reaching to as much as thirty-three feet in width in exposed sections, comprising fortifications so substantial that the Assyrian army took three years to take the city.[20] The more splendid palace, built of limestone and boasting a strong rectangular tower and an extensive outer court, which has hitherto been assigned to Ahab, almost certainly belongs to Jeroboam II.[21] The jasper seal of " Shema, servant of Jeroboam ", discovered by Schumacher in his excavations at Megiddo, is to be identified with Jeroboam II, as is now epigraphically certain, and the life-like and magnificently wrought lion, which appears on it, furnishes evidence that art had greatly advanced.[22]

In addition to archaeology Amos' prophecies shed light on the vastly increased commerce and wealth of Jeroboam's realm and the consequent luxury and moral and social decline of the era. Jeroboam's reign gave ample opportunity for the collected tribute of a greatly augmented territory to flow into the coffers of Samaria and to create a very wealthy class, largely no doubt of the ruling strata and court favourites, while glaring social and economic inequalities were fostered by the selfish and unscrupulous conduct of the rich.[23] Simple dwellings of unburned brick were replaced in many instances by " houses of hewn stone ", and Ahab's ivory palace (decorations only are meant) was imitated by many of the wealthy of the land.[24] Luxurious feasts and entertainments were the order of the day among the rich.[25] Religious observances, although maintained at the central shrine at Bethel, and at Gilgal and Beersheba, which had associations with the early history of the nation and where worshippers from both Judah and Israel would attend, had degenerated into a hollow ritualism devoid of righteousness and morality.[26]

As Amos had foreseen, this unhealthy prosperity, engendering a false sense of security and built upon a flimsy foundation of moral injustice and social inequality, was not destined to be permanent. The house of Jeroboam is to be visited with the sword[27] and the people of Israel are to be carried "into captivity beyond Damascus"[28]—predictions which the next quarter century was to justify fully. Somewhere about 746 B.C., or perhaps a few years earlier, Jeroboam II died, and was interred with his ancestors at Samaria. His son Zechariah succeeded to the throne, but after a very brief reign of only six months was murdered by a usurper, thus initiating a period of sharp decline and destructive civil strife. Precisely about the same time momentous events were transpiring in Assyria. Another usurper, the great king Tiglathpileser III (745–727), came to the throne, who, in the course of the next two decades was to build up a mighty empire that would eventually spell the doom of both Damascus and Israel.

II. DAMASCUS UNDER REZIN

After the events recounted in the Zakir Stele, complete obscurity prevails concerning Benhadad II and his successor on the throne at Damascus. Rezin (c. 750?–732), whose name occurs as *Raṣunnu* in the Assyrian monuments, is the next Aramaean king met with in our sources. He first appears in the Annals of Tiglathpileser III,[29] leaving a gap in our knowledge as to who[30] reigned in the interim, or precisely when he succeeded to the throne. One circumstance, however, is apparent. Whoever[31] headed the Damascene state during Jeroboam II's reign, if perchance the kingship might not have practically been abolished during the acme of Israelite power, which is not impossible, was a mere puppet of the strong Israelite monarch. With the latter's death the Northern Kingdom rapidly declined from its position as the leading power in middle and southern Syria. The civil confusion and weakness incident upon the extinction of the Jehu dynasty by assassination, and the subsequent murder of the usurper Shallum after a rule of only a month, gave the dependent Syrian states, especially Damascus, opportunity to shake off Israelite control. The Aramaean state, now under Rezin, once more, after several decades of almost total political eclipse, assumed sufficient importance again to appear in contemporary records. Although its rise was only for a brief period before its conquest by Assyrian arms, it gave signs of its old aggressive leadership in Syrian independence.

The moment called for the formation of a new coalition of Syrian and Palestinian states after the older models once more to turn back the dangerous threat of a newly awakened Assyria again on the march. But a change had come in the political complexion of Syria-Palestine. The balance of power had shifted much farther to the south. The north Syrian states, which never seemed able or inclined to furnish leadership in movements for Syrian solidarity, do not do so now. Hamath, apparently not above a tributary status under Jeroboam II and subject to Assyrian campaigns in 772, 765 and 755, even during the years of Assyrian decline, was in no position to undertake the initiative. Damascus, just emerging from a period of practical vassalage to Israel, was too weak to assume the lead. Israel, harrassed by regicide and internal strife, was hard-pressed to maintain its own stability. Judah under Azariah, in the light of the previous prosperous decades of its history, and according to the biblical representations, is to be considered by far the strongest and most influential state in Syria-Palestine at the time,[32] and in the imminent need for concerted action to meet a mutual peril would appear as the natural leader of a new confederation.

But the question of moment remains—is there any evidence in the Assyrian records to suggest such a coalition headed by Azariah of Judah? The answer must be in the affirmative. Tiglathpileser III makes clear reference in his Annals to *Azriyau* of *Yaudu* (genitive, *Yaudi*) in connection with what is obviously just such an uprising of Syrian-Palestinian states.[33] The earlier Assyriologists such as George Smith, Eberhard Schrader, Rogers, and others naturally and correctly assumed that they had found in an Assyrian document the account of the activities of Azariah of Judah not dwelt upon in the Old Testament. The appearance, however, of Winckler's *Altorientalische Forschungen*[34] promulgating the unhappy idea that *Azriyau of Yaudi* had no connection with Azariah of Judah, but referred to a king of a small state in North Syria, has misled many, but fortunately not all scholars.[35]

It is now established that Winckler's identification of *Y'dy* (the name of a district of northern Syria in the Sham'al inscriptions) with *Ya-u-di* (Judah) of the cuneiform texts is philologically untenable.[36] It is doubtful if Winckler's hypothesis would have fared so well with its linguistic defects if apparently serious chronological difficulties had not seemingly stood in the way of identifying *Azriyau of Y'dy* with Azariah of Judah.[37]

However, Edwin R. Thiele in his study, "The Chronology of The Kings of Judah and Israel "[38] has, as the result of a painstaking analysis of the records of Tiglathpileser III,[39] substantially removed the chronological impediments, and demonstrates that Azariah of Judah appears in connection with the events of 743, instead of 738, according to the old erroneous view, which gave rise to so much confusion, and helped to countenance Winckler's false theory. Thus Azariah employed his prestige and power to organize and promote a plan of concerted resistance against Assyria. His disappearance from the Assyrian records with no mention of his fate, except that the far-reaching coalition was smashed by the military prowess of Tiglathpileser III, certainly indicates that he died shortly thereafter, probably not later than 742, but in any case before the Assyrians were ready for punitive action against him.[41] There are no grounds whatever, though, to postulate an Assyrian invasion of Judah and an attack on Jerusalem at this juncture, as Luckenbill does.[42] The failure of united action against Assyria, nevertheless, did eliminate Azariah as a political and military figure so far as Syria was concerned, as the speed with which the allies came to terms with the invader proves. Subsequent events in Ahaz's reign show that Damascus and the other Syrian states had merely been foul-weather friends of Azariah, as Benhadad I and Ahab had been more than a century before.[43]

Tiglathpileser III's relations with Israel, which are to be dated in 743 B.C., the same year as his contacts with Azariah,[44] found Menahem (c. 745–738, Albright's dates) on the throne. The latter seems to have been an officer in command of the royal troops in Tirzah when the Jehu dynasty was brought to an end by the usurper, Shallum. Like Omri, by avenging his sire, he was able to seize the royal power and establish a new dynasty.

To consolidate his shaky throne he found it necessary to make a public example of the recalcitrant city of Tiphsah, in the vicinity of Shechem,[45] which failed to submit to him, and also servilely to court the favour of Tiglathpileser " to confirm the kingdom in his hand ".[46] This is corroboratory evidence that his payment of an enormous tribute of 1,000 talents of silver to the Assyrian monarch took place in the earlier part of his reign in the neighbourhood of 743 B.C. rather than the commonly accepted date 738 B.C., by which time his throne, if ever, must have certainly been established in his hand.

A careful analysis of the lists of places from which and to which the Assyrians transported captives at that particular time points substantially to the same conclusion. Places from which captives were transported at the time of Menahem's payment of tribute to Tiglathpileser were places captured in or shortly before his third year.[47] The same is true of the places into which these captives were settled.[48] These data are very important for fixing the date of the payment of Menhem's tribute by virtue of the fact that captives were usually transported at the time of conquest or shortly thereafter.

Moreover, among those enumerated with Menahem as paying tribute to Assyria are: Kushtashpi of Kummuh, Rezin of Damascus, Hiram of Tyre, Urikki of Kue, Pisiris of Carchemish, Tarhulara of Gurgum and Sulumal of Melid.[49] It is noteworthy that all of these are likewise included among the Syrian and Palestinian states said to have been conquered and under a tributary status to Assyria in connection with Tiglathpileser's campaign against Urartu in his third year,[50] and that the tribute was received from the latter group "in Arpad".[51] The eponym canon, moreover, names Tiglathpileser "in Arpad" in this pivotal year, 743. Hence it seems reasonable to conclude that Menahem's payment of tribute to Tiglathpileser is to be dated with the events of the third year[52] and it is very probable that the Israelite king appeared in Arpad along with Kushtashpi of Kummuh, Rezin of Damascus, Hiram of Tyre, Urikki of Kue, Pisiris of Carchemish, Tarhulara of Gurgum and Sulumal of Melid to present his tribute with them in 743 B.C.

The fact that II Kings xv, 19, 20 names Pul as the Assyrian monarch to whom Menahem paid tribute is now no longer an occasion of difficulty.[53] Schrader[54] long since correctly maintained that the two were one and the same person, and there can now be no question as to their identity in view of the evidence furnished by a Babylonian King List and the Babylonian Chronicle.[55] In the King List *Pulu* appears as succeeding a certain *Ukin-zer*, who became a vassal king of Assyria, while in the Babylonian Chronicle Tiglathpileser is said to succeed him. Additional confirmation is furnished by Ptolemy's Canon, which lists Chinziros (clearly *Ukin-zer*) and Poros (a Persian corruption of Pul) as Babylonian kings for 731 B.C., the seven-

teenth year of the Nabonassar Era.[56] It is thus evident that
Pulu was the name assumed by Tiglathpileser as king of Babylon,
just as Shalmaneser V was known in Babylon as Ululai.

With the death of Menahem, which is possibly to be dated
as early as 742 or 741 as a result of the new analysis of the
records of Tiglathpileser,[57] his son Pekahiah scarcely ruled two
years before he was assassinated by his general Pekah, who
seized the throne and inaugurated a pro-Damascene policy.
The exorbitant and oppressive tribute under which Assyria had
placed Menahem[58] and doubtless his son, who was a mere
vassal of Asshur, must inevitably have produced a strong anti-
Assyrian party in Israel which demanded a change in policy,
even if it required deposition of the present king. There is no
evidence that Damascus and other Syrian states fared any better
at the hands of Assyrian tribute collectors, so the time was ripe
for revolt and the formation of a new anti-Assyrian coalition.
Pekah had no difficulty in finding a ready ally in Rezin, if
indeed the latter was not the real moving spirit and promulgator
of the new combination.[59] Tyre, Sidon, and Samsu, queen of
the Arabs, also found the movement to their own interests, and
were not hard to win over. But other Phoenician cities and
Palestinian states were necessary to the alliance if effective
resistance was to be offered to Tiglathpileser.

A breathing spell was afforded for the consolidation of
such a coalition by Assyria's campaign in Urartu (737–735).
Whatever Philistia and Edom did, and they seemed to have
joined under pressure, Judah under Jotham's son Ahaz (*c.*
735–715), remained adamant. To cripple Judah as an effective
opponent or to force Ahaz into the anti-Assyrian coalition,
Pekah and Rezin took advantage of Tiglathpileser's momentary
preoccupation with Urartu to advance against Jerusalem in the
early part of Ahaz's reign, perhaps the first year,[60] and thus
precipitated the Syro-Ephraimite war. The allied army laid
siege to Jerusalem as II Kings xvi, 5 indicates. Rezin had to
content himself meanwhile in a campaign to the south. He
captured the harbour of Elath, Judah's seaport on the Gulf of
Akabah, and restored it to the Edomites,[61] doubtless as a reward
for action against Judah[62] or for promised participation in the
coalition against Assyria.

The Chronicler records a great slaughter wrought by Pekah
and Rezin and the removal of large bodies of Judaean captives

and quantities of booty to Damascus and Samaria.[63] The scene is illuminated by the prophet Isaiah, whose encouraging announcement of the imminent doom of Damascus and Samaria was ignored by Ahaz, who immediately dispatched an embassy with tribute to summon the aid of Tiglathpileser[64] against Pekah and Rezin. Ahaz's momentous decision was to have far-reaching repercussions, and inaugurated a series of events that eventually led to the downfall of Damascus and Israel, as well as of Judah itself. Although the Assyrian did not respond at once, Pekah and Rezin were forced by circumstances to lift the siege of Jerusalem and to retire to the north to prepare for the inevitable clash with Assyria.

Ahaz's plea must have fitted in well with Tiglathpileser's own ambitions in Syria-Palestine, if indeed it did not furnish him with new ideas for rapid conquest. His response, which we may be sure was made in his own self-interest, took the form of a campaign to Philistia in 734. It was a move evidently aimed at splitting the allies, isolating Damascus, opening a way through northern Israel to the coastal plain, and effecting contact with Ahaz. In all probability it was on this expedition to the Philistine plain that Tiglathpileser struck his first blows at the Israelite kingdom and captured the cities of northern Israel in Dan and Naphthali, deporting the inhabitants to Assyria as II Kings xv, 29 recounts, although his own records leave the exact date ambiguous.[65]

With Israel duly castigated by loss of its northern territories, Tiglathpileser now turned to Damascus to punish the other prominent rebel, Rezin. Events centre there in the next two years (733 and 732) when Damascus again appears in the eponym list. Despite the mutilated and fragmentary condition of Tiglathpileser's records dealing with the siege and fall of Damascus, the salient facts stand out clearly. The Assyrian achieved the overthrow of the city and the Aramaean state of which it was the capital, a feat his predecessors had been vainly trying to accomplish for more than a half-century. The clash with Rezin clearly resulted in the shattering of Aramaean power, which had so frequently thwarted the Assyrian advance in times past. According to a section of the Annals[66] which in all probability refers to these events, Rezin fled into the city, his chief advisers were impaled, and the picturesque gardens and orchards of the fertile Ghutah were completely ravaged.[67]

In the long siege, of which little is known, for not even Tiglathpileser's description of it is extant, Panammu of Samal, one of the loyal Syrian tributaries of the Assyrian king, lost his life,[68] thus supplying a hint how intense the struggle was. The city finally capitulated in 732. Making due allowance for hyperbole on the part of the Assyrian annalists, the destruction in the Damascene region must have been terrific. Some 591 towns of the " sixteen districts of Aram " the Assyrian says "I destroyed like mounds left by a flood".[69] Ḥadaru, some fifty-two kilometres south-west of Damascus, said to be the birthplace of Rezin, was besieged and taken, and 800 of its citizens with their movable property were deported. Other cities suffered a similar fate.[70]

The concise but comprehensive biblical notice closely links the fall of the city with Ahaz's appeal and payment of tribute to Tiglathpileser. " And the king of Assyria hearkened unto him . . . and went up against Damascus and took it, and carried the people of it captive to Kir, and slew Rezin ".[71] Thus terminated the career of the last of the Aramaic rulers at Damascus, bringing to an end a long line of powerful kings who for almost two centuries were the inveterate foes of Israel, and who exerted an indelible influence on both the Northern and Southern Kingdom and the Syro-Palestinian world in general. With Rezin's death the Aramaic kingdom of Damascus passed away for ever.[72]

CHAPTER X

DAMASCUS AND THE LAST DAYS OF ISRAEL

WITH its fall to Assyria Damascus lost its political importance and entered upon a period of comparative insignificance. For the next several centuries references to it are very few and inconsiderable. The heyday of its political prestige as a virile Aramaean state of the ninth and eighth centuries B.C. had past, but the city continued its commercial prosperity[1] under Assyrian and especially under Persian rule. Not until the establishment of the Seleucid Kingdom, with its capital at Antioch, did Damascus lose its position as the chief city of Syria.

I. DAMASCUS AS AN ASSYRIAN PROVINCE

With the capture of Damascus in 732 its entire territory was incorporated into the Assyrian Empire and out of its area four new Assyrian provinces were carved—Ṣubutu, Dimašqu (Damascus), Qarninu and Haurena. The province of Ṣubutu lay north of Damascus between the latter and Hamath. Eastward it extended beyond the Lebanon to the independent kingdom of Gublu (Byblus) and Ṣurru (Sidon) on the coast, and southward it bordered on Damascus, which in turn extended on the west to Lebanon, and on the south to the district of Qarninu. The latter extended from the Jordan between the Waters of Merom and the Sea of Galilee eastward, with the province of Haurena to the south-east, and the province of Gal'aza (Gilead) to the south.[2] In addition to these conquests of 733–732 must be added Galilee and the Plain of Sharon, which were, in all probability, taken in the campaign to Philistia in 734. The province Du'ru (Sharon) was ruled from Dor and the province Magidu (Galilee) from Megiddo.[3]

With these seven new provinces added to the six which Tiglathpileser had already formed in Syria, namely: Arpad, Kullani, Ṣimirra, Ḫatarikka and Manṣuate the Assyrian Empire rapidly expanded in the West. However, Gebal, Sidon

102

and Hamath, besides the southern kingdoms, still remained autonomous. Judah under Ahaz, on the other hand, showed its vassalage by the appearance of its king at Tiglathpileser's court established in the newly conquered city of Damascus. There Ahaz offered his homage to Assyrian might, probably soon after the city fell in 732.

Shalmaneser V (726–722), who before the death of his father had received supreme command over the West, had doubtless by virtue of his position developed ambitions to extend the sway of the Assyrian Empire in that region even before he came to power. Accordingly, he undertook to expand toward the south. Samaria was besieged, with the result that probably already in 723 under Shalmaneser, or at any rate by the assession year of Sargon II (722–704) the city had fallen, and Israel was added to the growing list of Assyrian provinces.

It is in connection with the records of Sargon that the last reference of importance for our purpose is made concerning Damascus, and it is significant that it is in the consistent role of a fighter for freedom from Assyrian domination that the city last appears. Since a revived Assyria began marching toward the Westland under Ashurnasirpal II and Shalmaneser III, Damascus had consistently opposed Asshur's vaulting ambitions in Syria: now taking the lead in a coalition to defend Syrian independence, as under Benhadad I (Adadidri); now standing alone against Assyrian aggression, as under Hazael. The fact that the city-state as an Assyrian province, with perhaps the bulk of its loyal patriots removed and supplanted by Assyrians from other parts of the Empire, in accordance with the policy of Tiglathpileser, yet found strength and courage for a final struggle to throw off the Assyrian yoke, proves how virile was the Aramaean love for freedom and the city's spirit of independence.

Moreover, the last attempt at revolt against Assyria under Sargon, which took place in 720, apparently was not the first uprising of which the city was guilty after the loss of its independence in 732. In this connection it is surprising that for the year 727 the eponym canon lists an expedition against Damascus, which seems to indicate some sort of civil commotion there and consequent weakness of the provincial administration in the city, but scarcely furnishes evidence for the theory that a native line of kings was continued after the death of Rezin.[4]

Whatever the nature of the revolt of 727, it could hardly have occurred in connection with the death of Tiglathpileser, which occurred late in the year. It was without doubt speedily crushed. The revolt of 720, on the other hand, was in the nature of a coalition, and was more dangerous to Assyria.

Although the status of Damascus as an Assyrian province rendered leadership of a new Syrian combination practically impossible, Hamath, despite reduction in size, was still independent,[5] and under Ilubi'di (Yaubi'di)[6] furnished the necessary point of contact in middle Syria with Ḥanun of Gaza in Philistia,[7] who, having fled to Egypt in 734, had returned to his kingdom after Tiglathpileser's death and was now also ready to strike for freedom from Assyria. In consequence of new problems incident upon Sargon's usurpation of the throne, and with trouble in Babylonia and Elam, Syria had been somewhat neglected for several years. The moment was opportune for Ilubi'di to stir up the Assyrian provinces Arpad, Ṣimirra, Damascus and Samaria in revolt.[8] Amassing his forces, he took up his position at the historic fortress of Karkar, where over a century and a quarter previously the famous Irḫulenu had figured prominently in the Syrian coalitions under Damascus which had effectually stopped the incursions of Shalmaneser III. Doubtless he dreamed that similar success would crown his efforts. If so, his hopes were soon shattered, for Sargon struck very swiftly before his foes could consolidate their full strength and completely defeated them. Karkar was captured and burned. Ilubi'di was cruelly tortured and the accomplices of his revolt were put to death in their cities.[9] Hamath was also taken and made a province under Assyrian administrators.[10] Loyal Assyrians to the number of 6,300 were settled there, and a military levy was imposed.[11]

After crushing revolt in central and southern Syria, Sargon advanced to the south-west to meet Ḥanum of Gaza and Sib'u of Muṣri.[12] A battle ensued at Raphia at the very borders of Egypt, culminating in victory for the Assyrians. Sib'u escaped, but Ḥanum was captured and carried to Assyria in chains with 9,033 of his people and their possessions. Raphia was destroyed, but Gaza was apparently spared. Egypt was again in peril, as under Tiglathpileser III. Probably nothing but her traditional reputation and the memory of the days when she ruled Asia with the Ninevite kings courting her favour with gifts, kept

Sargon from pushing over her frontiers to see how miserably weak and divided she was under the different dynasts.[13] However, Sargon may have deemed that further advance upon Egypt was unwise until a greater consolidation of Assyrian power was effected in Syria. Hence the next several years witnessed much attention devoted to the settlement of its affairs.[14] City-states not directly implicated in the revolt were allowed autonomy under their local kings. Others, such as Hamath and Samaria, soon appear with Assyrian governors.[15] Those such as Damascus, Arpad and Ṣimirra, which had already been Assyrian provinces, and as such must have enjoyed a certain degree of autonomy to be free to join in a general uprising against Assyria, were now, we may be sure, placed under a most rigid administration. With the putting down of the rebellion of 720, the autonomy of both Damascus and Hamath were definitely past. The relations which henceforth existed were those of two Assyrian chief district cities.[16]

II. DAMASCUS AND THE FALL OF THE NORTHERN KINGDOM

Left with but a fraction of his former kingdom,[17] evidently comprising little more than the hill country of Ephraim, with the anti-Assyrian league broken up, with his main ally probably already put to death by the Assyrians, and Damascus and the greater part of his own realm under Assyrian control,[18] Pekah necessarily became very unpopular with his subjects toward the end of his reign. Although the wave of invasion from the north had spent itself, the extremity in which he as a consequence found himself made it almost inevitable that he would fall a victim to some plot that would accomplish his removal, and that would replace him on the throne by a successor who would be little more than a satrap of Assyria. The whole affair was doubtless instigated by pressure from Assyria, which seems the more likely inasmuch as Tiglathpileser claims that *Ausi'* (Hoshea) was his own appointee to the throne,[20] and inasmuch as the biblical notices name " Hoshea the son of Elah " not only as a conspirator, but as the actual murderer of the king.[21]

As the ruler of a greatly diminished territory, under heavy tribute, Hosea was placed in a strictly dependent and peculiarly difficult position to guard the interests of his sovereign Tiglathpileser. With the country impoverished by oppressive exactions, a political party arose in Samaria which advocated forming an alliance with Egypt in hope of finding some relief or even a measure of independence from Assyrian domination. Hoshea doubtless found himself essentially in sympathy with the patriotic movement, and yet all the while was faced with his prime duty as Tiglathpileser's appointee of keeping his people from disloyalty to Assyria. A similar situation of political intrigue seems to have existed in Damascus at this time, whether under a governor or a local king. Tiglathpileser's appointee there must have been won over, or felt himself naturally in sympathy with the local patriotic movement that apparently led to an uprising of some sort, and an Assyrian expedition to the city in 727.

The prophet Hosea gives us a glimpse into the political duplicity of the time at the court of Samaria when the people "call unto Egypt", and at the same time "go to Assyria"[22]; when "they make a covenant with Assyria, and oil is carried into Egypt".[23] The death of Tiglathpileser in 727 greatly increased the temptation to treasonable action, and Hoshea yielded, apparently at first refusing to render tribute to the new Assyrian monarch Shalmaneser V, but presumably relenting upon a demonstration of Assyrian military might.[24] Grave suspicions were thus aroused concerning Hoshea's loyalty, and with the discovery of secret intrigues with "So king of Egypt"[25] and further failure to pay tribute, he was arrested and put into prison by Shalmaneser, who thereupon invaded the land and began the siege of Samaria.

The most important date in the reign of Hoshea is the siege and capture of Samaria by the Assyrians and the end of the Northern Kingdom. Biblical data place the beginning of the siege in the seventh year of Hoshea and the capture of the city three years later in his ninth year.[26] Since Hoshea succeeded Pekah in 732/731, the fall of Samaria must have taken place in 723/722, with the siege occurring 725/724 to 723/722. Following the biblical data Olmstead places the capture of the city in 723, and accordingly by Shalmaneser V rather than by Sargon.[27] But Sargon claims to have taken the citadel himself and deported its citizens in the *resh sharruti* or part of his reign before his first New Year.[28] If we accept his claim as genuine, then, following Albright and Begrich,[29] Samaria must have fallen between the accession of Sargon in December, 722, and the end of his accession year in the spring of 721. On the other hand, following the biblical data, if Samaria did not capitulate until the very last days of the final month of Hoshea's ninth year, there would still remain an interval of at least nine months between the capitulation of the city and Sargon's accession, since the Northern Kingdom would still have collapsed before the first of Nisan, 722.[30] It is thus obvious that if 732 is taken as the accession year of Hoshea, and the biblical notices are followed, Sargon could not possibly have captured Samaria in his accession year, though of course he could have been the one who transplanted the inhabitants.

It is well known that the biblical account makes no reference to Sargon in connection with the last days of Samaria. According to II Kings xviii, 9 Shalmaneser is specified as the king who commenced the siege, and according to II Kings xvii, 1–6 is presumably intended as the ruler who took the city, although, it is true, he is not expressly named as such. With regard to the relative reliability of the two sources, the Hebrew and the Babylonian, Olmstead[31] notes that II Kings xvii, 1–6 is apparently a trustworthy passage, going back to practically contemporaneous records, and that there existed no personal element to hinder the Hebrew writer from stating the facts as they were, for it was inconsequential to him or to the reputation of his people whether Shalmaneser V or Sargon was the captor of Samaria. He, therefore, either made a mistake, which is very improbable, or he gave the facts. In Sargon's account, however, there was present a tempting " personal equation " and the royal annalist would have every reason to carry over events which took place in the closing year of his predecessor into the initial year of his royal master. Olmstead[32] further maintains that in view of the " somewhat untrustworthy " character of the Annals and allied records, as well as the fact that no reference occurs to any capture of Samaria in the earlier documents, the accuracy of Sargon's own claim may well be viewed with scepticism.

Olmstead notes added corroboration of the accuracy of the Hebrew historian in the evidence supplied by the Babylonian Chronicle, in which the sole event of the reign of Shalmaneser noted is the taking of the city of Shamarain, equated with Samaria,[33] which, by reference to the Assyrian Chronicle is limited to the three years 725–723,[34] and only these three years, when expeditions are mentioned. The fact that the siege of Samaria according to the biblical data is said to have lasted three years, and the Babylonian Chronicle knew only of the capture of Shamarain for Shalmaneser's reign, the natural assumption is that this Assyrian king took Samaria in 723. Since the Assyrian Chronicle in its mutilated condition for the years 725–723 retains only the word "against" seems to Olmstead to warrant supplying "Samaria" from the Babylonian Chronicle. In the eponym chronicle, Luckenbill, from the above-mentioned evidence, likewise has restored the word "Samaria" for these three years.[35]

On the other hand, if Sargon actually took Samaria, as he claims, he did so between the last of December, 722, and the first of April, 721, the winter rainy season, which would have made it very difficult for the Assyrian army to march and when such an expedition would be very unlikely.[36] However, the siege may of course have been continuous. By way of summary, Olmstead's hypothesis contends that for the capture of Samaria by Sargon there is only his own claim recorded in a late series of documents which have frequently been proved inaccurate. Against it there is the silence of his own earlier accounts; also two other authorities, the Hebrew and the Babylonian, widely separated and unprejudiced; while a third, the native Assyrian, gives information which fits well into the chronological framework for the year 723. Olmstead therefore contends that to Shalmaneser is to be given the credit for the capture of Samaria in 723 rather than to Sargon between December, 722 and the spring of 721. Be that as it may, Sargon lists the taking of Samaria as the outstanding event of his first year, claiming to have deported 27,290 of its inhabitants (which he doubtless did, even if Shalmaneser really took the city) and settled other peoples in their place, appointing one of his officials as governor, and imposing tax and tribute.[37]

Thus the Northern Kingdom came to an end. By only a bare decade did it survive the Aramaean state of Damascus, with whose history it had run its course side by side for almost two centuries. For a good century and a half of this period, which was so closely interwoven with the destines of both kingdoms, the two rival states had been implacable foes. However, their final relations were amicable, although dictated by common distress and connected with their mutual decline.

Assyrian power, which for over a half-century had begun to loom up as a threat to Syrian independence, finally overwhelmed both nations, and the futile revolt of 720, in Sargon's second year, supplied sufficient proof that Assyrian might had come to stay.

NOTES TO CHAPTER I

1. John L. Myres, "The Ice Age in the Near East", *The Cambridge Ancient History*, Vol. I, p. 43.

2. The occurrence of *Timasku* in Thutmose III's list of conquered Asiatic cities belonging to his first Asiatic campaign (*c.* 1468) is the first definitely attested appearance of the name of the city in ancient contemporary records (cf. chapter II, n. 18). Albert T. Clay's identification of Damascus with *Qi-mash-qi* of the inscriptions of Gudea and Dungi is rejected by all competent scholars today (*Amurru The Home of The Northern Semites*, p. 128). Despite the fact that the city is very ancient, it was evidently not of sufficient importance to be mentioned in early Babylonian texts, at least in those that have survived.

3. *Mesopotamian Origins*, 1930, p. 154, n. 113. Cf. AASOR XIII, 1933, p. 33, n. 70.

4. "Ethnic Movements in the Near East in the Second Millennium B.C.", AASOR XIII, 1933, p. 25. Speiser bases his new interpretation on the practical absence of Hurrian names in the old Akkadian tablets from Gasur, referring to preliminary studies by T. J. Meek (AASOR 48, 1932, pp. 2–5, and in AASOR XIII, 1933, pp. 1–12. Cf. I. Gelb, Hurrians and Subarians, pp. 7 f., 52 f). Götze, too places the Hurrian migration after 1900 B.C. (AASOR XIII, p. 25, n. 47).

5. Speiser, *op. cit.*, pp. 32 f.

6. Cf. W. F. Albright, "The Egyptian Empire in Asia in the Twenty-First Century B.C.", *Journal of the Palestine Oriental Society* VIII, p. 254.

7. Speiser cites *Mat-qa*, near Kimash, and Mount *Bidir-gi* in Zamua as parallels (*op. cit.*, p. 154, n. 113). Among other place names of the district he assigned to the Hurrian-Zagros groups are *Saniru* (Hermon), the mountain of Damascus, and Aleppo. Evidence for the latter he adduced from a then recently published text (*Royal Inscriptions from Ur*, 275, 1, 5–10, ed. Gadd and Legrain, publications of the Joint Expedition of the British Museum and the Museum of the University of Pennsylvania to Mesopotamia, Philadelphia, 1928), according to which Naram-Sin was the first to sack the western

centres, Arman and Ibla, in an expedition which took the king from the Euphrates to the city of Ulisu (later Ulaza, which has a sibilant suffix of the type occurring in the districts of Arrapkha and Lullu). Sidney Smith, the editor of the above-mentioned text, considered it probable that the pronunciation Arman, *Ialman*, or *Halman* (cf. Speiser, *op. cit.*, pp. 89, 92) resembled the city of the same name in Lullu. If the variants be admitted as a rendering of Arman in Amurru, it would obviously represent the earliest name of Aleppo (Halpa of the Hittite texts). Speiser accepts the correctness of Smith's theory, and maintains the name must belong to a language related to that of the Lullu, as peculiarities of form and pronunciation could not be accidental (Speiser, *op. cit.*, p. 154, n. 113).

8.   In new excavations at Nuzi 1930/31 the level of the old Akkadian period was reached, yielding more than two hundred tablets written in the dialect of that era. Of some five hundred personal names found in the tablets many were Akkadian, some Sumerian, practically none Hurrian (Gelb, *op. cit.*, pp. 7 f.; 52 f. Cf. T. J. Meek, " Old Akkadian, Sumerian, and Cappadocian Texts from Nuzi ", *Harvard Semitic Series* X, 1935, for copies of the texts, list of names, with introduction). Cf. Gelb, *op. cit.*, p. 53 for his dating of the Gasur documents in the middle of the third millennium B.C., as had been well noted already by Meek (*ibid.*, p. XII).

9.   Genesis xi, 2.

10.   Shamash was also extensively employed as the name of the sun-god of the Aramaeans and the Amorites as both the Amarna letters and the Mari tablets show.

11.   Cf. note 10 Chapter V for evidence of importation of western deities into Mesopotamia at an early period. Also Dhorme, *Syria*, 1927, p. 40.

12.   A. T. Clay, *Amurru the Home of the Northern Semites*, pp. 77, 126; 128–131.

13.   Clay's theory, for example, assumes that the deity's habitat was in the mountain *Mash* and was called *Sha-Mash*, i.e. " He of Mash ", equivalent to "The God of Mash", or *El Shammash*. While numerous parallels, it is true, may be cited for such a use of *sha* in Akkadian-Babylonian both in common nouns and in proper names (for example *shabru* means "man of seeing", and *Sha-Addu* is a proper name) yet to assume such a derivation of Shamash is unwarranted inasmuch as the location of the mountain of Mashu is uncertain, and may not have been considered as the

god's habitat at all. Moreover, a totally different derivation may have been at the basis of the god's name (e.g. from the triliteral root שׁמשׁ. Besides there are philological difficulties following the parallel use of the Arabic relative, in offering an explanation of Damascus, *Dimashqu* similar to Shamash, as Clay ventures to do. The sibilant in Dammeseq, too, is clearly different from that in Shamash. The further assumption that the name Mesheq arose from the cuneiform writing of the name *Mash(qi)* is extremely precarious inasmuch as *Qi-mash* (*qi*) of the inscriptions of Gudea and Dungi is located probably in the Zagros mountains rather than in the Antilibanus.

14. Paul Haupt (ZDMG 63, p. 528), arbitrarily assuming an original form *Dar-mashqi*, connects with the Hebrew root שׁקה. But the name משׁק cannot well have anything to do with " well-watered country," despite Hebrew *Mashqê*, " well-watered terrain " (Gen. xiii, 10), and the town of *Meshqu* (*âl Me-iš-qí*, a perfectly good place name) in the Jordan Valley, which occurs in a little under-stood Amarna letter of Mut-Ba'lu, prince of Pella, to Yanhamu (Albright, BASOR, 89, p. 14). The modern Arabic place-name, *Mesqī*, offers a similar usage (*loc. cit*. n. 39).

15. Both *Dammeseq* and particularly *Darmeseq* may be Aramaic forms. It is significant that all the transcriptions from cuneiform are with one *m* (Kraeling, *Aram And Israel*, p. 47). משׁק (*meseq*) may be Arabic مشق *mišq*, meaning "terre rouge, Rötel, red chalk". The full name would be *dhu* (*dhî*) *mišq* (*mašq*), like *Di-zahav* for *dhî-dhahav*, " abounding in gold " (Deut. i, 1) and *Dhū-raidân*, *Dhū-rauyân* in South Arabic. Ugaritic offers names of gods formed with *dh*, as *'el d . p'ed*. Amarna forms *Dimashqa* and *Dumashqa* (Egyptian, *Ti-mś-gi*) also point to original *Dhi-mashqa*, with the feminine form for a land or town.

16. If the *hapax legomenon*, *mesheq* (Gen. xv, 2) means " acqui-sition, gain ", which is doubtful, then Dimashqu would mean " the one of acquisition ", "the place of gain ", a fit designation for a city on a commercial highway. Although the Arabic root دَمشَق (" to be quick, alert, active ") cannot reflect the origin of the city's name in its busy trade and industry for which it has been perennially famous, it probably does represent a later formation from the Arabic designation of the town, Dimashq, long after it had established a reputation as a busy emporium.

17. *Aram And Israel*, p. 47. Kraeling is incorrect in following W. M. Müller's erroneous identification of *Srmsk* (*Tiramaski?*) of

Ramesses III's list with Damascus (*Asien und Europa nach altägyp-
typtischen Denkmälern*, pp. 234 f.). This city has no connection
with Damascus, and, of course, cannot furnish evidence that the
Damascene region was already Aramaized by the end of the thirteenth century B.C. (cf. chapter II, n. 104).

18. This hypothesis would explain the form *dar* (*dum*, perhaps
from *dur*) as equivalent to Aramaic *der*, Babylonian *dûr*, "fortress",
from the Aramaic stem דור " to enclose, surround ". On the other
hand, it is possible that the *mm* under Aramaic influence came to
be naturally dissimilated to *rm* without assuming the initial idea
of *dar*, signifying " fortress " or " wall ".

19. ZDMG 69, p. 169. Interpreting *kur*, which interchanges
with *alu* (city) before the ideogram, as "mountain", Haupt maintains a reference to Antilebanon at the foot of which Damascus
was situated.

20. V. Scheil, *Textes élamites-anzanites*, XI, series 4, 1911, pp.
41–42.

21. This is the view of W. F. Albright in unpublished comments
on Gen. xv, 2 f. Albright offers the parallel שלם for ירושלם.

22. As the Massoretic text stands the passage is to be rendered
" a son of Mesheq is my family (house) " with the following words
" that is, Damascus—Eliezer " being a gloss to explain to a later
period that *Mesheq* is *Dammeseq*, and that " son " refers to Eliezer.
This old gloss (like a half dozen in Gen. xiv) is very likely correct,
and gives us the earlier name of the ancient city.

23. *Ben* with a genitive of place denotes a native of that locality,
one born or reared there. " Shallum ben Jabesh " (II Kings xv,
10, 13) is tantamount to " Shallum of Beth Jabesh ". " Shamgar
ben Anath " (Jud. iii, 31; v, 6) signifies "Shamgar of Beth Anath".
" Hadadezer ben Rehob " (II Sam. viii, 3, 12) is equivalent to
" Hadadezer of Beth-Rehob " (cf. W. F. Albright, *Archaeology and
the Religion of Israel*, p. 219, n. 104). Cf. the plural " sons of Zion ",
Zionites (Ps. cxlix, 2); " sons of the East ", the inhabitants of the
Arabian Desert (Jud. vi, 3; vii, 12; Is. xi, 14, etc.); "sons of Babylon",
Babylonians (Ez. xxiii, 15, 17). Ball is correct (*International Crit.
Com.*, *Genesis*, rev. ed. 1925, p. 279) in rendering *ben Dammeseq
Eliezer*—" a Damascene—Eliezer " and Skinner's criticism that the
singular *ben* with the name of a city is contrary to Hebrew idiom
(*lòc. cit.*) is thus unsustained. Cf. *mâr Bâbili*, *mâr Barsip*, etc. in
Accadian.

24. For example Skinner views 2b as " absolutely unintelligible " and regards the text as so corrupt that even the proper names are doubtful. He contends that there is only a presumption that the sense agrees with 3b (Skinner, *op. cit.*, p. 278). The *hapax legomenon*, *Mesheq*, is variously treated by the versions: the LXX takes it as Eliezer's mother; Aquila's Greek Version as mashqeh (ποτίζοντος); Theodotion, the Vulgate, Targum Onkelos, Targum of Jonathan, as " steward ". Modern commentators regard the word as a modification of *meshek* (Job xxviii, 18), meaning " possession "—so *ben meshek* would be " son of possession ", or " possessor, heir "; but this view lacks philological justification and traditional support. The root *mshq*, despite Zeph. ii, 9, is very doubtful (*op. cit.*, p. 279). R. Kittel construes " Damascus of Eliezer " as equal to " Eliezer of Damascus " (*Hist. of the Hebrews*, translated by J. Taylor, Edinburgh, 1895, Vol. I, p. 137).

25. Cf. note 22.

26. Cf. Ball: " And he who will possess my house " (*û môshēq bêthî hu' ben-dammeseq 'Eliʿezer*) " is a Damascene—Eliezer", is plausible, but involves too violent emendations. The same is true of R. Kittel's effort (*Biblia Hebraica, in loc.*).

27. Albright (unpublished comments on Gen. xv, 2 f.) assumes both a haplography and a transposition. Thus *ûbēn bethi* [*ben*] *méseq*—"and the son of the house is the son of Meseq". However, it seems to me to be necessary only to assume the dropping out of one *ben* from the Massoretic text, without a transposition. Thus *ûbēn Méseq* [*ben*] *bêthî* " and the son of Meseq is the son of the house ". By homioarkton it would be easy for one *ben* to drop out, which, however, occurred, some time before the third century B.C. Of course, the words *hu' Dammeseq—'Eliʿezer* are the explanatory gloss. The occurrence of *bēn bêthî* in 3a greatly strengthens the above-mentioned reconstruction.

28. Unless the gloss is appended as an explanation of the peculiar Semitic idioms it was originally designed to clarify, and unless these idioms are rendered in baldly literal and unidiomatic English, it is impossible to give the clear sense of the entire passage as in an idiomatic translation.

29. Cyrus H. Gordon, " Biblical Customs and The Nuzi Tablets ", *The Biblical Archaeologist* III, Feb. 1940, pp. 2 f.

30. Gen. xv, 4.

31. The submission of Asshur, according to Sidney Smith, took place under Ur-Nammu's son, Dungi (Shulgi), *Early History of*

Assyria, 1928, p. 131. Gelb, however, contests this (AJSL 55, 1938, p. 69).

32. De Vaux, *op. cit.*, pp. 336 f.

33. Cf. I. J. Gelb, "Studies in the Topography of Western Asia", AJSL 55, 1938, pp. 66 f., a study devoted to a group of geographical names from the tablets of the Ur III period.

34. Cf. F. Thureau-Dangin and Maurice Dunand, *Til Barsip*, 1936, pp. 112 f.

35. Harold Ingholt, *Rapport préliminaire sur la première campagne des fouilles de Hama*, 1934, pl. II, 1.

36. *Syria* VIII, 1927, p. 24.

37. M. Dunand, *Fouilles de Byblos* I, 1939, No. 4183. An Ur III cylinder has been recovered on the same site in the foundations of a Twelfth Dynasty temple (De Vaux, *op. cit.*, p. 337, n. 9).

38. A good translation of the biography of Khu-Sebek is given by Ranke in Gressmann's *Altorientalische Texte zum Alten Testament*, 81, 82).

39. W. F. Edgerton, "Chronology of the Twelfth Dynasty", JNES I, 1942, pp. 307–314. Cf. W. F. Albright's dates 1882–1843 (BASOR 81, p. 16, n. 2).

40. De Vaux, *op. cit.*, p. 339; Breasted, *Ancient Records of Egypt* I, p. 304. The Brussels inscriptions, dating between 2000–1800 B.C. (cf. W. F. Albright, "New Egyptian Data on Palestine in the Patriarchal Age", BASOR 81, pp. 16–21) more precisely placed between about 1850–1825 B.C. in the first half of the reign of Amenemhet III (BASOR 83, pp. 32 f.) include Shechem (Balâṭah) spelled *Skm'm'*, perhaps indicating a dual form *Sakmâmi* or *Sakmêmi*, the *s* instead of *š* reflecting original initial *ṭ* (*th*). The new data seem to disprove Albright's view that the *Skmm* of Sebekkhu's stele reflects a pronunciation *Sakmum* (with mimation), which occurs in a number of new cases where the orthography makes it certain (Albright, *op. cit.*, pp. 18 f., n. 11). For the later orthography *Sa-ka-ma* equals Amarna *Sakmi*, Heb. שְׁכֶם for *Šakm* (see *The Voc. of the Egypt. Syll. Orth.*, p. 55). Posener, followed by Alt (" Herren und Herrensitze Palästinas im Anfang des II Jahrt. v. Chr." ZDPV 64, pp. 35 f.), correctly identified *Skm'm'* with Shechem (*Sakmâmi*, " the two shoulders ") (BASOR 83, p. 33).

41. De Vaux, *op. cit.*, pp. 339 f. John A. Wilson, "The Egyptian Middle Kingdom at Megiddo," AJSL, July 1941, p. 236. Cf. Albright, *Archaeology and the Religion of Israel*, p. 62, BASOR 83, pp. 30–36 with quoted references.

42. Cf. Sidney Smith, *Alalakh and Chronology*, pp. 14, 15, note 51, Albright BASOR 81, pp. 18 f. The statuette of the Egyptian official and priest, Thuthotep, found at Megiddo, as well as that of Sesostris-enekh uncovered at Ras Shamra, seem to furnish clear evidence that the foreign relations of the Twelfth Dynasty were not only commercial and cultural but also military and administrative (J. A. Wilson, *op. cit.*, pp. 231, 236).

43. Smith, *op. cit.*, pp. 13 f.

44. *Ibid.*

45. *Syria* IX, pp. 10 ff.

46. Schaeffer, *Ugaritica* I, pp. 20 ff.

47. Smith, *op. cit.*, p. 15.

48. *Ibid.*

49. Cf. BASOR 83, pp. 30–36, also No. 81, pp. 16–21.

50. Cf. note 46 for Albright's datings.

51. For the list with identifications by Posener, Albright and Alt see BASOR 83, pp. 33, 34.

52. For the general evidence of an Egyptian Asiatic Empire under the Middle Kingdom see Wilson, *op. cit.*, pp. 225–236. Cf. note 48 above. The execration texts not only confirm such an Empire, but enable us to fix definitely the sphere of authority (Albright, BASOR 83, pp. 33, n. 6).

53. Albright, *op. cit.*, p. 33.

54. For Albright's identification see *op. cit.*, list number E 33/4.

55. J. A. Knudtzon, *Die El-Amarna Tafeln*, 53: 63; 107: 28; 197: 21. Cf. Chapter II, n. 34. The later Egyptian spelling *'U-pi* shows that the name has hitherto been erroneously read with *b* instead of *p*. *U* was employed as there was at that time no graphic *o* in either cuneiform or Egyptian. It follows that there was a long *â* in *Apum* which was obscured to *o* between the eighteenth and fifteenth centuries, along with the phonetic change that affected all other normal cases of accented long *â* in South Canaanite. The *um* is, of course, the nominative ending with the old mimation. In the Amarna age the nominative was *'Ôpu*, genitive *'Ôpi*, written *Upi*, except in the north, under Amorite influence, where the form *Apu(i)* survived (Albright, *loc. cit.*). Cf. A. Alt, *Kleine Schriften* I, 226.

56. Chapter II, p. 20, and also n. 14 of that chapter.

57. George Dossin, *Syria*, 1939, p. 109 gives the list of kings and the cities over which they ruled. See Dossin's article, " Les Archives économiques du Palais de Mari " (pp. 97–113).

58. Albright, *op. cit.*, p. 35.

59. Written *Ḫa* which is frequently used for '*a* in Old Babylonian, even in Accadian words (Albright, *op. cit.*, p. 35, n. 17).

60. JPOS VIII, p. 239. The name reappears in the Amarna era as a prince of Pella, *Ayab*. The correct vocalization is '*Ayyâbum* (BASOR 83, p. 36).

61. Like Zippor, "sparrow", etc., since this name could be either *Zuz* or *Ŝûŝ* in Hebrew.

62. Cf. Ili-Kabkabu (" The Star-god is my God ") the Amorite name of the father of Shamshi-Adad I of Assyria, which offers an excellent parallel. *Kabkab* in Ugaritic means " star " (Accadian, *Kakkab*) Albright BASOR 83, p. 36.

63. W. F. Albright, *From the Stone Age to Christianity*, p. 150. Cf. R. P. R. DeVaux, *op. cit.*, p. 329, who places the Twelfth Dynasty (*c.* 1989–1776), following the medium dates proposed by W. F. Edgerton, " Chronology of the Twelfth Dynasty " (JNES I, 1942, pp. 307–314), and the Hyksos invasion a little before 1700 (*op. cit.*, p. 328). Cf. also " The Kahun Papyrus and the Date of the Twelfth Dynasty," Lynn Wood (BASOR 99, pp. 5–9). See also Alexander Scharff and Anton Moortgat, *Agypten und Vorderasien im Altertum* (München, 1950), pp. 95–115.

64. Albright, *loc. cit.* Albright dates the historical background of Genesis xiv, for instance, between 1900–1700 B.C. (BASOR 67, p. 30).

65. Albright, *op. cit.*, p. 180. The name of Abraham, moreover, is found in Mesopotamia at the beginning of the second millennium under the forms *A-ba-am-ra-ma*, *A-ba-ra-ma*, *A-ba-am-ra-am* (DeVaux, *op. cit.*, p. 323).

66. C. J. Gadd in *Iraq* VII, 1940, p. 38, n. 5. For an account of the Mari finds see André Parrot, *Studia Mariana* (Leiden, 1950) with extensive bibliography.

67. Isaac and Jacob are apocopated theophorous names whose complete form would be *Yiṣḥaq-'el* and *Ya'qub-'el,* and belong to types known in the environment from which the ancestors of the Hebrews came. As DeVaux has noted, their meaning necessitates their being considered as the names of persons, two of them being borne by people in profane documents. For DeVaux's use of the recent archaeological material in attesting the historicity of the Hebrew patriarchs, and for disproving the various theories that the patriarchs were lunar or astral figures, ancient Canaanite divinities, mythical heroes, personifications of clans or tribes, legendary founders of Canaanite sanctuaries, or fictitious characters in cycles

of legends, which were finally organized into a unified whole by a fiction of blood relationships, see *op. cit.*, pp. 321–328. The fact that in Israel the names of Abraham, Isaac and Jacob are strictly confined to the first ancestors and were not commonly borne by the masses, as would have been the case in tales and legends which were later woven together, is a weighty presumption in favour of the biblical tradition and conducts us back to Hebrew origins, as DeVaux points out (p. 327).

68. Cyrus Gordon, *op. cit.*, pp. 1–12.

69. Albright, *loc cit.*

70. Kraeling, *op. cit.*, p. 33.

71. Josh. xii, 4, 5.

72. Deut. xxvi, 5.

73. Albright, *op. cit.*, p. 182.

74. Cf. E. G. Kraeling, " The Origin of the Name ' Hebrew ' ", AJSL 58, 1941, pp. 237–253. Julius Lewy, " Habiru and Hebrews ", *Hebrew Union College Annual* XIV, 1939, pp. 587–623.

75. BASOR 77, p. 32.

76. See Albright's view (*The Voc. of the Egyptian Syllabic Orthography*, 1934, p. 42, VII, B, 4 and *Archaeology of Palestine and the Bible* [1932–35], pp. 206 ff.).

77. *Revue de l'Histoire des Religions*, p. 118; pp. 170–187.

78. BASOR 77, p. 32.

79. Albright, *From the Stone Age to Christianity*, pp. 182 f.

80. Albright, BASOR 77, p. 33.

81. Albrecht Goetze, " The City Khalbi and the Khapiru People ", BASOR 79, pp. 32 f.

82. Goetze, *op. cit.*, p. 34.

83. Cf. E. Speiser, " Ethnic Movements in the Near East in the Second Millennium B.C.", AASOR XIII, p. 43. For a comprehensive survey of the Habiru (Hapiru) problem see Moshe Greenburg *The Hab/piru*, Vol. 39 of the American Oriental Series (1955), pp. 1–96. See Philip K. Hitti, *History of Syria* (New York, 1951), pp. 160–161.

84. Albright has a discussion of this difficult document in JSOR X, pp. 231 ff. Cf. also Franz Böhl, " Das Zeitalter Abrahams ", *Der Alte Orient* 29, 1931, pp. 12 ff.

85. Gen. xiv, 15. " The Hebrews defined the quarters of the heavens with their faces to the East; hence the left-hand is northward " (John P. Lange, Genesis, 1869, p. 404). We now know from documentary sources that *sim'al*, " left " meant " north " in

Syria about 1700 B.C. (Dossin, *Mélanges Dussaud*, II, 1939, p. 983). The name of Benjamin, "son of the south", like Mari *Banû (Bin)-yamîna*, demonstrates that the use of "right" for "south" and "left" for "north", which subsequently became regular in Arabic, was already known in early Israel (Gen. xiv, 15. Cf. Job xxiii, 9. Josh. xix, 27; Ez. xvi, 46). Cf. Albright, "The Oracles of Balaam", JBL, 63, 1944, p. 223, n. 109.

86.   Gen. xv, 2. Cf. note 23, and Sidney Smith, *Alalakh and Chronology*, p. 34.

NOTES TO CHAPTER II

1. George Steindorff, Keith C. Seele, *When Egypt Ruled the East*, p. 36. It is possible that since the Twelfth Dynasty Hyksos kings may have controlled Damascus.

2. For the archaeological evidence of the Twelfth Egyptian Dynasty in Syria see Sidney Smith, *Alalakh and Chronology*, 1940, pp. 13–16. For the evidence at Ras Shamra see Schaeffer, *Ugaritica* I, pp. 20 ff.; at Qatna see *Syria*, IX, pp. 10 ff. The "Execration Texts", which belong to this period and not to the Eleventh Dynasty, as Capart and Posener have shown (*Comptes rendus de l'Academie des Inscriptions et belles Lettres*, 1939, p. 69) point to Egyptian rule not only in Palestine, but also in Syria, as is also true of the story of Sinuhe.

3. W. Max Müller, *Asien und Europa nach altägyptischen Denkmälern*, pp. 144, 154 f. Cf. A. Scharff, A. Moortgat, *Agypten und Vorderasien im Altertum* (München, 1950), pp. 116–140.

4. James Henry Breasted, *Ancient Records of Egypt* II, p. 170.

5. Müller, *op. cit.*, p. 146.

6. *Op. cit.*, p. 144. Although Naharên did at times include parts of North Syria, it was strictly speaking the Canaanite-Aramaic and Egyptian term for Mitanni in Mesopotamia (cf. Sidney Smith, *op. cit.*, p. 37, Ignace J. Gelb, *Hurrians and Subarians*, pp. 74 ff. See note 22 below). M. Noth (ZDPV 60, 1937, p. 202) and scholars in general equate it with נַהֲרַיִם of the Old Testament.

7. The term *Rtnw* equals Palestine (and Syria) and must have been well known to the Egyptians before the middle of the Twelfth Dynasty since it presents the older orthography (cf. W. F. Albright, *The Vocalization of the Egyptian Syllabic Orthography*, p. 12, sect. 21). For the development of the meaning of the terms *rtn ḥrt* and *rtn ḥrt*—" Lower Retenu " and " Upper Retenu " in the New Empire and for the history of the orthography cf. A. Alt, ZDPV 47, 1924, pp. 170 f.

8. Müller, *op. cit.*, pp. 143 ff.

9. It is singular that this list includes places in central Palestine. Unless " Upper Retenu " is regarded as including Palestine, this must be explained by the fact that the superscription introducing

the enumerated cities is the work of a second scribe, as the contradiction in the range of the list and the diverging orthography of the name " Megiddo " may indicate. This second copyist may have had the entire campaign in mind, and could not persuade himself that only a limited number of cities were to be included under the caption " Upper Retenu ".

10.   *Loc. cit.* See Scharff and Moortgat, *op. cit.*, pp. 129 ff.

11.   Campaigns six and eight, years thirty and thirty-three.

12.   Müller, *op. cit.*, p. 145.

13.   Müller, *loc. cit.*

14.   M. Noth, " Der Aufbau der Palästinaliste Thutmoses III ", ZDPV, 61, 1938, p. 55.

15.   Breasted, *Ancient Records of Egypt* II, p. 51.

16.   G. A. Reisner and M. B. Reisner, " Inscribed Monuments from Gebal Barkar ", ZAS 69, 1933, pp. 31–33. The biblical Kadesh on the Orontes, present-day Tell Nêbî Mendû south-west from Höms, appears as al Kinza in the Amarna documents (EA 54: 22, 27; 174: 12); mât Kinza 175: 10; 176: 10) also as al Kidsa, Kidsi, Gidsi, Gizza (151: 60; 162: 22; 189: 11; 197: 27, 32), and as mât al Kinza in the Boghazköy documents (cf. E. F. Weidner, *Boghazkoï-Studien*, Heft 8, p. 14, note 2; Weber, *Vorderasiatische Bibliothek* II, p. 1118 f.). The alteration between the forms Kidša and Kinza furnishes an illustration of nasalizing common in Hurrian territory (cf. Albright, *Journal of Egyptian Archaeology*, 23, 1937, p. 195).

17.   Reisner, *loc. cit.*

18.   *Ya-nu-ʿa-m(a)* equals Canaanite **Yanô-ʿam(ma)*, Amarna *Yanuamma* (Albright, *The Vocalization of the Egyptian Syllabic Orthography*, pp. 36, IV, 4; 47, 9, 1); Albright locates it at *Tell* en-Nâʿmeh in the Hûleh Plain (" The Jordan Valley in the Bronze Age ", AASOR VI, pp. 18–24). *Nu-ga-sa* is equivalent to cuneiform Nukhashshe, first identified by Dhorme with Aramaic לעש (Albright, *op. cit.*, p. 46, C, 3; also JEA 10, p. 6, n. 3).

19.   A. T. Olmstead, *History of Palestine and Syria*, p. 135. Although Thutmose III's record furnishes the first non-biblical historical reference to the actual city of Damascus, archaeological discoveries of the Brussels figurines and the Mari Tablets from Tell El-Harrîrî on the middle Euphrates give a much earlier glimpse into the land of Damascus between 1850 and 1750 B.C. in which the famous ancient town of Abraham's day was located (Albright, BASOR, 83, p. 35).

20.   The name is variously rendered in the records. The oldest

cuneiform spelling *Ma-i-ta-ni* (not *Ma-i-te-ni* as read by Speiser, JAOS, XLIX, 1929, p. 271, cf. E. R. Lacheman, BASOR 78, p. 22) is employed by Shuttarna I (cf. Sidney Smith, *The Antiquaries Journal* XIX, p. 42). The writing with the single consonants is more characteristic of the older orthography (Gelb, *op. cit.*, p. 70, n. 167). Later the name is written *Mitanni, Maitanni, Mittanni*. The Egyptian forms *M ì t n* and *M ì t n* occur in Thutmose III's lists, and in the records of Amenophis II and Amenophis III (1413–1377). Ramesses II (1301–1234), Ramesses III (*c.* 1195–1164) and even later. The history of Mitanni can be sketchily outlined for about two hundred years from obscure beginnings about 1500 B.C. until absorbed by Assyria. As a political unit the term Mitanni is paralleled by its much rarer use as a geographical entity (EA 54: 40; 56: 39, etc.), but the usage is not always synonymous. While the country itself was situated in northern Mesopotamia, the state of Mitanni at different periods often embraced regions far beyond the bounds of geographic Mitanni. Mitannian ambition is proved by the fact that Saushshatar, one of the early Mitannian kings, not only became overlord of northern Syria, controlling Alalakh in Mukish, but also imposed his sway as far as Arrapkha, east of the Tigris (Sidney Smith, *Alalakh and Chronology*, pp. 40, 41). Accordingly, his empire included large areas beyond Mitanni proper, controlling other smaller kingdoms, all of which had their local kings (Gelb, *op. cit.*, p. 71, 76). Cf. A. Scharff and A. Moortgat, *op. cit.*, pp. 327 ff., 341 ff.

21. Archaeological evidence (cf. S. Smith, *op. cit.*, p. 36) suggests that Shutarna I (and not Saushshatar as was frequently supposed) was the Mitannian king whom Thutmose III defeated. Besides, the fact that Saushshatar dominated northern Syria furnishes proof that he cannot have been contemporary with Thutmose III (*loc. cit.*, p. 41).

22. *Naḥrima, Nahrina* is the " Canaanite-Aramaic " and Egyptian term for Mitanni, corresponding roughly with Mesopotamia, but at times included parts of north Syria. For example Tunip (*Tw-n-p*) in the time of Ramesses II was said to be " in the land of Naharin (*N-h-r-n*) " (Breasted, *Anc. Rec. III*, sec. 365). Sidney Smith, therefore, would include in the term " the land from the Orontes to the Euphrates " (*op. cit.*, p. 37). Cuneiform *Naḥrima* with variants (for *Nahrima*) attested only in the Armarna letters is a " Canaanitic " plural form with *m* and final *a* corresponding to *Nahrina*, the " Amorite " form in *n* with final *a* apparently employed by the

Egyptians. Phonetically it is practically identical with Egyptian *Nhr(y)n* appearing commonly in texts from Thutmose I to Ramesses III. That the Egyptians identified their *Nahrina* with Mitanni (in the political and not merely in the geographical sense) is demonstrated by one of the Amarna letters of Tushratta to Amenophis IV, which an Egyptian scribe in an appended note written in hieratic, described as a " copy of the Nh(r)yn letter " (EA 27, p. 1065). West Semitic (Amorite) *Nahrên* (*Nah(a)rên(a)*, " the Two Rivers " (Amarna Canaanite Nahrima for *Nah(a)rêm*. Hebrew נַהֲרַיִם. Cf. Albright, *The Voc. of the Egyptian Syllabic Orthography*, p. 45, A, 3). Further evidence for the definition is furnished by the wife of Amenophis III, Kelu-Khepa, who was the daughter of Shuttarna II of Mitanni and a sister of Tushratta (EA 17: 5, 24 f.; 19: 6, 29: 18 ff.) and who in an Egyptian scarab inscription is described as *Krgp*, daughter of *Strn*, prince (*wr*) of *Nhrn* (Breasted, *op. cit.*, II, sect. 867; EA p. 1043).

23. Sidney Smith, *op. cit.*, p. 38. Cf. *Ancient Records of Egypt* II, sect. 512, where Smith corrects Breasted's Arrapachitis to Alalakh.

24. B. Maisler, " Canaan and the Canaanites ", BASOR, 102, p. 9 f., where the stela is discussed.

25. W. F. Albright, " Mitannian Maryannu ' Chariot Warrior ' and The Canaanite and Egyptian Equivalents ", AfO, VI, 1930–31, pp. 217–221.

26. Diversity of opinion prevails as to the precise signification of Khanigalbat. The usual view is to interpret the term as another name for the same state (cf. F. Bilabel, *Geschichte Vorderasiens und Agyptens*, p. 6, etc.). Gelb's conclusion, for example, is that the name is normally the Akkadian equivalent of geographic Mitanni proper, which in later Assyrian records displaces Mitanni as a political term (*Hurrians and Subarians*, p. 75). For Gelb's arguments see pp. 72, 73. Sidney Smith (*op. cit.*, pp. 40, 41) and Götze (MAOG IV. 64) maintain that the preamble to the treaty of Rim-shar of Aleppo precludes the interpretation that the two countries are identical in view of the clear distinction there said to be made between the king of Khanigalbat and the king of Mitanni.

27. Artatama I's daughter married Thutmose IV. During the reign of Artatama's son, Shuttarna II and his grandson, Tushratta, friendly relations with Egypt were maintained, the Mitannian princesses, Kelu-Khepa and Tatu-Khepa, being wedded to Amenophis III (1413–1377), the latter also to Amenophis IV (1377–1361). For the dates of the pharaohs of the Eighteenth Dynasty, and

especially those of the Amarna age, see Borchardt's new astronomic and calendaric chronology, *Die Mittel zur zeitlichen Festlegung von Punkten der ägyptischen Geschichte und ihre Anwendung*, Cairo, 1935 and Albright, *The Journal of Egyptian Archaeology*, 23, 1937, p. 193, n. 8. See also Viktor Korošec, *Hethitische Staatsverträge*, 1931, p. 11, who follows E. Meyer's dates (*c.* 1405–1370 for Amenophis III and 1370–1352 for Amenophis IV).

28. A. T. Olmstead, *Hist. of Pal. and Syria*, p. 140. E. Meyer, *Gesch. des Altertums*, I, 2, 1913, p. 675.

29. EA 53: 40–43.

30. EA, nos. 53 and 55.

31. Heretofore, in the absence of decisive details from contemporary records, the city of Qatna has been variously located. However, M. Dossin, as a result of his brilliant work on the Mari texts, has now shown beyond dispute that Qaṭana (*c.* 1725 B.C.) was the later Qaṭna, present-day el-Mishrifeh north-east of Höms (Emesa) in central Syria, and just south of Hamath on the Orontes (BASOR 77, p. 32, 78, p. 23). Count du Mesnil du Buisson excavated at intervals there between 1925 and 1929 (cf. René du Mesnil du Buisson, *Le Site archéologique de Mishrifé-Qatna* 1935, cf. also Sidney Smith, *Alalakh and Chronology*, p. 11, n. 41). Biruaza (equals Biriawaza, EA, pp. 1026, 1109), the high Egyptian official who exercised jurisdiction over Qaṭna may have had his headquarters in this place (EA 52: 44–46) some ninety miles in a north-easterly direction from Damascus. At the time of Zimri-lim, during the First Dynasty of Babylon, the city was the capital of an important kingdom, for the powerful king of Assyria, Shamshi-Adad I, did not disdain to desire the daughter of Ishkhe-Adad, the king of Qatna, as a wife for his own son Iasmakh-Adad, so famous was the house of *Qatanum* (G. Dossin, R. A. XXXVI, p. 54). By the Amarna age the city had apparently lost much of its political importance, and the Amorite form of the name *Qatana*, shortened to Qatna, occurs instead of the more Akkadianized *Qatanum* (Dossin, *op. cit.*, p. 53). As with Damascus, the city appears first in Egyptian records in the inscriptions of Thutmose III (R. du M. du Buisson, *op. cit.*, pp. 28 f.) who retook the city for Egypt (*c.* 1468) and initiated the period of stable Egyptian occupation (*op. cit.*, p. 39). Cf. A. Scharff and A. Moortgat, *op. cit.*, p. 359.

32. Following the almost universal practice R. du Mesnil du Buisson construes the letters of Akizzi as addressed to Amenophis III. He dates them *c.* 1400 to 1395, and places the destruction of

Qatna by Shuppiluliuma c. 1385 or 1380. See for his reasons (op. cit., p. 33). But the name of the addressee in Akizzi's letters has been misread as *Nammuriya*, instead of *Nam-khur-ia* (Sturm, *Wiener Zeitschrift für die Kunde des Morgenlandes* 41, 1934, p. 167). Akizzi's corrected *Namkhuria* is to be equated with Napkhuria (Amenophis IV), the nasalizing being common in Hurrian territory (Albright, *The Journal of Egyptian Archaeology* 23, 1937, p. 195). The letters of Akizzi are, therefore, to be dated not long before the final destruction of Qatna, either in the second or third campaign of Shuppiluliuma, i.e. in the middle of Amenophis IV's reign or at the conclusion of it (Albright, *loc. cit.*).

33. EA 53: 23 ff.

34. *al Timašgi* (EA 53: 63) is, of course, the celebrated city of Damascus (*Dammeseq*), identical with Egyptian *Tmšḳ* in Thutmose III's list of Syrian conquests. It is an Egyptianized form of the more common renderings *al Dimaška* (EA 197: 21) or *al Dumaška* (EA 107: 28) in the current Akkadian *lingua franca*. Besides the regular transcription of ד by *d* there are numerous cases in Egyptian where *t* is substituted, not because the Semitic sound was foreign to the Egyptians, as in the case with ט, but because the language itself began to confuse the *d* and *t*, two dentals, which are identical, except that the one is surd and the other sonant (Müller, *op. cit.*, p. 97). Variation of form is by no means surprising in intercourse involving such diversity of social and cultural forces as the Amarna letters present to us. The intricate ethnic and linguistic complexion of Palestine-Syria in the late Bronze Age demanded some common medium of converse not only to facilitate trade, but especially to expedite the administration of government with the rise of the Egyptian Empire in the Near East. In the Akkadian language Egypt found the vehicle needed, and Palestine-Syria adapted and moulded the language to meet the needs of its heterogeneous populations. In the Hittite texts from Boghozköy occurs *Damašḫuna(š)* (*Dam-ma-aš-ḫu-na-as*) which J. Garstang maintains simulates Damascene, and the identification is perhaps possible, for the context contains Khalep (Aleppo) (L. A. Mayer, John Garstang, *The British School of Archaeology in Jerusalem*, " Index of Hittite Names ", *Supplementary Papers* I, 1923, pp. 12, 53).

35. 53: 63–65.

36. Also variously written Etakkama, *Edagama*, *Etagama*, *Etaḳkama*, *Attakkama*, *Itakama*, *Itâtkama*, *Ittaḳkama* (EA 174: 11; 151: 39, 189: 2, 56: 23, 140: 25, 189: 20; 197: 31).

37. EA 53: 24–34. *Namiawaza* (*Namiaza* 53: 34) equals *Biriawaza* (Biruaza). For *nam* equals *bir*, see Thureau-Dangin, *Le Syllabaire acadien* (1926), *bir*, (𒉿𒊭𒉿), p. 54, equals *nam* p. 61; *Revue D'Assyriologie* 37, p. 171.

38. EA: 35–39. Cf. R. du Mesnil du Buisson, *op. cit.*, p. 31.

39. So correctly Cavaignac, *Subbiluliuma et son Temps*, p. 26.

40. So Otto Weber in Knudtzon, EA p. 1109.

41. E. Mayer in *Ägyptiaca*, pp. 71 f. correctly equated Upe with Egyptian Opa, and locates it in the plain of Damascus. Dhorme (*Revue Biblique*, 1908, pp. 505 f.) accepted the earlier equation Ube equals הוֹבָה (Gen. xiv, 15). But this identification is impossible and modern Ḥoba situated some sixty miles north-west of Damascus cannot be identical with the ancient biblical site " on the left hand ", i.e. to the north of Damascus. Notwithstanding, compare René Dussaud: " Dans *ḫbt* nous avons la mention du Ḥobah biblique, le Ube des Egyptiens" (*Les Découvertes de Ras Shamra et L'Ancien Testament*, 1941, p. 39, n. 2. Cf. *Syria*, 1935, p. 228). '*Apum* (spelled '*a-p-w-m*) of the Brussels figurines, which was so large it was divided into two districts in the nineteenth century B.C., is, of course, to be equated with *Ube*, *Abi* (*Upe*, *Api*) of the Amarna records (Albright, BASOR 83, p. 35) and with *Apum* (written in the genitive *A-pi-im^{ki}*) of the Mari archives from the eighteenth century B.C. (Albright, *loc. cit.*, George Dossin, *Syria*, 1939, p. 109). Cf. A. Alt, *Kleine Schriften zur Geschichte des Volkes Israels* I, p. 226.

42. The precise location of the city-states, Lapana and Rukhizzi, must remain conjectural in view of present available sources. Always appearing in closest connection with each other in the two letters of Akizzi of Qatna to Amenophis IV (EA 53 and 54) they were probably located somewhere on the slopes of the Antilebanon, in the vicinity of the fountain heads of the Orontes (EA 1111).

43. Weber, EA, p. 1290.

44. EA 53: 60 ff.

45. Albright, *The Jour. of Egypt. Arch.*, 23, 1937, p. 195.

46. Since they were obviously written by the same scribe, showing similar peculiarities, even of handwriting, Albright's tentative dates for these letters are *c.* 1365–1358 B.C. (*op. cit.*, p. 196), by which time the Egyptian court had likely moved from Akhetaton.

47. EA 189:9 ff.

48. Breasted, *Hist. of Egypt*, p. 387.

49. EA 195: 27 ff.

50. EA 107: 28.

51. EA 107: 30 ff.

52. Ernst F. Weidner, *Politische Dokumente aus Kleinasien, Boghazkoï-Studien*, Heft 8, p. 14, lines 40 ff.

53. Otto Weber, EA, p. 1113.

54. Pierre M. Purves, *Nuzi Personal Names*, p. 194. Friedrich maintains these names are Indo-Aryan (i.e. belong to the Aryan languages of India), rather than Iranian (*Reallexikon der Assyriologie*, hreg. von Erich Ebeling und Bruno Meissner I, 1932, pp. 144–148). So also Dumont; see Albright JNES, Jan. 1946, p. 7.

55. Cf. Pierre M. Purves, *op. cit.*, pp. 193 f. and Ephraim A. Speiser, *Mesopotamian Origins*, p. 176. Besides references in the Amarna letters to this ruling class, Hittite tablets from Boghazköy mention Indo-Iranian princelings. Compare Dumont and Albright's investigation of a Hittite source which refers to four kings of the Hurrians. The three names which are fully preserved were found to be Indo-Iranian (BASOR 78, pp. 30 f. Cf. Stanley A. Cook, *The Cambridge Ancient History*, II, p. 331).

56. EA 194–197.

57. EA 194: 9 f.

58. So correctly Ranke in Knudtzon, EA, p. 1289.

59. EA 194: 20 f.

60. EA 52: 45.

61. Flinders Petrie offers a similar explanation of the circumstances connected with the parents of Queen Teye, whose father he views as a North Syrian prince, and whose mother as an Egyptian princess (*History* II, pp. 182 f.). But this view is now rejected by all Egyptologists.

62. EA 52: 44 ff.

63. Little is known of Artatama I except that he was Tushratta's grandfather and that his daughter, a sister of Shutarna II, was given in marriage to Thutmose IV (EA 24 III 52 ff., 29: 16 ff. Cf. Gelb, *op. cit.*, p. 77).

64. EA 19: 17 ff., 20: 8 ff., 21: 13 ff., 23: 7 ff., etc.

65. EA 27: 1 f., 28: 1 ff., 29: 1 ff.

66. Gelb, *op. cit.*, pp. 77 ff.

67. EA 17: 30 ff.

68. Albright, *The Jour. of Egypt. Arch.*, 23, 1937, p. 195.

69. *Boghazkoï-Studien* VIII, no. 1, lines 1 ff.

70. Gelb is doubtless correct in maintaining that the terms Mitanni and Khurri are synonymous (*op. cit.*, pp. 73 f.) and that the difference between them in the treaty should be explained from

the Hittite (not the Mitannian) point of view, according to which the Hittites probably considered Tushratta as a king who had usurped for himself the kingdom of Mitanni, regarding Artatama II, on the other hand as the legitimate ruler over all the Khurri lands (*op. cit.*, p. 79 and note 241). However, Winckler (*Mitteilungen Deutsche Orient Gesellschaft*, no. 35, 1907, p. 35 and *Mitteilungen Vorderasiatische-aegyptische Gesellschaft* XVIII 4, 1913, pp. 64–66) followed by Weidener (*Boghazkoï-Studien* VIII 2, n. 1 and 16, n. 1) and others, construes Tushratta's predecessors Saushshatar, Artatama I, and Shuttarna II as kings of great Khurri (Khurri plus Mitanni), who were followed originally by Artatama II and by his son Artatama III. Tushratta is considered a usurper, who snatched Mitanni away from its rightful rulers, restricting Khurri to a small area in Armenia. But the discovery that Shuttarna I and Saushshatar called themselves in their seals kings of Mitanni, but not kings of Khurri, which in turn implies that Artatama I and Shutarna II, who ruled between Saushshatar and Tushratta, were likewise kings of Mitanni, renders the hypothesis implausible.

71.   Washshukanni is taken as the capital of Mitanni (perhaps unwarrantedly) solely because Saushshatar is said to have had his palace there (*Boghazkoï-Studien* VIII, n. 2: 9). Besides Washshukanni (*Ibid.*, no. 1: 26 f.), Shuta, Irrite, Taida, Kakhat and Kharran are listed as cities of Mitanni (*Ibid.*, rev. 28: 36; no. 2: 37–64). Cf. Scharff and Moortgat, *op. cit.*, p. 341.

72.   For more precise location see Sidney Smith, *Alalakh and Chronology*, p. 31.

73.   So Weidner, who identifies Niya with Apamea (present-day Kal'at el Mudîk). For an improbable location east of Aleppo, see S. Yeivin, JPOS, XIV, pp. 218–225. S. Smith, *op. cit.*, p. 37, n. 102.

74.   Cf. M. Noth (ZDPV 52, pp. 139 ff.) who correctly following Dhorme and others, identifies Nukhashshe with Lu'ash of the Zakir Stela, and locates it south-west of Aleppo, and north of Hamath. Cf. Scharff and Moortgat. *op. cit.*, pp. 356, 360.

75.   So correctly Weidner. *Boghazkoï-Studien*, VIII, p. 14, n. 1, Weber, *Vorderasiatische Bibliothek* II Leipzig, 1907 ff., pp. 1110 ff. Cf. also *Keilschrifturkunden aus Boghazkoï*, III, 57, rev. 4. The suffix -*na* in *Api-na* is clearly a Hurrianizing element introduced into the Akkadian *lingua franca* in which the treaty between Shuppiluliuma and Mattiwaza was written. In the Nuzi texts *Tar-pa-áz-ḫi* (R. A. 28, no. 4: 2) occurs as a place name, and also as a plural formation *uru Tar-ba-az-ḫé-na* (R. A. 28, no. 5: 9) cited by Johannes

Friedrich, *Kleine Beiträge zur Churritischen Grammatik*, Leipzig, 1939, p. 4. Also *Tup-pa-ku-u-uš-ḥe-na* (*meš*) *šu-ú-al-la-ma-an* II, 21, and *Tu-pa(-ku-u-u)š-ḥe-na* (*meš*) *du-pè-na-a-ma-a-an du-u(al-l)a-ma-an* II, 29 (Friedrich, *op. cit.*, p. 5. Cf. E. A. Speiser, "Introduction To Hurrian", AASOR, Vol. XX, 1940–41, pp. 98–103, for the Hurrian noun suffixes in *ni* and *na*. Thureau-Dangin construes *na* as the plural of the definite suffix *ni* (cf. Syria XII, p. 256, just as *ni* signifies French *le* and *na* French *les* (" Tablette ḥurrite provenant de Mari ", R. A. 36, no. 1, p. 19). Hattina in North Syria, which H. Hrozny locates just north of the Orontes as it turns toward the sea (see *Archiv Orientální* VII, 1935, p. 176), furnishes a linguistic parallel to Apina, apparently.

76. *Topographie historique de la Syrie*, p. 513.

77. These names are probably Hurrian or Indo-Aryan (Iranian).

78. *Op. cit.*, no. 1, 11. 43 f.

79. *Op. cit.*, no. 1, 1. 45.

80. *Op. cit.*, no. 1, 11. 17–47. So Weidner, *op. cit.*, p. 6, n. 1 and Gelb. *op. cit.*, p. 78.

81. Weidner, *ibid.*, lines 45 ff. and 77 ff.

82. *Keilschrifttexte aus Boghazköi*, I, 4, I: 1 ff.

83. *Boghazköi-Studien* VIII, no. 1: 48.

84. Weidner, *op. cit.*, p. 15, n. 3.

85. *Boghazköi-Studien* VIII, no. 2: 35–38. Cf. the fragmentary document, *Hittite Texts in the Cuneiform Character from Tablets in the British Museum* (London, 1920), no. 21, KUB VIII 80, where these events are described. They are discussed by J. Friedrich, " Ein Brüchstuck des Vertrages Mattiwaza-Šuppiluliuma in hethitischer Sprache?" (*Archiv für Keilschriftforschung II*, 1924–25, pp. 119–124).

86. Gelb, *op. cit.*, p. 80.

87. *Boghazköi-Studien* VIII, no. 1, rev. 14–21. Later sources refer to the same area only by the name Khanigalbat (Gelb, *op. cit.*, p. 81).

88. Breasted's *Ancient Records of Egypt* III, p. 71. Breasted is incorrect in placing this Kadesh in Galilee.

89. E. Kraeling, *Aram and Israel*, p. 35.

90. Breasted (*op. cit.*, III, p. 40) is incorrect in assuming this was the Galilean Kadesh.

91. Breasted, *ibid.*

92. Breasted, *op. cit.*, p. 39. For a discussion of the lists of Sethos I see M. Noth, " Die Wege der Pharaonenheere in Palästina und Syrian " (ZDPV 60, 1937, pp. 210–229).

93. Steindorff and Seele, *op. cit.*, p. 250.

94. *Apa* (*KUR A-pa*) is of course *Api* or *Upe* of the Amarna letters, that is the plain of Damascus (Albrecht Götze, " Zur Schlacht von Qadeš ", *Orientalistische Literaturzeitung*, XXXII, 1929, p. 837. *Keilscrifturkunden aus Boghazkoï* XXI, 17). In Hittite cuneiform *b* and *p* were not distinguished.

95. Breasted's identification (*op. cit.*, III, pp. 159 f.) is impossible, both geographically and phonetically.

96. Müller, *op. cit.*, p. 221.

97. Breasted, *op. cit.*, III, pp. 41, 161 f.

98. *Boghazkoï-Studien* VIII, Zweiter Teil, pp. 112–123. See also, E. Edel, " Weitere Briefe aus der Keiratskorrespondenz Ramses' II " in *Geschichte und Altes Testament* (Tübingen, 1953), pp. 29–63.

99. E. Cavaignac, " L'histoire politique de l'Orient de 1340 à 1230 ", *Revue Hittite et Asianique* 3, 1934–36, p. 125.

100. Kraeling (*op. cit.*, pp. 35 f.) is incorrect in placing this Kadesh in Galilee.

101. *Loc. cit.*

102. Müller, *op. cit.*, p. 227 f.

103. William F. Edgerton and John A. Wilson, *Historical Records of Ramses III*, Vols. I, II, plate 101, p. 109.

104. With the failure of Müller's identification of *Srmsk* with Damascus, his conclusions, of course, regarding the non-Amorite character or non-Egyptian control of Damascus at this period are completely invalidated (cf. *op. cit.*, pp. 227 f.).

105. S. Schiffer, *Die Aramaer*, p. 25 and n. 2.

106. Breasted, *Ancient Records* of Egypt IV, sect. 59 ff.

107. More precisely the Aryans (Thraco-Phrygians) composed of Peoples called Tabal, Mushke (Cf. Gen. x, 2) and Kashka (Gashga).

108. Müller, *op. cit.*, p. 222. For vocalization '*A-ar-mu*, cf. Albright, *The Voc. of the Egypt. Syll. Orth.*

109. Breasted, *Ancient Records of Egypt*, IV, pp. 59 f.

110. George A. Smith, *The Historical Geography of the Holy Land*, 1903, pp. 426 ff.

111. Cf. Breasted, *A History of Egypt*, p. 260. Almost three millennia later, during the period of the Crusades, the armourers of Damascus had become famous in history for their swords. Their flourishing trade in arms was not brought to an end until Tamerlane carried the craftsmen away to Samarcand in 1399. By that time the " Damascene blade " had become a proverbial phrase for a weapon

of finely tempered steel skilfully inlaid by a process called " damaskeening " or " damascene work ".

112. Breasted, *A History of Egypt*, p. 260.

113. *Loc. cit.*

114. Steindorff and Seele, *op. cit.*, p. 48. The modern English word " damask " to the present day perpetuates the renown of the textile industry of the ancient city.

115. René Dussaud, *Topographie historique de la Syrie*, p. 293.

116. Helbon (Ezek. xxvii, 18), *Ḥilbûm* of Neo-Babylonian texts, is commonly identified with *Khalbūn* (Albright, AASOR VI, p. 21), thirteen miles north-west of Damascus, a locality still renowned for its wine produce. The village is situated in a narrow valley shut in by steep, bare cliffs and long shelving banks two thousand to three thousand feet high. Orchards spread over the floor of the glen, and far up the mountain slopes are terraced vineyards. The wine was celebrated in Assyria, Babylonia and Persia (Henry S. Gehman), *Westminster Dictionary of the Bible*, 1944, p. 235.

117. W. F. Albright, *From the Stone Age to Christianity*, pp. 155 f. A. T. Olmstead, *History of Palestine and Syria*, pp. 143 ff.

118. Albright, *op. cit.*, p. 156.

119. Gen. xv, 16; Lev. xviii, 24–28.

120. EA 7: 73 ff.

121. J. Breasted, *The Cambridge Ancient History*, II, pp. 96 ff. Cf. Philip K. Hitti, *History of Syria* (New York, 1951), p. 168.

NOTES TO CHAPTER III

1. Cf. chapter II, pp. 42–45.
2. Cf. Friedrich Bilabel, *Geschichte Vorderasiens und Agyptens*, p. 10, A. Dupont-Sommer, *Les Araméens* (Paris, 1949), pp. 14–19.
3. The *Sutû* appear in contemporary records " as desert nomads in documents from the time of Rim-Sin *c.* 1743 B.C., on down, and they are mentioned in literary texts from the end of the third millennium or the beginning of the second " (W. F. Albright, " The Oracles of Balaam ", JBL, 63, p. 220, n. 89. Çf. Landsberger, *Zeit. f. Assyr.*, 35, p. 233). *Šûtû* (*Šwtw*) are also listed in the Egyptian execration texts of the twentieth and nineteenth centuries B.C. as a nomadic folk somewhere in Palestine (Albright, *ibid.*). However, the name is not to be connected with Egyptian *Sttyw* signifying "Asiatics". In the Amarna letters the *Sutû* appear in function as so many *ʿApiru*. With the *Akhlâmu* they make debut in Assyrian sources at the time of Arik-den-ilu (1316–1305). Despite the close association of the *Sutû* with the Aramaeans in time, place and mode of life, there is no concrete proof as yet to identify them with the Aramaeans (Bilabel, *op. cit.*, p. 10, n. 4). Cf. also S. Schiffer, *Die Aramäer*, p. VII. Cf. also Philip K. Hitti, *History of Syria* (New York, 1951), pp. 162 ff.
4. The term *Akhlâmu* is ostensibly etymologically a broken plural, خِلْم a singular *qitl* form, meaning " companion " or " friend " with plural أَخْلَام. The name is likely a simple appellative denoting "allies" or "confederates". This is the common view, and it agrees with the cuneiform usage of the word from the late fourteenth to the late eighth centuries B.C. Just as the roving Bedawin tribes are settling in the sown, the name *Aram* significantly appears. They are, moreover, the only branch of the Bedawin to whom the more generic term is applied.
5. *Reallexikon der Assyriologie* II, 1929, p. 131.
6. " Alteste Geschichte der Aramäer ", *Klio* VI, pp. 193 ff.
7. *Die Aramäer*, pp. 15–18.
8. " Aramu ", *Reallexikon der Assyriologie* II, 1929, p. 131, cf. A. Alt, *Kleine Schriften* I, 174, No. 1.

9. Thureau-Dangin, RA, VIII (1911), pp. 199 ff.

10. Dhorme, *ibid.*, p. 488.

11. Albright, *From the Stone Age to Christianity*, pp. 181 ff.

12. Albright, *Archaeology and the Religion of Israel*, pp. 96–100.

13. The meaning of the name *Aram* is unknown. Hebrew tradition presents the Aramaeans as independent groups in Genesis x, and also as the descendants of Abraham. Possibly Aramu may first have been a place name, possibly Arma, a mountain city mentioned by Shalmaneser I (*Keilschrifttexte aus Assur historischen Inhalts*, 14, col. II, 6 ff.). The designation doubtless spread to a tribe, and finally to a larger confederation. The name Aramaean appears under numerous forms *Arayu, Arimi, Arumu*, with later spellings such as *Aramu, Arami*, preceded by the determinative *amêl* in Assyrian inscriptions. Kraeling's view that *Armayu* presents the more original form is doubtless correct (*Aram and Israel*, p. 21), for the writings *Arimi* and *Arumu* are clearly cases of vowel harmony. A. Sachs first pointed out that in middle Assyrian when the vowel of the penultimate syllable is a short *a*, it is regularly assimilated to the vowel of the nominative and genitive endings (BASOR, 67, p. 27, n. 6). E.g. *Ṣubutu* (for *Ṣubatu*), *Ṣubiti, Arubi, Aribi*, etc. Much later (from the seventh century on) the Aramaic form, which was *Aram* all the while, seems to have replaced the form *Arumu* completely, because in late Assyrian the old phonetic law of vowel harmony had ceased to operate and the current Aramaic custom was adopted, yielding Aramu (cf. R. T. O'Callaghan, *Aram Naharaim* (Rome, Pontificum Institutum Biblicum, 1948) p. 95, note 6).

14. Attempts to reconstruct this ambiguous name are futile. The name as it stands means " double wickedness " and may represent a fruitless effort to reconstruct a word already corrupted by transmission.

15. R. Kittel, for example, considers the substitution of *Edom* for *Aram* in Judges iii, 8 ff. very tempting (*Geschichte des Volkes Israel* II, p. 82, n. 2). Marquart tenuously proceeds still farther to make the very unlikely identification with the Edomite prince חֹשֶׁן (Gen. xxxvi, 34 f.) and views *Rišʿaṭaim* as a corruption of ראש עתים. This, however, is pure speculation, despite the fact that there existed a south Jordanic *Kushan* as we know from the archaic passage in Hab. iii, 7 (cf. BASOR, 83, p. 34, n. 8) in addition to the Cushan in North Syria (cf. note 16), and despite the additional singularity that Cushan bears the *an* ending frequent among those tribes related to Abraham through Ketura (Gen. xxv, 2) such as Zimram, Madan,

Midian, Jokshan, etc., which were situated to the east and south-east of Israel.

16. A territory in northern Syria in the thirteenth and twelfth centuries B.C. designated *Qusana-ruma*, perhaps *Kushan-rôm*, "Kúshan is high". It is enumerated in the list of Ramesses II (no. 89), so that the name is attested for the region called Naharaim (*Nhr(y)n* of the Egyptian sources). Cf. Wm. F. Edgerton, John A. Wilson, *Historical Records of Ramesses* III, plate 101, p. 110; also Albright, *Archaeology and the Religion of Israel*, p. 205, n. 49.

17. *Aram Naharaim*, a Ph.D. dissertation (1945) The Johns Hopkins University, published by Pontificum Institutum, Rome, 1948, p. 143. O'Callaghan notes that in a few instances both in Egyptian inscriptions and in the Bible the term Aram Naharaim appears to have received a political meaning, but "in the vast majority of cases, not only the use of Egyptian and Akkadian determinatives, but the very contexts themselves make us see in it a geographical designation" (*Op. cit.*, p. 143).

18. As to the extent of the term O'Callaghan puts "the heart of it in the region from the Khabur westward to a line from Aleppo to Carchemish". He interprets the Egyptian and biblical data as suggesting "a southward extension as far as Tunip and perhaps Kadesh on the Orontes" (pp. 143–144).

19. *Asien und Europa nach altägyptischen Denkmälern*, pp. 250–252. Müller is unwarranted in insisting on a plural as the original form, and in rejecting the dual of the Massoretic text as a hyper-refinement of the Massoretes (*op. cit.*, p. 252). The dual vocalization of the Massoretic tradition is obviously correct and follows the manner of many place names as *Yerushalaim, Kiryathaim, Karnaim*, etc. As the Greek·Μεσοποτομία it fixes attention on the two great rivers, the Tigris and the Euphrates, rather than on the territory watered by many rivers (the Euphrates, the Tigris, the Khabur, as well as the Orontes) according to Müller's view (*ibid.*). Συρία ποταμῶν (Judges iii, 8, 10), plainly reflects the plural *neharîm*, which likely gave rise to the opinion that such was the original form. This theory may now safely be dismissed since dual forms are found in Amorite or early West-Semitic. For example, from the region of Mari in the eighteenth century B.C. come such place names as *Qaṭṭumân* "the two little places", *Ḥimarân*, "the two asses", etc. Cf. Albright's review of Zellig Harris' *Development of the Canaanite Dialects*, JAOS 60 (1940), p. 415. Accordingly, *Naharaina (the dual) is original. In Hebrew and Canaanite the form, of course, received

an *m* ending, but retained its dual character, *Nahrêma*, since the Canaanite diphthongs contract. Cf. A. Alt, *Kleine Schriften* (München, 1953), I: 237 f.

20. Judges xviii, 7, 28.

21. *Ibid.*

22. It is very likely we are to read אָדָם following the LXX GAL (Codex Alexandrinus, and the recensio Luciana, also Symmachus, Latin (Codex Lugduensis, ed. Ul. Robert, 1881, 1900), and *versio syriaca hexaplaris.*

23. Judg. xviii, 28 בָּעֵמֶק אֲשֶׁר לְבֵית רְחוֹב while the Septuagint gives ἐν τῇ κοιλάδι τοῦ οἴκου ʿΡααβ "In the valley of the house of Raab". This Beth Rehob has no connection with the city in the tribe of Asher (Josh. xix, 28; xxi, 31 and Judg. i, 31). Cf. *The Westminster Historical Atlas to the Bible*, Wright, Filson, Albright, p. 42, plate VI, which is most likely the *Ra-ḫ-bu* of the Thutmose list no. 87 (Müller, *op. cit.*, p. 135).

24. Num. xiii, 21.

25. Cf. E. Forrer, *Provinzeinteilung*, pp. 62, 69 and W. F. Albright, *Archaeology and the Religion of Israel*, p. 130 f. for the evidence supplied by the analysis of the Assyrian provincial organization.

26. II Sam. viii, 3. Cf. S. Schiffer, *op. cit.*, p. 76, Meyer, *Geschichte des Altertums* I, p. 364.

27. Cf. Schiffer, *ibid.*, W. F. Albright, *Archaeology and the Religion of Israel*, p. 219, n. 104.

28. *Geschichte Israels* I, pp. 141 f.

29. E. Kraeling, *op. cit.*, p. 39.

30. Fr. Delitzsch, *Wo lag das Paradies?* I, p. 141.

31. H. Winckler, *Geschichte Israels* I, p. 141. H. Guthe, *Bibelatlas* (1926), no. 3. Basing their hypothesis on the Annals of Asshurbanipal and the Assyrian geographical lists, their conclusions are invalidated, because no consistent order is observed in these Assyrian records.

32. S. Schiffer, *op. cit.*, pp. 144 f. and E. Kraeling, *op. cit.*, p. 40 f. It may well be, of course, that Zobah, in the heyday of its power before David, extended southward to a considerable extent into Coelesyria, just as it certainly embraced Damascus in the Antilibanus region.

33. Cf. note 13 of this chapter. The variant readings Ṣubatu and Ṣubiti illustrate the normal vocalic dissimilation of the middle Assyrian dialect, and point to an original Ṣubatu Ṣubutu (Albright,

Archaeology and the Religion of Israel, p. 211, n. 6, BASOR 67, p. 27, n. 6. Cf. Fr. Delitzsch, *Wo lag das Paradies?* pp. 62, 69. Also see Julius Lewy, *Hebrew Union College Annual*, XVIII, p. 447, n. 100.

34. Albright, *op. cit.*, p. 130 f., E. Forrer, *Provinzeinteilung*, pp. 62, 69. Le P. F. M. Abel, *Géographie de la Palestine* II, carte VI.

35. Albright, *op. cit.*, p. 211, n. 7.

36. II Samuel viii, 3.

37. II Samuel viii, 5, cf. v. 9.

38. I Samuel xiv, 47 (LXX).

39. I Chronicles xviii, 8.

40. Albright, *op. cit.*, p. 131.

41. Cf. Genesis xxii, 24.

42. Schiffer, *op. cit.*, pp. 142 ff. Cf. II Sam. viii, 8, I Chron. xviii, 8. The root *ṣhb* occurs in the Old Testament in the sense " to glitter, to shine " (as copper or gold)—" to be reddish or yellowish " like the human hair (Lev. xiii, 30; xxxii, 36) and in Ezra viii, 27 מָצְהָב " polished, glittering ", describing the colour of bronze utensils. The Arabic has a similar meaning " to be red like a fox ".

43. II Chronicles viii, 3, 4.

44. Julius Lewy, " Ḥamât-Ṣôbâ and Ṣubat-Ḥamâtu " (*Hebrew Union College Annual*, XVIII, 1944, pp. 443–454). For example, Lewy assumes the root *ṣ-h-b* originally meant " to be hot " (equals *ḥ-m-m*) and connects it with a " sun-god " *Ṣôb*. On this presumption he equates Ḥamât/Ḥamatu with Ṣôbâ/Ṣubatu, two names by which he maintains the Assyrians knew the modern town of Baʻalbek (*op. cit.*, p. 451). The theory is ingenious but because of its weak links is hardly to be taken seriously. For the location of Baʻalbek (Heliopolis) see Dussaud, *Topographie de la Syrie*, carte XIV.

45. Deut. iii, 14; Josh. xii, 5; xiii, 11.

46. Deut. iii, 14; Josh. xii, 5; xiii, 11, 13. The Geshurites mentioned in connection with the Philistines in south-western Palestine offer a problem (Josh. xiii, 2).

47. G. E. Wright, *Westminster Historical Atlas*, Philadelphia, 1945, plate VII A.

48. Abel, (*op. cit.*, p. 10) connects Tob of Judges xi, 3–5 and II Samuel x, 6–8 with *tb* (*toubi*) of Thutmose III's list, no. 22, north of Gilead, " l'actuelle eṭ-Ṭaiyibé sur la route de Boṣra à Derʻā."

49. Abel, *ibid.*

NOTES TO CHAPTER IV

1. W. F. Albright, *Archaeology and the Religion of Israel*, p. 130. For a discussion of David's reign see M. Noth, *Geschichte Israels* (Göttingen, 1950), pp. 155–177.

2. Eduard Meyer, *Geschichte des Altertums*, II 2, 1931, pp. 366, 373. See A. Alt's discussions of David's conquests in *Kleine Schriften* II, pp. 68–75.

3. I Sam. xiv, 47. See Noth, *op. cit.*, pp. 142–155.

4. *Ibid.* There is no reason to doubt the historical value of this passage. It fits remarkably well into the general historical context of the period, and is precisely what one would expect in the general conditions prevailing. For a critical discussion of the historical worth of the Biblical notices covering the period of Saul, David and Solomon see Albrecht Alt, *Die Staatenbildung der Israeliten in Palästina*, Leipzig 1930, pp. 42–45. Cf. C. H. Gordon, *Introduction to O.T. Times* (1953) pp. 145–168.

5. II Sam. x, 1–6.

6. Is *Ishtob* a personal name or a place? Cf. ARV איש טוב "men of Tob", Kraeling (*Aram and Israel*, p. 42, cf. n. 1) construes Ishtob as the king of Maacah.

7. II Sam. iii, 3; xiii, 37.

8. II Sam. x, 1–6.

9. II Sam. x, 15–19.

10. The name also occurs as Hadarezer (II Sam. x, 16, 19; I Chron. xviii, 3, 5, 7, 9, 10, 16, 19 Massoretic text, Syriac and Vulgate). But the form Hadadezer (II Sam. viii, 3 ff. and I Kings xi, 23) is original, as we know from the common divine name Hadad, the West Semitic storm god. The confusion between *daleth* and *resh* in script is doubtless the explanation of the variant, although assimilation of the *daleth* to the final sonorous *resh* may have encouraged the change. Cf. *Adramelek* (*Adarmelek* II Kings xvii, 31) which most certainly was developed from *Adadmelek*. Did a similar influence of the sonorous *mem* through dissimilation bring about the form *Darmeseq* for *Dammeseq*?

11. The expression is scarcely more than a geographical designation, and must be understood from its context. In the case of

II Samuel x, 16 the reference is to the country east of the Euphrates. However in I Kings v, 4 the allusion is patently to the region west of the river.

12. I Chron. xix, 6. This is the last biblical occurrence of the term *Aram Naharaim* (date *c.* 400 B.C. for the book of I Chronicles). Yet the events refer to David's reign, after which period the term no longer occurs. Cf. Roger T. O'Callaghan, *Aram Naharaim* (Rome, Pontificum Institutum Biblicum, 1948), p. 143, accounts for this singularity by the fact that Damascus meanwhile had assumed control in northern Syria, constituting a deadly menace to Israel. The thoroughly political complexion of affairs, he maintains, was enough to establish state names as the proper terms for natural and ready reference. O'Callaghan is correct in locating Aram Naharaim of I Chron. xix, 6 and Psalm lx, 2 approximately in the region south-west of the Euphrates and not narrowly " beyond the River " in Mesopotamia proper (*op. cit.*, p. 141).

13. II Sam. x, 16 (?), 17. Is this place identical with *Ḥl'm* of the Brussels Figurines dating from about 1850–1825 B.C., located by Albright north of Gilead (BASOR 83, 1941, p. 33)? However, I Chronicles xviii, 3 seems to place the battle חֲמָתָה " to " or " by " Hamath, unless we are to construe this encounter as a victory of David subsequent to the clash at Ḥelam.

14. These structures cannot be as late as Solomon's reign when a different style of construction was in vogue. Since these two towns were outposts of Judah, they point to construction in the early reign of David.

15. I Chron. xviii, 3. Does this verse describe a later military expedition of David to extend his power northward? However that may be, it can hardly be identical with the battle of Ḥelam, unless Ḥelam is located in the vicinity of Hamath, for the powerful city on the Orontes is assuredly meant. David could easily have by-passed Damascus to make the attack possible.

16. Albright, *From the Stone Age to Christianity*, p. 120 ff. *Archaeology and the Religion of Israel*, pp. 132 ff.

17. I Kings x, 15.

18. Albright, *Archaeology and the Religion of Israel*, p. 133.

19. James A. Montgomery, *Arabia and the Bible*, p. 175.

20. Cf. *The Palestine Exploration Fund Quarterly Statement*, 1933, pp. 138, 183 f.

21. Nelson Glueck, *The Other Side of the Jordan*, 1940, pp. 93 ff. BASOR 79, pp. 3 ff.

22. Glueck, AASOR XV, 1934–35, p. 50.

23. I Kings xi, 14–22.

24. Glueck, AASOR XV, 1934–35, " Explorations in Eastern Palestine II ", p. 50. Cf. J. A. Montgomery, *op. cit.*, pp. 52, 73, 175–179.

25. EA 107: 25–28.

26. I Kings iv, 24.

27. II Chron. viii, 4.

28. Albright, *Archaeology and the Religion of Israel*, p. 133.

29. E. Kraeling, *Aram and Israel*, p. 47 f.

30. Cf. Chapter III, n. 44 for Julius Lewy's location of Hamath-Zobah in the lower Biqaʿ, Greek Heliopolis, modern Baʿalbek. However, we maintain Hamath on the Orontes, north of Damascus, is meant. The geographical distinctions between Zobah and nearby Hamath (II Sam. viii, 9, 10) doubtless had long since passed away at the time of the Chronicler, so that the double name is to be taken as a loose designation for the general region which Hadadezer had dominated at the height of his North Syrian empire (cf. II Sam. viii, 9 f.).

31. II Chron. viii, 3, 4.

32. II Sam. viii, 9, 10.

33. Albright, *op. cit.*, p. 154.

34. I Kings iv, 24.

NOTES TO CHAPTER V

1. Cf. W. F. Albright's reconstruction of the Benhaded inscription in BASOR 87 (October 1942), pp. 23–29; further discussed by Levi della Vida in BASOR 90 (April 1943), pp. 30–32; Albright, *Ibid.*, pp. 32–34; also M. Maurice Dunand's " Stèle araméenne dediée à Melquart" in the *Bulletin du Musée de Beyrouth*, Vol. III (*c*. 1941), pp. 65–76. See also de Vaux, *Bulletin du Musée de Beyrouth* V (1943 or 1944), pp. 7–20 and " Psalms and Inscriptions of Petition and Acknowledgment", *Louis Ginsberg Jubilee Volume*, New York, 1945, pp. 159–171.

2. *Bir-hadad*, of course, stands for later *Bar-hadad*, Hebrew, *Ben-hadad*. The earlier vocalization is supported by a number of Assyrian transcriptions, particularly *Bir-dadda* (i.e. *Bir-dad*), Albright (BASOR 87, p. 26, n. 6); cf. also AJSL XLIV, 1927, p. 33.

3. This name is identical with Hebrew-Canaanite *Ḥzyn* for the old *Ḥzyn*, i.e. *Hezion* of I Kings xv, 18. The Aramaic *d* appears in Hebrew as *z*, as the former sound no longer existed in South Canaanite. Cuneiform *Ḥadiânu*, Ugaritic *Ḥdyn* fix the original consonants of the name as *ḥdw* or *ḥdy* (Albright, JPOS, 1935, p. 229). Albright suggests a likely etymology from the Arabic. *Ḥaḍyân* equals *ḥaḍwâ*, " a person having pendulous ears " (BASOR 87, p. 26, n. 7).

4. Albright, *op. cit.*, p. 26.

5. From the LXX (B,L) of I Kings xi, 23, which has *Εσρων(μ)* (Esron) it has been supposed that Hezron was the correct form. Kraeling was, of course, right in positing Hezion as the correct spelling long before the evidence from the royal inscription of Benhadad was available (*Aram and Israel*, p. 48). G^B gives *Αζειν*, G^AL *Αζαηλ* (influenced by חזאל for Hezion of the Massoretic text of I Kings xv, 18, from which Winckler (*Altestamentliche Untersuchungen* 1892, p. 62) erroneously deduced the original name as Hazael. There is no decisive proof that Hezion was king of Damascus. He may have been only a tribal chieftain.

6. Albright, *op. cit.*, p. 26, n. 7. An inscription from Tell Halaf reads thus: ^m *Ka-pa-ra mâr* ^m *Ḥa-di-a-ni*. The *zain* and the *daleth* representing a Hebrew-Aramaic phonetic correspondence, now well

established from many other examples, as Hebrew *Hadad-ʿezri* for Aramaic *Hadad-ʿeḏri*. There is a possibility that the kingdom of Kapara and Damascus may have been related not only by racial affinities, but also by family ties. Both families could conceivably have belonged to the same clan *Bêt Haḏyân*.

7.   II Kings xvi, 6, 9; xv, 37; Is. vii, 4, 8.

8.   E. Meyer (*Geschichte des Altertums* II 2, 1931, p. 269), Rudolph Kittel (*Geschichte des Volkes Israel* I, 1909, p. 221) and others agree that Rezon established the strong Aramaic kingdom of Damascus. The data giving these facts (I Kings xi, 23 ff.) are brief. As Meyer notes the account is mechanically inserted in the story of Hadad of Edom by the redactor, and the source employed obviously had more to say concerning the matter (*op. cit.*, p. 269, n. 2).

9.   The brevity and fragmentary character of our information, and the circumstances of its insertion in the episode of Hadad's Edomite uprising, are, however, no arguments against its historicity.

10.   The name stands for *Ṭâb-Rimmôn*, " good is Rimmon " (*Ṭab-Rammân* of the Benhadad stele). The formation offers no difficulty, being illustrated by many parallels in Aramaic and Assyrian names of the neo-Babylonian period (Albright, BASOR 87, p. 26, n. 6). Rimmon, the national god of the Aramaeans, whose temple was located in Damascus (II Kings v, 18) is identical with Hadad (Baʿal), the great West Semitic storm god, variously called Alʾiyân-Baal at Ugarit, Hadad-Rimmon at Megiddo, and Adonî, " my lord " (Greek Adonis) ·at Byblus and Cyprus (Albright, *Archaeology and the Religion of Israel*, p. 80), and Melcarth, " king of the city ", at Tyre. The conquerors who founded the dynasty of Accad early transported Hadad to Mesopotamia, where he was popularly connected with *ramâmu*, " to thunder ", and received the permanent epithet *Ra-mi-nu*. Dussaud imagines the Massoretes altered *Rammân* to *Rimmon* (pomegranite) in II Kings v, 18 and Zechariah xii, 11 where the complete expression occurs Hadad-Rimmon—" Hadad the Thunderer " (René Dussaud, *Découvertes de Ras Shamra et L'Ancien Testament*, second ed., Paris, 1941, pp. 99, 101, 134). However, by natural phonetic change *Rammânu* (" Thunderer ") would appear in Hebrew as *Rimmon*, synonymous with the Semitic word for " pomegranite " (cf. *arimânu* in Accadian). From the first centuries of the second millennium B.C. Accadian texts recognize Hadad as specially the god of Aleppo, and thus, according to Dhorme, the deity is to be considered as a western

importation (cf. Dhorme, " La plus ancienne histoire d'Alep", in *Syria*, 1927, p. 40).

11. I Kings xiv, 25, 26.

12. I Kings xv, 16–22.

13. II Chron. xvi, 1–14.

14. W. F. Albright, AASOR, XXI, XXII, Chapt. I, n. 13.

15. BASOR 87, p. 27.

16. Cf. W. F. Albright, "The Chronology of the Divided Monarchy of Israel" (BASOR 100, pp. 16–22). On the antedating system the total number of regnal years of Judah from Rehoboam to Ahaziah, inclusive, must equal the corresponding total of the kings of Israel from Jeroboam I to Joram, inclusive. Since these totals do not tally, the alternative is either to increase drastically the Israelite numbers, or reduce the reign of Rehoboam from the traditional seventeen to eight, allowing him not more than three years of rule after Shishak's destructive incursion into Judah.

17. The other regnal years of Asa mentioned by the Chronicler; namely, the fifteenth, thirty-fifth, thirty-ninth and forty-first all confirm his citation of the thirty-sixth year (BASOR 100, p. 20, n. 14). In particular, the fifteenth year (II Chron. xv, 10), when Asa initiated his reform after deposing the queen-regent Maachah, is so plausible that it is even critically accepted by Julian Morgenstern (*Heb. Un. College Annual* XV, p. 111).

18. *Encyclopaedia Biblica* I, p. 531 f.

19. Cf. E. Kraeling, *op. cit.*, p. 50.

20. Vol. III, pp. 65–76.

21. Albright dates the script somewhere between 875 and 825 B.C. as extreme limits, with a preferred date about 850 B.C., or slightly earlier. M. Dunand (*Bulletin du Musée de Beyrouth*, III, 75, 76) arrives at a later date (end of the ninth or beginning of the eighth century) but he did not have access to the Phoenician inscriptions of the first half of the ninth century. The script fits neatly into the period between the type represented by the inscriptions of Cyprus and Sardinia (first half of ninth century), and the Gezer Calendar (late tenth century), on the one hand, and the steles of Mesha (*c.* 840 B.C.) and Kilamuwa (*c.* 825 B.C.) on the other (Albright, BASOR 83, pp. 14–22). *Beth, zayin, yodh*, and *nun* are shown to be more archaic than these characters are in inscriptions dating after 840 B.C., and the *mem* and *kaph*, as well as the particular stance of the letters, exhibit the characteristic slope of later times. These epigraphic criteria strongly oppose any dating appreciably earlier

than the middle of the century, and render it extremely unlikely that Benhadad I is not to be identified with Benhadad II (BASOR 90, p. 32).

22. BASOR 87, pp. 23–29. (Cf. H. L. Ginsberg, "Psalms, and Inscriptions of Petition and Acknowledgement", *Louis Ginsberg Jubilee Volume*, 1945, p. 160, n. 4). De Vaux, however, reports that after an examination of the original, the restoration of Benhadad's patronymic does not seem feasible to him (*Bulletin du Musée de Beyrouth* V, 1943 or 1944, p. 9, n. 1). Notwithstanding de Vaux's scepticism, H. L. Gingsberg is correct in saying "Albright's chronology and his ascription of the stele commend themselves" (*op. cit.*, p. 160, n. 4).

23. Cf. F. X. Kugler, *Von Moses bis Paulus*, pp. 134–189; Julius Lewy, *Die Chronologie der Könige von Israel und Juda* (Giessen); J. Begrich, *Die Chronologie der Könige von Israel und Juda* (Tübingen); Sigismund Mowinckel, "Die Chronologie der Israelitischen und jüdischen Könige" (*Acta Orientalia*, X, pp. 161–277); Max Vogelstein, *Biblical Chronology*, Part I (Cincinnati); Edwin R. Thiele, "The Chronology of the Kings of Judah and Israel", (JNES III, 1944, pp. 137–186); W. F. Albright, "The Chronology of the Divided Monarchy of Israel" (BASOR 100, pp. 16–22).

24. Continuous revision downward has been necessitated since the third quarter of the last century as a result of the flow of new evidence from the Assyrian documents. The well-known tendency of chronological numbers to increase with time is due to the prevalent custom among ancient Oriental scholars and scribes of including in the text variants which had come down to them. In consequence their chronological lists show swelling regnal and dynastic totals (Albright, *From the Stone Age to Christianity*, p. 45). They made every effort to do justice to the variant readings—frequently including them in a new total by direct addition, or choosing the larger of two alternatives (BASOR 100, p. 19, n. 12).

25. BASOR 100, p. 20, n. 14.

26. These two pivotal synchronisms were fixed precisely, so any years between them deducted from the kings of Judah must likewise be deducted from the kings of Israel. The synchronisms in Kings were calculated for the most part by later Jewish scholars from the table of kings and the synchronisms available. There are no indications, however, that such a series of synchronisms in terms of Israelite regnal years as was at the disposal of the Chronicler was available to the Deuteronomic editor of Kings. These synchronisms

were likely computed secondarily by the latter or a precursor. Babylonian Chronological tablets furnish precise parallels. The method of dating by the years of the reigning monarch is always followed in the Babylonian Chronicle, with no cross datings as in Kings. But the accessions of Assyrian and Elamite kings are dated in terms of Babylonian regnal years. However, synchronistic lists of Assyrian and Babylonian kings from Asshur display a number of correct synchronisms. But the greater majority were the work of later compilers (cf. Albright, *Revue d'Assyriologie* XVIII, 10 f., BASOR XXI–XXII, Ch. I, n. 13).

27. It is apparent from I Kings xvi, 29 that there is considerable secondary confusion as to the twelve years allotted Omri's reign in verse 23. The synchronisms with Asa of Judah in verses 23 and 29, calculated on the antedating system consistently employed, would allow Omri no more than eight years—six years at Tirzah (v. 23) and two at his new capital Samaria (as Crowfoot's excavations at the latter site corroborate). The apportionment of twelve years to Omri's reign must be construed as a calculation based mistakenly on the reigns of Tibni and Omri as successive instead of contemporaneous, which became fixed in the text of Kings before the synchronisms were added by a later scholar.

28. The evidence of the synchronisms is manifestly in favour of this reduction, as recent chronologists (Lewy, Kugler, Begrich, etc.) have taken into account.

29. Any appreciable increase above eight years is highly improbable for the reign of Joram. The transmitted regnal span of a dozen years can be squeezed into the period between 853 B.C., when, according to the Assyrian annals, Ahab was confederate with Benhadad in the battle of Qarqar, and 841 B.C., when Jehu was already king, but it is unreasonable not to assume an interval of at least a year or two before Ahab would go to war with Syria. The double chronology in the case of Joram (II Kings i, 17; iii, 2) in itself casts doubt on the twelve-year period.

30. But it is clear from II Chronicles xiii and I Kings xv, 19 that Judah under Abijah (and possibly under Rehoboam) had concluded an alliance with Tabrimmon, Hezion's son, king of Damascus, thereby inaugurating a policy later pursued by Asa of putting pressure upon Israel whenever the latter's aggression toward the south became dangerous (A. T. Olmstead, *Hist. of Palestine and Syria*, pp. 356 f.).

31. E. Kraeling, *op. cit.*, p. 48.

32.   I Kings xiii, 32; xviii, 2; xxi, 1; Amos iii, 9, etc.

33.   Many parallels from Western Asia may be cited where the name of the capital and the country are identical. For example, Asshur, Khatti, Damascus, Hamath, Sidon (Tyre, the capital), etc.

NOTES TO CHAPTER VI

1. Cf. A. Alt, ZDMG, 88, 233 ff.; "Völker und Staaten Syriens", *Der Alte Orient*, 34: 4.

2. I Kings xviii, 18. It is highly probable that this royal marriage actually took place during the reign of Omri. If Ahaziah of Judah, the son of Joram and Athaliah, at his accession in 842 B.C. was twenty-two years old (II Kings viii, 26), his birth is to be fixed 864/863, and his mother, the daughter of Ahab and Jezebel, accordingly must have been born around 880 (E. Meyer, *Geschichte des Altertums*, II, 2, 1931, p. 278, n. 2). Meyer (*op. cit.*, p. 279), whose chronology places Omri's reign 885–874 B.C., allowing him the full traditional twelve years, would then put the event about the fifth year of Omri's rule. Albright's chronology (876–869 for Omri) would not provide for this event, which, according to the reduced dating, would occur four years or more *before* the accession of Omri. Albright considers Athaliah as the daughter of Omri (II Kings viii, 26) rather than Ahab (II Kings viii, 18). He views the בת־אַחְאָב of the latter passage as a copyist's slip, following the mention of אחאב two words previously in the same verse. According to this view Athaliah would be a young girl when her father, Omri, became king. In any event the marriage almost certainly occurred before Ahab's entrance upon the kingship.

3. Ittobaal of Tyre. At this phase of history Sidon and Tyre comprised but one state, as shown by Albright, *Studies in the History of Culture*, 1942, pp. 33–34.

4. The practice of importing foreign deities on political rather than on religious grounds, so pronouncedly true of Solomon almost a century before (I Kings xi, 4–8), evidently originated as a policy of the Northern Kingdom with Ahab. It was doubtless initiated in accordance with the general ancient Near Eastern custom, whereby an alliance or the establishment of an amicable relationship was consummated between two kings by marriages in the royal houses and by the adoption of each other's deities (G. Levi Della Vida, BASOR 90, p. 31). However, the extremely unfavourable light in which Omri was regarded by pious Jahwists in later tradition (I Kings xvi, 25, 26), coupled with the ominous reference to "the statutes

of Omri ", which are linked with " all the works of the house of Ahab " (Micah vi, 16), would suggest that he not only laid the foundation for the religious syncretism of his son's reign, but that he may actually have had a share in the importation of foreign deities for political purposes.

5.   Lines 4–8.

6.   II Kings iii, 4.

7.   I Kings xvi, 16.

8.   I Kings xvi, 17, 18.

9.   J. W. Crowfoot's excavations at Samaria (1931–33) under a joint expedition including Harvard University, the Hebrew University in Jerusalem, the Palestine Exploration Fund, the British Academy, and the British School of Archaeology in Jerusalem, with further work done in 1935 by the three last-named institutions, have cleared up the stratigraphy of the Israelite period (J. W. Crowfoot, Kathleen M. Kenyon, and E. L. Sukenik, *The Buildings at Samaria*, 1942). Strata I and II, belonging to the Omri-Ahab dynasty, but indistinguishable as to " Omri " and " Ahab " phases, demonstrate that Omri merely began constructions which were carried forward by Ahab (Cf. Albright, BASOR 100, p. 20, n. 15; Jack Finegan, *Light from the Ancient Past* (1946), pp. 154–155).

10.   It is unnecessary to assume from I Kings xx, 34 that Omri was a vassal of Aram, as Kraeling does (*Aram and Israel*, pp. 50, 51). Alfred Jepsen is correct in pointing out that the portrait of Omri who vanquished his internal opponents, concluded a treaty with Tyre, built a new capital, and impressed the Assyrians as the representative Israelite, and yet in spite of all this is said to be a vassal of Aram, is more than contradictory (*Archiv für Orientforschung*, XIV, Berlin, 1942, p. 157, n. 17). However, his attempt to resolve the difficulty by referring the events of I Kings xx, in so far as they reflect generally recognizable historical happenings, to the Jehu instead of the Omri dynasty, furnishes an escape, but scarcely a solution to the problems involved (*op. cit.*, pp. 156, 157).

11.   It is significant that no mention is made of Israel or of Damascus in the records of Ashurnasirpal II (883–859) in his victorious sweep to the Mediterranean (I. M. Price, *The Monuments and the Old Testament*, 1925, p. 267). He kept clear of Damascene territory, striking at the Aramaean and Hittite states to the north, and then advanced southward along the coast (R. Kittel, *Geschichte des Volkes Israel*, II, p. 335, n. 1) reducing Tyre, Sidon, Byblus, and

Arvad to the state of tributaries. But there is no evidence that Israel was subdued, or paid tribute, at this time.

12. For the use of *ben* with a genitive of place to denote a native of that place see Chapter I, n. 23. Hence Jehu, who overthrew the Omride dynasty, is called *Ja'ua apil Ḥumrî*, "Jehu son of Omri", on Shalmaneser III's black obelisk (ARAB, I, 590).

13. ARAB, I, 816.

14. I Kings xvi, 34; xxii, 39. E. Meyer, *op. cit.*, p. 327. Like Solomon, by cultivating close affinity with Tyre, Ahab displayed a pronounced taste for architecture in Phoenician style (I Kings xxii, 39). The " ivory house " which he built being imitated in the following century by many of the wealthy nobles of his realm (Amos iii, 15; Meyer, *op. cit.*, p. 327). See A. Scharff and A. Moortgat, *Ägypten und Vorderasien im Altertum*, (München, 1950), p. 440.

15. Amos i, 9.

16. W. F. Albright's final rendering of the Benhadad Stele, incorporating suggestions by H. L. Ginsberg and Levi Della Vida, runs thus: " (This is) the stele which Bir-Hadad, son of ⌈Ṭab-Ramman son of Khadhyân⌉, king of Aram, set up for his lord Milqart, to whom he vowed it because he heard his voice " (BASOR 90, p. 32). The god, as he is seen on the Benhadad Stela (BASOR 87, p. 24, fig. 1) wears a Syrian loin cloth, and appears in warlike character, with composite bow and battle axe, reflecting pre-Assyrian art of the cultural milieu of the older reliefs from Senjirli and Carchemish, as Albright has observed (*op. cit.*, pp. 28, 29). There can be no doubt that the deity itself was cosmic in character (cf. Albright, *Archaeology and the Religion of Israel*, pp. 80, 81 ff.; JBL, 1940, pp. 102–110) and was but the local Tyrian adaptation of the great West-Semitic storm god, Baal, Baal Hadad, Baal Rimmon, or Aliyan Baal, etc. The name "Milk-qart", whence "Melqart", Graeco-Roman "Melcarth", signifies "king of the city", that is, doubtless originally "king of the Netherworld", (Ras Shamra, B VIII, 11, quoted by Albright, AJSL 53: 11; *Archaeology and the Religion of Israel*, pp. 81, 196, n. 29); Henri Seyrig, " Antiquités Syriennes ", *Syria*, XXIV, 1944–45, pp. 62–80. There is, in addition to the Ugaritic material, ample evidence furnished by Sumero-Accadian practice, which greatly influenced Canaanite religious concepts, for both the idea and nomenclature for the use of *qartu* (Hebrew, *qeret*) " city " in the sense of the underworld (Ps. lxxii, 16). However, with the ascendancy of Tyre to the prevailing position in

Phoenician maritime trade and colonization, there can be no reasonable doubt, it appears to me, that the Tyrian deity assumed a popular meaning "King of the City", that is, "King of Tyre", from which alone as the mother city, so far as we know, Phoenician colonies went out. Hence everywhere Melqart, the city god, was current as the founder and protector of the colonies—in Cypress, Malta, as well as in North Africa and Spain (E. Meyer, *op. cit.*, pp. 81, 82). This seems indubitably the case inasmuch as the kings of Tyre sought to hold their colonies in a state of permanent dependence. The religious connection with the mother city, which was expressed by gifts and tribute to the temple of Melqart at Tyre, for example, was dutifully maintained by Carthage even when it had attained to a position of great power (Meyer, *op. cit.*, p. 113).

17.   This is the view of both W. F. Albright and G. Levi Della Vida (BASOR 90, p. 32). Ethbaal was obviously prompted by the same reasons to enter into a family tie with the king of Damascus as he was to give his daughter in marriage to the king of Israel. He doubtless not only wished to guarantee the flow of trade on his side, but more particularly to protect the exposed borders of his maritime state from attack from the inland kingdoms. Peace with such a powerful neighbour as Damascus was of the greatest importance.

18.   It seems wholly unnecessary in maintaining the cosmic character of Melqart to assume that Benhadad I worshipped this deity independent of his rank as the patron god of Tyre, or that the new deity was honoured by any proportion of his Aramaic subjects. It is best to explain the peculiar nature of the stela in being composed in Aramaic, but bearing a Phoenician flavour (following Della Vida, BASOR 90, p. 31), by surmising that the Syrian monarch added a foreign god to his pantheon, and had the dedicatory words composed in the distinctive style of the deity's original home.

19.   I Kings xviii, 19, 21, etc.

20.   Albright considers this as Omri's act, not Ahab's (cf. n. 2 above).

21.   E. Meyer, *op. cit.*, p. 332.

22.   E. Kraeling, *op. cit.*, p. 51.

23.   The thirty-two kings of the Massoretic Text (I Kings xx, 1), confirmed by the LXX, has commonly been taken as an exaggeration since at the important battle of Karkar in 853 the Monolith Inscription of Shalmaneser III mentions only a dozen kings (and actually numbers but eleven) as allies with Damascus. The Zkr stele mentions

from twelve to eighteen allied kings, the number depending on the restoration of the figures in question in lines 4–5 of the inscription (Noth, ZDPV, 52, 1929, p. 132). On the other hand, the figure in I Kings xx, 1 may be exact, but may have included names of persons who were not much more than provincial governors, feudal princes (cf. I Kings x, 15; xx, 24), or Arabian shiekhs, like Gindibu, who furnished Benhadad's federation at Karkar one thousand camels. A. T. Olmstead construes the data as indicative of the considerable size of the empire the Syrian kings had already built up at this time (*History of Assyria*, 1923, p. 133).

24. This is now known to be mediaeval Afîq, modern Fîq east of the Sea of Galilee in southern Jôlân, on the road from Damascus to Beisān (Abel, *Géographie de la Palestine* II, p. 246. Cf. Forrer, *Provinzeinteilung des Assyrischen Reiches*, p. 62, Albright, *Archaeology and the Religion of Israel*, p. 209, n. 84). R. Kittel, however, locates it in the valley of the Kishon in Esdraelon (*op. cit.*, p. 358, n. 3), where Meyer likewise identifies it with the battle ground there known from the Philistine wars (*op. cit.*, p. 332).

25. The 100,000 enemy infantry slain in one day of the Massoretic Text (I Kings xx, 29), and also of the LXX, is to be taken in all probability as a round number for a very great multitude. In any case it could not be more than an estimated aggregate (cf. n. 42).

26. I Kings xx, 30.

27. Olmstead, *op. cit.*, p. 134.

28. Meyer, *op. cit.*, p. 333.

29. I Kings xx, 34.

30. Called "Adâ, a city of Urḫileni of Hamath", on band IX of the gates of Balawat, and identified with Tell Dānīt south-west of Idlib (*Revue Archéologique*, 1908, p. 225; cf. Kraeling, *op. cit.*, p. 73). Dussaud (*Topographie historique de la Syrie*, p. 243) suggests " le Dana, près Tourmanin, d'oû par Sermin ou Idlib on gagne le Roudj qui représente évidemment Argana ". For a study of the topography of Syria see Karl Elliger, " Sam'al und Hamat in ihrem Verhältnis zu Hattina, Unqi und Arpad " in the Eissfeldt *Festschrift*. This is an excellent discussion and bears on Damascus.

31. Dussaud (*ibid.*) rejects the identification of Barqâ (Parqâ) with Bargylus (a mountain, not a city) or with " Bargash ou Bargoush ", and connects it with " Barquom près de Zeitan et de Zirbé, au nord-ouest d'Alep ".

32. For Dussaud's location see n. 30. Kraeling, on the other hand, connects the place with the site of modern Rīḥā on the north

side of the mountain bearing this name (*Revue Archéologique*, 1908, p. 225; Kraeling, *op. cit.*, p. 73).

33.   It is now quite unnecessary, in the light of the new evidence supplied by the Melcarth Stela from the region of Aleppo, to engage in the old controversy as to whether Benhadad I is the same person as Hadadezer (Adadidri), whom the Assyrian records mention as on the throne at Damascus in the years 853, 848, and 845. The new monument solves the heretofore vexing problem of the succession of Syrian kings, and proves that Benhadad who invaded Israel in the thirty-sixth year of Asa (*c.* 879 B.C.) is the same ruler who met his death at the hands of the usurper, Hazael (II Kings viii, 7–15), some thirty-six years later about 843 B.C. (Albright, BASOR 87, p. 28, n. 16). The occurrence of the double nomenclature, one a personal and the other a throne name, is illustrated in the case of at least seven kings of Judah, by pharaohs of Egypt (AASOR XXI–XXII, ch. II, n. 9), as well as by Hazael's son, Benhadad II (the Birhadad of the Zakir Stele), who was commonly styled *Mari'* by the Assyrians, which was, in all likelihood, an abbreviation for a name like *Mari'-Hadad*,—" Hadad is my Lord " (Albright, *loc. cit.*).

34.   Alfred Jepsen, " Israel Und Damaskus ", AfO, XIV, p. 166. Cf. AsO XVI, pp. 315 ff.

35.   AfO XIV, p. 167.

36.   Unhappily, almost nothing is known of the internal organization of the Damascene state at this time. Later, at the period of Tiglathpileser III (744–727), there is a notice of sixteen districts in the land of Damascus (ARAB, 777; P. Rost, *Die Keilschrifttexte Tiglath-Pilesers* III, p. 36 f.). How old this organization was, which was well established at that time, of course, is not known. It likely dates from the period of ascendency, and could scarcely have arisen at the time of the fall of the city to Assyria, nor in the preceding period of decline (cf. Jepsen, *op. cit.*, p. 167; Forrer, *Provinzeinteilung*, p. 62).

37.   Meyer, *op. cit.*, p. 333.

38.   ARAB I, 611.

39.   Jack Finegan, *Light from the Ancient Past*, p. 172.

40.   A. T. Olmstead, *History of Palestine and Syria*, p. 384.

41.   The absence of Judah, Edom, and Moab from the list indicates their virtual state of vassalage to Ahab, with whose contingent their troops must have been included (Olmstead, *loc. cit.*). It is very doubtful that Egypt is included in the coalition. The 1,000 soldiers " of the land of Musri ", enumerated in the Monolith

Inscription, probably refers to a small kingdom in the Cilician-Cappadocian region of Asia Minor, rather than to the land of the Nile (cf. A. Alt, ZDMG, 88, p. 255). For the general cuneiform sources see Ernst Michel, *Die Assur-Texte Salmanassars III* (858–824), which appeared in *Die Welt des Orients* I (1947), pp. 5–20, 57–71; (1948), pp. 205–222; (1950) pp. 385–396; (1952) pp. 454–475; (1954), pp. 27–45. Although a survey of the cuneiform evidence seems not to include Egypt, nevertheless, Meyer (*op. cit.*, p. 333), Montgomery (*Arabia and the Bible*, p. 94) and Olmstead, etc., construe the reference to Egypt, the latter referring to a fragment of a large two-handled jar of Egyptian alabaster, which was discovered in Ahab's courtyard, and which is marked with the cartouche of Osorkon II (874–853), as an indication that the pharaoh had an interest in the coalition (Cf. Reisner, Fisher, Lyon, *Harvard Excavations at Samaria*, 1924, p. 247, Olmstead, *loc. cit.*).

42. The number of the slain increased with the passage of time from 14,000 (the conservative figure of the Monolith which itself is doubtless exaggerated) to 20,500 Annals (66), to 25,000 of the Bull Inscription from Nimrud, to 29,000 of a recent statue from Ashur. " Man sieht was von diesen Zahlen zu halten ist " (Meyer, *op. cit.*, p. 333, n. 2).

43. Gilzau may be the Seleucid Larissa (Qal'at Seǧar) where the Orontes River runs through a steep narrow valley (Kraeling, *op. cit.*, p. 75). Its banks at this juncture would furnish a natural site for the battle. Cf. Bell, *The Desert and the Sown*, p. 235. Dussaud (*op. cit.*, p. 242) would connect Gilzau with " Asharné où se trouve un pont antique ". But Thureau-Dangin (*Comptes-rendus Acad.*, 1924 p. 168) would connect the site with Qarqar.

44. Meyer, *op. cit.*, pp. 333, 334. Cf. M. Noth, *Geschichte Israels*, p. 213.

45. I Kings xxii, 1.

46. I Kings xxii, 3.

47. I Kings xxii, 31.

48. II Kings iii, 5.

49. Of course, in the light of the Melcarth Stela Luckenbill's theory that Benhadad is not identical with Adadidri, but is rather the latter's predecessor (AJSL, 27, 277 ff.) is to be rejected. Adadidri is the Assyrian rendering of the Aramaic form of the personal name, pronounced Hadadezer in Canaanite dialect, as in the case of the King of Zobah (II Sam. viii, 3 ff.). Benhadad, Hebraized from Barhadad (Birhadad) can be nothing more than the more popular

throne name. Where the Bible reads Benhadad e.g. (I Kings xx, 22; II Kings vi, 24; viii, 7 f.) the Assyrian records give (ilu) IM-idri. Before the reading of " Adad " for the ideographically written name of the deity was established, although the god-lists show clearly that *Addu* and *Dadu* were the names of the god *IM* in Amurru (*Cuneiform Texts from Babylonian Tablets*, 1896 f., XXV pl. 16: 16), the strangest combinations were offered with a supposed Aramaic deity called *Bir*, (Meyer, *op. cit.*, p. 332, n. 1). For example, *Birhadar* was held by many to be the more original form of Barhadad (*Bir*, an imaginary deity, *hadar*, meaning " glory ") since the LXX renders Benhadad " son of Ader " (cf. Zimmern, *Hilprecht Anniversary Volume*, p. 303). The LXX usage, however, can be much more satisfactorily explained as a later substitution of *hadar* for Hadad to avoid mentioning this heathen deity, or simply as a copyist's error הדר for הדד. An ingenious but unsuccessful theory to equate Benhadad with Hadadezer assumes the full name to be Ben-Hadadezer of which the Assyrians dropped the first element, and the Hebrews the last (cf. *Zeitschrift für Keilschriftforschung*, II, 167).

50. ARAB I, 654. Cf. A. Scharff and A. Moortgat, *Ägypten und Vorderasien im Altertum*, pp. 403–405.

51. Olmstead, *Hist. of Assyria*, p. 138.

52. ARAB I, 659.

53. Kraeling, *op. cit.*, p. 78.

54. From a comparison of the monuments, it does seem that Shalmaneser views himself as opposed by a Syrian confederation which remained substantially the same from 853–845. Only the Monolith Inscription actually mentions Ahab of Israel in the coalition at Karkar in the sixth year of the Assyrian' kings reign, while the later Bull Inscription gives " Hadadezer of Damascus, Irḫuleni of Hamath together with the kings of the Ḫatti and the seacoast " (ARAB I, 647). Similarly, upon the Black Obelisk " Hadadezer of Damascus, Irḫuleni of Hamath together with the kings of the Ḫatti and the seacoast " (*op. cit.*, 563). Since the confederated kings against whom Shalmaneser fought in his tenth, eleventh, and fourteenth years are designated with similar or identical words, and since such designations in the later Annals tended to become more general and unprecise, there is reason to surmise that essentially the same circle is intended. But however plausible the arguments from the Assyrian records for Israelite participation in the later coalitions of Shalmaneser's reign may be, it must always be borne in mind that concrete proof is lacking.

55. While Jepson clearly recognizes the possibility of defection among one or the other of the members of the coalition, he is manifestly arbitrary, owing to his critical presuppositions, in insisting that there are no data to this effect giving us the right to such a surmise (*op. cit.*, 154, 155). So far from the evident success of the federation in achieving its desired result of thwarting Shalmaneser's designs in Syria-Palestine making such a defection more improbable, as Jepsen maintains, the effectual check of Assyria's advance at Karkar gave four or five years of respite to allies who were intrinsically enemies at heart to become embroiled again in old feuds and rivalries. Accordingly, Ahab's struggles with Damascus after Karkar offer no insuperable difficulties.

56. Assuming II Kings iii–viii to belong to the reign of Joram, it is difficult to see how the Israelite king, with a full-scale Moabite revolt on his hands, could have assisted the Syrian league, at least to any appreciable extent. The threat of Assyria doubtless explains why conflicts with Syria at this time are represented for the most part as predatory incursions in the nature of robbing bands, rather than as invasions by the regular Syrian army (II Kings v, 2; viii, 9, 23). On the other hand, Benhadad I's invasion of the country and his unsuccessful though pitiless siege of Samaria, could only have occurred in the interim between the Assyrian advance, probably after 845.

57. The general situation embracing a state of war between Israel and Syria (*c.* 850) as presented in I Kings xxii, some three years after the battle of Karkar, is not to be summarily dismissed as unintelligible at the time of Ahab on the grounds that the Syrian federation was in force, and that there was ever an imminent possibility of Shalmaneser's return. This was precisely the time when the Assyrian avoided Syria for an extended period of some four years, and in the light of instances of hostility and the sudden nature of the attacks before Karkar, it is rather presumptuous for Jepson to say that " sufficient grounds for such a struggle are scarcely to be named " (*op. cit.*, p. 156), and to insist that reasons adduced in favour of such an attack, for instance, the typical disunity of the Syrian principalities, etc., " are generalities . . . which prove nothing " (*loc. cit.*, n. 10).

58. Lacking the evidence of the Melcarth Stela, on the basis of a new critical examination and evaluation of the sources, Jepsen labours to dispose of a king Benhadad of Damascus for the era of Ahab and his sons. Accordingly, he lists I Kings xx, 1–34 among

the sources for the Aramaean wars of the Joash period, and maintains that the name of Ahab was subsequently inserted (*op. cit.*, p. 157), and that either the author did not have Benhadad's accession clearly in mind, or a later redactor gave this name to an otherwise nameless king, which alone seemed to fit the defeat described (*op. cit.*, p. 160).

59. *Eucharisterion*, p. 191.

60. *Op. cit.*, p. 185.

61. An examination of I and II Kings and I and II Chronicles discloses the correctness of Hölscher's comment. The phrase he " slept with his fathers ", as employed in connection with the demise of kings, is consistently used of those who died a natural death (e.g. I Kings i, 21; ii, 10; xi, 43; xiv, 20, 31; xv, 8, 24, etc.) and never in the case of decease by assassination, accident, or war (e.g. I Kings xv, 31; xvi, 14, 20; II Kings i, 18, etc.), except in the sole case of Ahab (I Kings xxii, 40).

62. Why the author of this chapter and the Judaean pre-exilic prophetic circle in general should have been so eager to picture the period of Ahab as a time of Aramaic struggles as to distort facts, and to resort to a pseudo-historical setting for the representation, Jepsen does not explicitly say (*op. cit.*, p. 156). To assume throughout a legendary fabrication to supply a popular religious story which would depict an adequate punishment for Ahab's defection from Yahwism, and which would serve as a warning for the common people against the perils of religious syncretism, is in the highest degree arbitrary.

63. Jepsen, *op. cit.*, p. 156. Cf. Jepson, AfO XVI, pp. 315 ff.

64. II Kings xiii, 25, 26.

65. The theory of the later insertion of Ahab's name to fit the unnamed king of this chapter is pure supposition, without historical or documentary proof. Jepsen's contention (*op. cit.*, p. 157) that the narrative is not a unit, but that verses 35–42 as a later addition with its inimical attitude toward Ahab contradicts the first part of the chapter, which reports with glee Israel's successes over Aram, is manifestly a strained argument, for Ahab in the latter part is presented unfavourably not because of his triumph over Aram, but on account of his sparing Benhadad's life. Similarly Ahab's favourable attitude toward the prophets of Yahweh in this chapter is supposed to clash with his attitude in the prophet traditions (chapters 17–19). But here again the difficulty is magnified, as there must have been a decided change in both the royal and the popular

reaction towards the prophets of Yahweh after Elijah's victory over
the prophets of Baal (I Kings xviii). Besides Jezebel is represented
as their real enemy, and not Ahab (I Kings xviii, 4; 13, 20).

66. Jepsen, *op. cit.*, p. 157.
67. I Kings xxii, 2.
68. II Kings xiii, 12.
69. II Kings xiii, 14 ff.
70. II Kings xiii.
71. Cf. J. Morgenstern, JBL, 59, 1940, p. 390.
72. Jepsen, *op. cit.*, p. 169.
73. ZDMG, 88, p. 246.
74. I Kings xx, 24.
75. Jepsen, *op. cit.*, p. 169.
76. I Kings xxii, 3.
77. *Op. cit.*, p. 156.
78. *Op. cit.*, p. 79.
79. *Loc. cit.*

NOTES TO CHAPTER VII

1. See pp. 81, 82.

2. It is no longer necessary, now that the Benhadad-Adadidri problem has been solved by the new evidence from the Melcarth Stela, to assume that II Kings viii, 7–15 is inaccurate or unhistorical when it names Hazael as the successor of Benhadad. Benhadad is neither an error nor a gloss for Adadidri, as E. Kraeling surmises (*Aram and Israel*, p. 77, n. 1, 79), but is the same person (Albright, BASOR 87, p. 26).

3. On a pavement slab from Nimrud (Calah) Shalmaneser records his crossing the Euphrates river for the sixteenth time in the eighteenth year of his reign (841 B.C.) and his attack upon Hazael, *Haza'ilu* of Damascus (Albright, BASOR 87, p. 28, n. 16; Luckenbill, ARAB I, 663).

4. L. Messerschmidt, *Keilschrifttexte aus Assur historischen Inhalts*, Leipzig, 1911, no. 30: 25; Millar Burrows, *What Mean These Stones?*, 1941, p. 281; ARAB I, 681.

5. *Archiv fur Orientforschung*, XIII, pp. 233 f.

6. Hebrew tradition portrays quite an extensive influence of the Israelite prophetic movement under Elijah and Elisha (especially the latter) upon the court at Damascus. Elijah is said to have been commanded to anoint Hazael king over Aram (I Kings xix, 15). Benhadad's highly successful commander-in-chief, Namaan, is actually represented as being aided in his victories for Syria by Israel's God, Yahweh (II Kings v), besides applying in person to Elisha to be healed of leprosy (II Kings v, 1 ff.). Benhadad himself, well-acquainted through Namaan with Elisha, is also represented as appealing to the Hebrew seer for help in his sickness (II Kings viii, 8).

7. *Geschichte des Altertums*, II, 2, 1931, p. 337, n. 1).

8. II Kings viii, 7–15 quite unambiguously indicates that Hazael is the successor of Benhadad. Since the Melcarth Stele proves Benhadad and Adadidri to be identical, there is perfect accord between this passage and the Assyrian monuments. Lacking this evidence, Jepsen must resort to a wholly arbitrary hypothesis that still another king, Benhadad, must be inserted between Hadadezer

and Hazael. This imaginary king, a son of Hadadezer, is supposed to have been set aside by Hazael after a very brief rule of only a few months, somewhat after the fashion of Nadab, Elah, and Zechariah in Israel. This, in the face of the evidence of the Assyrian and biblical tradition, of course only increases the confusion. Under this wholly unnecessary theory it must be assumed that either the Assyrian record erred, and hence not Hadadezer, but his son Benhadad had been murdered, or that the Old Testament is wrong; in which case, Hazael would have assassinated Hadadezer but would not have ascended the throne immediately (AfO XIV, p. 158).

9. II Kings viii, 28; ix, 14.

10. Meyer, *op. cit.*, p. 337.

11. II Kings, chapters 9 and 10.

12. The Assyrians, doubtless because of Israel's reputation for power and prestige under the Omrides, retained the designation *Bît-Ḫumrî* for this realm, which had been the customary Assyrian term for the land of Israel from the days of king Omri to the time of Tiglathpileser III (ARAB I, 816) more than a century later (Jack Finegan, *Light from the Ancient Past*, pp. 173, 174). Shalmaneser's reference to Jehu as a " native of *Bît-Ḫumrî* is a significant tribute to the eminence of Omri's House (cf. Meyer, *op. cit.*, p. 341). *Bêth-'Omri*, Assyrian *Bît-Ḫumrî*, was the official Israelite name of Samaria, and an inhabitant of *Bît-Ḫumri* was *mâr-Ḫumrî* (cf. Chapter I, n. 23).

13. The situation could hardly have been otherwise in the light of Jehu's ruthless extermination of the line of kings who had been so intimately related to the royal house of Tyre, and in view of his drastic religious policy of complete extirpation of the Tyrian cult of Baal Melcarth (cf. A. T. Olmstead, *History of Assyria*, p. 141).

14. Israel's decision (together with Tyre and Sidon) to make a bid for Assyrian friendship, while obviously important in that these states thereby declared themselves the foes of Aram, yet scarcely furnishes evidence, as Kraeling maintains, that Jehu pursued the tradition of the Omride dynasty in fraternizing with Phoenicia (*op. cit.*, p. 80). Submission by rendering tribute, unlike the danger of facing a common attack (and there was no such present danger from Syria) does not require an alliance, but may, and often does, involve strict independence of action.

15. Whether the break-up of the Assyrian coalition is to be attributed to the death of Hadadidri as the real impelling personality and directing head, or because the former allies refused to recognize

a usurper, "a son of a nobody", or perchance because of subtle Assyrian diplomacy, or for some other reason, can scarcely be determined from our sources. Whatever the cause, the allies of Hadadezer became disloyal, seemingly without exception. From Tyre and Sidon (841, 837) Israel (841) and Gebal (837) the Assyrian received tribute.

16.   According to Deuteronomy iii, 9 Mt. Hermon (i.e. Hermon plus Antilibanus) was called Sirion by the Phoenicians and Senir by the Amorites. Phoenician usage is attested by a Ras Shamra text (reconstruction of H. Bauer II AB, VI, 19 and 21, *Les Découvertes De Ras Shamra et L'Ancien Testament*, R. Dussaud, Paris, 1941, p. 125, n. 5; p. 126, n. 1). Ezekiel xxvii, 5 employs the parallelism between Antilibanus and Hermon by making use of the synonym Senir (cf. Dussaud, *loc. cit.*).

" With cypress trees from Senir for your planks,
With cedars from Lebanon for your masts."

17.   Kraeling fixes Hazael's stand close to the Wadi Zerzer, on the present railroad from Damascus to Shtora, assuming that the Assyrians advanced upon Damascus via the Biqâ' by the very same route as does the modern traveller journeying from Beirût (*op. cit.*, 79, 80).

18.   Another shorter fragment from Calah contains an obviously exaggerated 16,000, with slightly variant 1,131 chariots (ARAB I, 663).

19.   ARAB I, 672.

20.   Layard discovered this very interesting monument in 1846 in the palace of Shalmaneser at Nimrod (A. H. Layard, *Ninevah and its Remains*, 1849, I, p. 282).

21.   ARAB I, 590. Cf. n. 12, below; also Chapter I, n. 23.

22.   ARAB I, 578. The eponym chronicle describes the campaign for this year "to the land of Danabi", which has been identified with the classical Danaba and the Dunip (Tunip) of the Amarna Letters (Knudtzon, *Die El-Amarna Tafeln*, 2, 1124 f.). But this identification is quite impossible. Tunip was nearby Hamath, and the location of Danaba is unknown.

23.   From 827, the beginning of the insurrection against Shalmaneser in Assyria, "the giant among the Semites" was so busy with domestic troubles that Syria was left quite undisturbed, and no longer needed to be concerned about paying tribute which was owing. Cf. the Saba'a Stele of Adadnirari III, published by E. Unger

("Reliefstele Adadniaris III, aus Saba'a und Semiramis"; ARAB I, 734).

24. II Kings x, 32, 33.

25. *Op. cit.*, p. 341. This observation is doubtless correct, and Meyer compares II Kings xiv, 25, 28.

26. Throughout we have followed W. F. Albright's revised "Chronology of the Divided Monarch of Israel" (BASOR 100, pp. 20–22). Here the seventeen years of Joahaz's reign are corrected to fifteen, following the synchronistic datings in II Kings xiii, 1, 10 (*Loc. cit.*, n. 20).

27. Meyer, *op. cit.*, pp. 341, 342.

28. Obviously this entire chapter dealing with the Joahaz-Joash era was frequently worked over and subjected to extensive editorial redaction. In verses 1–9, verses five and six are parenthetical, and very likely were added later, as also may be the case with verse four. But Jepsen's view that verses 3–6 belong to the following portion dealing with Joash's reign, and only inserted here on the basis of a scribal error (יהוֹאחז for יהוֹאשׁ) is arbitrary, and lacks documentary confirmation (*op. cit.*, p. 159). Of course, it is not to be denied that the basic historical facts of Joahaz's reign are to be gleaned from verses one, seven, nine (and twenty-two).

29. The figure 10,000 does seem to be disproportionate to the other numbers mentioned (cf. *Orientalistische Literturzeitung*, 1901, p. 144). But no concrete evidence is available that the number should be corrected to 1,000.

30. Amos i, 6–15; Is. ix, 12.

31. R. Kittel, *Biblia Hebraica*, 2nd ed., 1905, *in loc.*

32. Kraeling maintains that Arabia was close to Hazael's interest, and that it was to exercise a more complete control over the Arabs that he projected his conquests into Philistia where the Arabian caravan routes reached the sea (*op. cit.*, p. 81). This was doubtless at least one of many factors entering into the situation. It is interesting enough to surmise that Hazael may have been of Arabian extraction, but the fact that there was a king of the Arabs named *Hazaīlu* in the time of Esarhaddon (680–669) (*loc. cit.*) of course, proves nothing.

33. That the Philistine city was destroyed by Hazael is suggested by the fact that it no longer appears in the enumeration of Philistine towns (Amos i, 6–8; Zeph. ii, 4; cf. Meyer, *op. cit.*, p. 342). The destruction of Gath is narrated in Amos vi, 1–6. On the other hand, it is mentioned at the time of Sargon (724–705), having evidently been rebuilt by that time (ARAB II, 62).

34. II Kings xii, 17–18. For a summary of Hazael's power see Philip Hitti, *History of Assyria*, pp. 167 f.

35. II Chronicles xxiv, 23–24. It is highly probable that Hazael had died during the interim and the new king had come to the Damascene throne, here called "the king of Damascus", and known to us at Benhadad II (Mari'). The patent differences between II Kings xii, 17–18 and II Chronicles xxiv, 23–24 are not to be explained on the ground that the latter passage is based on the former, and has been "entirely rewritten" according to "the Chronicler's pragmatic construction of history" (E. L. Curtis, I. C. C., *in loc.*). While, to be sure, the pragmatic element in the Chronicler's notice is not to be denied, the two accounts are unquestionably supplementary, referring to different events, and both together give the full outline of Judah's contact with Syria at the time of Hazael's wars.

36. *Op. cit.*, p. 81.

37. *Op. cit.*, pp. 168, 169. A. T. Olmstead likewise would extend Hazael's hegemony "from Philistia and Judah through Israel and Central Syria clear to Hazrek" (*Hist. of Pal. and Syria*, p. 407).

38. ARAB I, 735.

39. *Loc. cit.*

40. Cf. Chapter VI, n. 73.

41. Meyer, *op. cit.*, pp. 342 ff. Cf. Dupont-Sommers, *Les Araméens*, pp. 45–48.

42. *Loc. cit.* Jepsen's contention that, since Benhadad appears as the real opponent and leader of the enumerated kings, a common opposition to Hamath could scarcely have been the occasion of the concerted military action loses all point in the light of Noth's discussion of the Zakir Stele (ZDPV, 1929, pp. 124–141) or under the hypothesis of an anti-Assyrian movement at the time. If Hamath was the one state loyal to Assyria, then its king chose to abandon his perilous allegiance to Asshur and to join the allies; the pro-Assyrian party in Hamath organized the rebellion which elevated Zakir to the throne in the stronghold of Hadrach. It was natural for the allied forces to attempt to suppress the rebellion, although defeated by an Assyrian relief expedition (Kraeling's theory, *op. cit.*, p. 102). Cf. also Jepsen's views in AfO XVI, pp. 315 ff.

43. ARAB I, 735, 739.

44. Amos i, 3, 4.

45. Kraeling's theory that Hazael's successor assumed the kingship in 804 B.C., at the latest, must disregard this bit of concrete evidence and treat the passage as inexact (*op. cit.*, p. 82, n. 1).

Following Kuenen (*Einleitung*, 25) the arguments he employs to place the siege of Samaria (II Kings vi, 24–vii, 20) about 806 B.C. in the time of an imagined resurgence of power under Joahaz, incident upon a change in rulers at Damascus, are extremely weak. It is arbitrary to assume that such an attack upon Israel was *à priori* unlikely during Joram's reign because of the Assyrian danger, for there was plainly a lull in Shalmaneser's activity in Syria at the time. To use the notice in II Kings vi, 32 that the king was the " son of a murderer ", as conclusive proof that Joahaz is meant is most unsound, as the epithet is applicable with perfect propriety to Ahab (I Kings xviii, 4, 13, 14; xxi, 10, 13).

46. *Op. cit.*, p. 159; cf. n. 24.

47. Mari' is likely the abbreviation of a name like *Mari'-Hadad*, " Hadad is my lord " (Albright, BASOR, 87, p. 28, n. 16). It is an old Semitic word, originally meaning " man of ", or the like.

48. F. Thureau-Dangin, A. Barrois, G. Dossin, M. Dunand, *Arslan Tash*, 1931, pp. 135–138.

49. C. C. McCown, *The Ladder of Progress in Palestine*, 1943, p. 198.

NOTES TO CHAPTER VIII

1. II Kings xiii, 24. See Chapter VII, n. 45. The mention of " Barhadad, king of Aram " on the Zakir Inscription, who was on the throne of Damascus in the first quarter of the eighth century B.C. (Albright gives 775 B.C. as the probable date of the erection of the stele, BASOR, 87, pp. 25, 26) confirms the biblical statement that Barhadad succeeded Hazael.

2. E. Meyer (*Gesch. des Alt.*, II, 2, 1931, p. 345, n. 5) is unjustified in saying concerning *Mari'*: " Whether he was a son of Barhadad, we do not know ". Although it is true we do not know precisely who *Mari'* was, we at least know from the evidence of the Zakir Stele and the Bible that he was not the son of Barhadad. Cf. likewise Stanley A. Cook's groundless supposition that *Mari'* may be the son of Barhadad (*The Cambridge Ancient History*, III, p. 376). Meyer ventures to proceed radically with a too-early date for the Zakir Stele, as he considers the data in II Kings xiii, 14 ff. (ostensibly not only the prophetic traditions in verses 14–21, but the Chronicler's notices in verses 22, 24, 25 as well) to be historically completely worthless. The reason he adduces is that the passage attributes to Joash, who did not enter upon the kingship until *c.* 800, three victories over Benhadad, the son of Hazael, and the recovery of the border territory, " whereas already in 805," says Meyer, " no longer Barhadad, but *Mari'* was king of Damascus " (*op. cit.*, p. 346, n. 1). Accordingly, it is clear that, unless the Chronicler's notices in II Kings xiii, 22, 24, 25 are rejected, for which there are no good critical reasons (cf. A. Jepsen, *Archiv für Orientforschung*, XIV, p. 160) *Mari'* must be construed as having reference to Hazael; in any case, unless the whole is viewed as historically worthless, to Benhadad II. Cf. the evidence from Arslan Tash (Chapter VI, n. 48).

3. II Kings xiii, 25. Besides a lack of critical reasons to reject the historical value of this notice, despite its indirect connection with the preceding Elisha prophetic tradition (vs. 14–21), the situation it describes admirably fits into the historical picture of the period (cf. n. 2 above). However, collating the other verses of II Kings xiii dealing concretely with Joash, the unusual position of verses 12 and 13, which we would normally expect after verse 25, furnishes further

evidence that this chapter has undergone extensive redactorial revision (cf. Chapter VII, n. 28). Attempting to restore the original order, it is plain verse 22 falls out. Verses 11 and 23 are apparently later redactorial additions, so that we arrive at the probable original order: vs. 9b, 10, 24, 25, 12, 13, which, if correct, supplies additional corroboration (besides verse 22) that Hazael died (to be sure soon) but in any case only after the death of Jehoaz (cf. Jepsen, *op. cit.*, p. 160).

4. II Kings xiii, 22. Cf. Chapter VII, n. 31. Jepsen, *op. cit.*, p. 168.

5. *Op. cit.*, p. 160. Jepsen of course is unwarranted in using the contents of the peace treaty in I Kings xx, 34 as between Joash and the Aramaeans, and holding that this circumstance is in precise agreement with his surmise.

6. Chapter VII, n. 25; also n. 27.

7. II Kings xiii, 12. Cf. xiv, 12. These two notices dealing with Joash's Judaean War are substantially the same. (Cf. xiv, 8–16 with II Chronicles xxv, 6–13; 17–24).

8. II Chron. xxv, 6 f. gives 100,000 mercenaries from Israel, compared with 300,000 of Amaziah's own troops (v. 5).

9. II Kings xiv, 11; II Chron. xxv, 21. In both cases the scene of the battle is said to be " Beth-Shemesh, which belongeth to Judah ". The modern site is Ain Shems or Tell er-Rumeileh some seventeen miles slightly south-west of Jerusalem in the Shepelah (Plate XVIII, B-5, p. 102); cf. 106 a, *The Westminster Historical Atlas to the Bible*, G. E. Wright, F. V. Filson, with introduction by W. F. Albright (1945). In 1911–12 the Palestine Exploration Fund undertook work there, and it was the last Palestinian Excavation before the First World War (R. A. S. Macalister, *A Century of Excavation in Palestine*; 1930, p. 69). Since 1928 Elihu Grant of Haverford College has carried out further diggings (E. Grant, *Beth Shemesh*, 1929; *Ain Shems Excavations*; 5 vol. 1931–39). The site appears to have been occupied by two cities; one from the Middle and Late Bronze Age (2000–1200 B.C.); the other from the Iron Age, earlier and late Israelite (1200–500 B.C.) or as is more consonant with the designations of classical archaeology, Early Iron I and II. (Cf. Elihu Grant, *Ain Shems Excavations*, Part I, p. 84). In Joash's day the unwalled city commanded a direct route to Jerusalem (A. T. Olmstead, *History of Palestine and Syria*, p. 416).

10. The imperfectly preserved number permits a restoration to 12, 13, 16, 17, or 18. Cf. Noth, " La'ash Und Hazrak ", ZDPV,

1929, p. 132, n. 1. Meyer, *op. cit.*, p. 343 would restore the number to 12 on the basis of Assyrian parallels. In any case only seven take part in the actual operations against the city of Hazrek. The break in line eight doubtless contained information concerning the activity of the other allies.

11. Zechariah ix, 1.

12. W. F. Albright, JPOS, 6 (1926) p. 86, Guthe, Bibelatlas, 2nd ed., leaf 5; Noth, *op. cit.*, p. 134. The place where the stele was found, long held secret by its discoverer Pognon, was finally divulged after his death in 1921 (Dussaud, *Syria* 3, 1922, p. 175 f.) and furnished pivotal evidence to discountenance such current erroneous views of a location for Hazrek-Lu'ash in South or Central Syria as that of Procksch, who located it somewhere east of Phoenicia (cf. Kraeling, *op. cit.*, p. 97); of Montgomery, who placed it in the region of Homs (JBL 28: 69); of Pognon, who, despite his knowledge of the place of discovery of the stele, argued for a location between Damascus and Hamath (*Inscriptions semitiques de la Syrie, de la Mesopotamie et de Mossoul*, p. 166); of Dussaud, who identified it with the land of Luḫuti in the Bargylus plateau (*Revue Archéologique*, 1908, p. 222 f.). The fact that the stele stems from Âfis, some forty kilometres south-west of Aleppo, furnished added proof to the internal evidence of the stele itself (cf. Noth, *op. cit.*, p. 133) that the location of Lu'ash-Hazrek is in North Syria.

13. Cf. Noth, *op. cit.*, pp. 138–141.

14. Bargush, following Schiffer (*Die Aramäer*, Introduction p. IV, n. 7) is mâr (A)gusi, that is a member of the dynasty of (A)gusi, its founder, which according to Asshurnasirpal's Annals (Col. III, line 77 f.), seems to have ruled over the land of Yaḫan in North Syria with its capital city at ancient Arpad (Tell Erfad) about 30 km. north of Aleppo (Schiffer, *op. cit.*, p. 90, n. 6; Forrer, *Provinzeinteilung*, p. 56; Dussaud, *Topographie*, pp. 236, 240). Alfred Jepsen (AfO, XIV, p. 164) connects Bargush with the Aramaean penetration of Syria, and interprets him as an Aramaic leader attempting by the help of others to push into the land and settle there. To this end he places his army at Benhadad II's command, and for this reason, according to Jepsen, appears as the only non-king in the coalition and enjoys a place of preference immediately after Benhadad himself because Zakir (supposedly) saw in him a direct opponent. Jepsen sees his status comparable to that of Rezon and his army before they conquered Damascus (I Kings xi, 23–25).

15. Noth, *op. cit.*, p. 132, 133.

16. *Op. cit.*, p. 126 f.

17. A. Alt, " Die Syrische Staatenwelt vor dem Einbruch der Assyrer ", ZDMG 88, p. 244.

18. II Sam. v, 5; I Kings i, 35; Noth, *op. cit.*, p. 126.

19. Lu'ash (the land) bears the same relation to Hazrek (the capital city), as Ya'di does to Sam'al. A parallel to the Lu'ash-Hazrek combination occurs in Ya'di-Sam'al. Bir-rakeb, on one occasion calls his father and predecessor, Panammu, " King of Ya'di " (Panammu Inscription, line 1); on another, " King of Sam'al " (Building Inscription, lines 2 and 3).

20. Noth is correct in maintaining that the solemn declaration of divine enthronement in Hazrek is not to be explained by a simple annexation of the city by Zakir (Cf. *op. cit.*, p. 130, n. 2).

21. Benhadad II's title, " King of Aram ", in the Zakir Stele, while indisputably indicative of the primacy of Damascus' power in Syria, at least before the battle of Hazrek, had become the traditional designation of the kings of Damascus since Benhadad I, who perhaps first bore the epithet (I Kings xv, 18) and who had lifted the Aramaean realm to the position of the foremost power in Syria. There is no reason to suppose that Hazael first earned the title. He is called " Hazael of Aram " (ARAB I, 675, 578, 663, 672; " son of nobody ", 681) but not actually " king of Aram " by the Assyrians. Jepsen, accordingly, has no grounds for his supposition that the use of the term in the Israel-Judaean Annal Work (I Kings xv, 18) relative to Benhadad I may be an anticipation of a title which only later (under Hazael?) became current (*loc. cit.*, n. 47).

22. Lidzbarski, *Ephemeris für Semitische Epigraphik*, III, pp. 8 f.; ZDPV, 1929, p. 130. Cf. also Kraeling's surmise (*op. cit.*, p. 98) that the pro-Assyrian party in Hamath revolted, and raised Zakir to the throne in Hazrek, in opposition to Hamath itself joining the anti-Assyrian coalition, Meyer (*op. cit.*, p. 344) holds the view that the respite from Assyria in the last days of Shalmaneser III and his son Shamšiadad furnished the occasion for the North Syrian principalities to join with Damacus as the most powerful Syrian state, but that the new Hamath-Lu'ash kingdom stood in the way. Meyer's date for the Zakir stele is, however, too early.

23. E. Ebeling (OLZ, 1913, p. 254). Cf. (*loc. cit.*) Thureau-Dangin's list of the occurrences of the god *mi-ir* (*wi-ir*) in Babylonian personal names.

24. Line 128, Cf. Gressmann, *Altorient. Texte*, 2nd ed., pp. 345 f.

25. Alt, *op. cit.*, p. 244.

26. Noth, *op. cit.*, p. 131; Cf. Forrer (*op. cit.*, p. 58 f.) who correctly locates the Assyrian province of Ḥatarikka in the general region south-west of Aleppo (cf. n. 12 of this chapter), but his identification of Ḥatarikka with Magaratarícha (present-day Mughâra, 22 km. south of Idlib in Djebel Riḥa), and more precisely with Riḥa on the north side of Djebel Riḥa, is impossible. Only archaeological research in this region, which is still largely a *terra incognita* to the archaeologist, can decisively settle the exact location of the city of Hazrek (cf. Noth, *op. cit.*, p. 134, n. 1). As an Assyrian province Ḥatarikka is met with occasionally in the Assyrian provincial catalogues (Forrer, p. 68). In the eponym list for 689 B.C., a certain Giḥilu is listed as the governor of Ḥatrika (ARAB II, p. 438).

27. Meyer, *op. cit.*, pp. 342 f., p. 373. For the Aramaean penetration of Syria in the ninth and eighth centuries B.C. see Alfred Jepsen, AfO, XIV, 1942, pp. 161–166.

28. Alt, *loc. cit.*, n. 2. However, Alt's conclusions are somewhat misleading, since Ingholt's excavations at Hamath have brought to light earlier Aramaic inscriptions.

29. Syria, 3 (1922), pp. 175 f.

30. JPOS, 6 (1926) p. 86.

31. M. Noth's rejection of the correct equation of *'pš* of the stele with modern Âfis was corrected by W. F. Albright (BASOR 87, p. 25, n. 2).

32. Cf. Kraeling, *op. cit.*, p. 102.

33. *Op. cit.*, p. 126, n. 3.

34. Cf. notes 1 and 2 of this chapter. It is extremely unlikely for other reasons besides the data concerning Hazael that Zakir's Relief is to be assigned to Adadnirari's campaign against Mari' in 803 (JBL 28: 62). As the king of 'Umq appears in the coalition, and this state most certainly was reduced from the kingdom of Ḥattina, which last appears in 832, the reduction could only have taken place because of hostility to Assyria and in connection with Adadnirari III's campaigns in Syria, for it is known not to have taken place in Shalmaneser's reign, nor in that of his son Shamšiadad (824–813), who made no recorded campaign in the Westland. The influence of Urartu, which had forced Arpad to resist Adadnirari in 806, must have likewise acted upon its neighbour Ḥattina, for in the next year (805) the Eponym List names a campaign against the Ḥattina city Ḥazaz (ARAB II, p. 443). It is not impossible, as Kraeling supposes (*op. cit.*, p. 101), that since the campaign against Damascus in 803 at least suggests the passive aid of Hamath, the

latter was rewarded by districts cut off from Ḥattina, which since then were called 'Umq. At any rate, it is almost certain that Zakir's Relief cannot be placed before the beginning of the eighth century B.C.

35.   BASOR, 87, pp. 24–25.

36.   Forrer, *op. cit.*, p. 59.

37.   ARAB II, p. 433.

38.   Cf. Kraeling, *op. cit.*, pp. 101–102, who supposes Benhadad II to have perished in the battle of Hazrek in 772 B.C.

39.   Jepsen, *op. cit.*, assigns Benhadad III (II) to the years 801–773, without, however, positing reasons for his *terminus ad quem*.

40.   Cf. notes 5 and 6 of this chapter.

41.   II Kings xiv, 25, 28 confirmed by xv, 29. Cf. I Kings xv, 20.

42.   Amos vi, 13, first recognized by Grätz (cf. Meyer, *op. cit.*, p. 347, n. 1); *l' dᵉbhar* equals *lô dᵉbhar* (cf. II Sam. xvii, 27; ix, 4 following the Massoretic Text; Greek Λωδαβάρ, Λαδαβάρ, Kittel, *Biblia Hebraica*, 1905, ed., *in loc.*).

43.   At the time of Tiglathpileser III, Qarnaim (Roman *Karnium*, present-day Šeḫ-Saʿad) was an Assyrian province (Qarnini), located east of the Jordan from the Waters of Merom to the Sea of Chinneroth with the province of Dimašqu (Damascus) bordering on the north, and the province of Galʾaza on the south and Ḥaurena on the south-west (cf. Forrer, *op. cit.*, p. 62; *The Westminster Hist. Atlas to the Bible*, plate VII, map c).

NOTES TO CHAPTER IX

1. Amos prophesied at Bethel during the latter part of Jeroboam II's reign, c. 760–750 (*The Westminster Historical Atlas to the Bible*, G. E. Wright, F. V. Filson, W. F. Albright, p. 49 a, b). For an earlier date for Amos c. 780 B.C. cf. Alfred Jepsen (AfO XIV, p. 170, n. 52). These arguments are not very conclusive, however. Hosea was a younger contemporary, who flourished between c. 750 and 720, and began his ministry several years before Jeroboam's death (cf. Hos. i, 4).

2. II Kings xiv, 25 is generally accepted as historical, while II Kings xiv, 28 is commonly rejected.

3. The corrupt state of the text of I Kings xiv, 28 is no decisive argument, of course, against its historical value, and the correct reading likely follows the Syriac version (cf. Kittel, Biblia Hebraica, 2nd ed., *in loc.*). However, D. D. Luckenbill (AJSL, XLI, 1925, pp. 227 ff.) gives a literal rendering: " And how he let Hamath and Damascus return to Judah against (to the disadvantage of) Israel ", assuming a decline in the latter part of the reign of Jeroboam II and his loss of prestige in central and southern Syria to the prosperous Azariah of Judah.

4. E.g. when he reports something more in detail, as concerning the ivory palace of Ahab (I Kings xxii, 39) or concerning the aqueduct and pool of Hezekiah (II Kings xx, 20, cf. II Chron. xxxii, 30). Numerous ivories were found in the excavations at Samaria (J. W. and Grace Crowfoot, *Early Ivories from Samaria*, 1938) which are of interest in view of Amos's denunciation of the " houses of ivory " (iii, 15) and the " beds of ivory " (vi, 4) of the opulent people of Samaria (J. Finegan, *Light from the Ancient Past*, pp. 156 f.). The ruins of the palace faced with white marble found at Samaria may have been connected with his "ivory house", which possibly means it was lavishly ornamented with ivory (cf. G. A. Barton, *Archaeology and the Bible*, 7th ed., p. 120). The great tunnel of Hezekiah was excavated in the solid rock (Finegan, *op. cit.*, fig. 68, cf. pp. 158–160) and connected the Gihon spring with the Pool of Siloam. The entire system of tunnels related to the Gihon spring was cleared by Capt. Parker in 1909–11, measured and photographed by Father

Vincent (Finegan, *op. cit.*, p. 159). On the right wall of the tunnel, about nineteen feet from the Siloam entrance the famous Siloam Inscription was discovered in 1880 (Barton, *op. cit.*, p. 476).

5. II Sam. viii, 3–6.

6. II Sam. viii, 9–11.

7. Cf. Wright, Filson, Albright, *op. cit.*, plate VII: A.

8. II Chron. viii, 3, 4. This campaign is commonly entirely ignored in histories of Israel or Solomon. Since it is not referred to in Kings, neither J. Benzinger nor R. Kittel discusses its historicity. Winckler, however, thinks it not at all incredible (*Geschichte Israels* II, p. 266, *Keilinschriften und Alte Testament*, p. 239).

9. The question of the precise topographical implications of the phrase " the entrance of Hamath " is much in dispute. Cf. the new discussion on this location between Noth and Elliger (ZDPV 58, pp. 242 ff.; PJB 32, pp. 34 ff.; 33, pp. 36 ff.). Wright and Filson (*op. cit.*, p. 47 b, plate VII: A) place it in the area between Riblah and Kadesh. Since Hamath is known to have extended to Riblah south of the lake of Homs (e.g. II Kings xxiii, 33), it is likely the ideal frontier included the southernmost limits of Hamath. Kraeling locates Labo Hamath as Libum (present-day Lebweh) where the Orontes River leaves the Biqâ' just south of modern il Harmel, which is equated with Harbelah of LXX (Num. xxxiv, 11) and Riblah of the Massoretic text (*op. cit.*, p. 96). Cf. B. Maisler, BASOR, 102, p. 9 and J. Lewy, *Heb. Un. Col. An.* XVIII, p. 445.

10. Josh. xiii, 5.

11. PJB 32, p. 43.

12. AfO XIV, p. 161.

13. Thus correctly Elliger (PJB 32, p. 43) against Noth (PJB 33, p. 50).

14. Wright, Filson, Albright, *op. cit.*, p. 49 a, cf. plate VII: A; cf. I Chron. xiii, 5.

15. *Loc. cit.*, plate VII: A. The northern limits of David's empire are not indicated in II Samuel, except that they are known to have bordered on Hamath (II Sam. viii, 9 ff.). The ideal northern boundary of Israel is represented as extending from Hazar-enen and Zedad to " the entrance of Hamath " (Num. xxxiv, 7 ff.; Ez. xlvii 16; xlvii, 1). This doubtless reflects David's actual northern frontier in the light of the persistent tradition that this was Israel's real boundary. Otherwise it would be difficult to account for the origin of the tradition.

16. II Sam. viii, 9–12.

17. A tributary arrangement between Hamath and Israel is perfectly understandable in view of the general state of affairs at the time. It is not at all unlikely that the Assyrian campaign of 772, or perhaps not until 765, offered the occasion for the Hamathites to purchase for themselves a certain protection, or even military aid by the payment of tribute to Israel.

18. II Kings xiv, 24.

19. Cf. J. W. Crowfoot, Kathleen M. Kenyon and E. L. Sukenik, *The Buildings at Samaria*, 1942.

20. II Kings xvii, 5; Wright, Filson, Albright, *op. cit.*, p. 49 a.

21. Finegan, *op. cit.*, p. 155.

22. Barton, *op. cit.*, p. 456, cf. plate II, fig. 27; Olmstead, *History of Palestine and Syria*, p. 420.

23. E.g. Amos ii, 6; viii, 6.

24. Amos iii, 15; v, 11; cf. I Kings xxii, 39.

25. Amos vi, 4–6.

26. Amos iv, 4; v, 5; viii, 14; cf. v, 21 ff.

27. Amos vii, 9. Amos did not say that Jeroboam himself would die " by the sword " as Amaziah, the priest at Bethel, the royal shrine, had reported to the king of Israel (v. 10). Meyer has no documentary authority for the contention that Amos " expected " Jeroboam to die in this manner (*op. cit.*, p. 360).

28. Amos v, 27.

29. ARAB I, 772, 777. Cf. A. Alt's *Kleine Schriften* II, pp. 150–162.

30. According to H. Winckler's surmise Tab'el (Is. vii, 6) is Rezin's father and predecessor (*Alttestamentliche Untersuchungen*, 1892, p. 74). This hypothesis, although of course, possible, is at most extremely uncertain. The name suggests that he was a Syrian. But Isaiah vii, 6 adds nothing more than that his son was a tool of Rezin of Damascus, whom the king of Israel and of Aram planned to place upon the throne of Judah.

31. Although we cannot say that Tab'el was Rezin's father and predecessor, we do know from the Annals of Tiglathpileser III (ARAB I, 777) that Hadara, present-day El-Hadhr, 52 km. south-west from Damascus (Forrer, *op. cit.*, p. 62) was Rezin's father's house, and the place of Rezin's birth. It is doubtful the Assyrians would have made reference to " the father's house of Rezin " if he had not preceded his son on the throne of Damascus. He was accordingly likely a usurper, and not the son of Benhadad II.

32. II Kings xiv, 21, 22, II Chron. xxvi; S. Cook, *The Cam. Anc.*

Hist., III, p. 378; I. M. Price, *The Monuments and the Old Testament*, 7th ed., 1925, p. 288; Luckenbill, AJSL, XLI, July, 1925, pp. 224 ff.

33. Thiele, *op. cit.*, p. 156, and n. 37; Albright, BASOR 100, p. 18, n. 8.

34. Vol. I, with a first study entitled " Das Syrische Jaudi und der angebliche Azarja von Juda ". Meyer (*op. cit.*, p. 433, n. 1) strangely enough follows Winckler's hypothesis contra Luckenbill.

35. For a discussion in favour of the identification of *Azriau of Yaudi* with Azariah of Judah, see Schrader, *The Cuneiform Inscriptions and the Old Testament* I, 208 ff. Also Howell M. Haydn, "Azariah of Judah and Tiglethpileser III ", JBL, 28 (1909) pp. 182–199; Luckenbill, *op. cit.*, pp. 217–232; cf. Forrer, *Provinzeinteilung*, p. 57.

36. Aramaic *Y'dy* would appear in Assyrian *Ya-'()di-i/ya*, in which short final vowels were no longer pronounced, and not *Ya-u-di*, the regular cuneiform rendering of *Yᵉ hûdāh* (Judah). See Albright (BASOR 100, p. 18, n. 8). As both the noun " Judah " and the gentilic " Judaean ", *Ya-u-da-ai* occur a number of times in Tiglathpileser, Sargon and Sennacherib's records, there is no doubt as to the Assyrian form. The substitution of *aleph* for *he* would not be likely, but if the *aleph* had a long *u* after it, this would appear in the writing. The Zenjirli inscriptions regularly write Assyria אשׁוּר and Panammu פֿנמוּ. Western ע,א and ח are almost invariably rendered in Assyrian cuneiform by (ˀ), while western ה is not so rendered; cf. מוֹאָב *Ma'ba*; חֲזָאֵל *Haza'ilu*; יִשְׂרָאֵל *Sir'ilai*, but cf. יֵהוּא *Ya-u-a*; חִזְיָהוּ *Ḥa-za-ki-a-u*; הוֹשֵׁעַ *A-u-si-'a*.

37. Cf. S. Cook (*op. cit.*, p. 378) who stresses the " serious chronological and other difficulties in connecting the two ". Olmstead (*History of Assyria*, p. 186) speaks of the north Syrian Azriau as " so certainly an Azariah that it is small wonder he was identified by earlier scholars with the *almost* contemporary king of the better-known Judah to the South ".

38. JNES 1944, pp. 155–163.

39. The datings of Tiglathpileser's contact with the kings of Syria-Palestine have heretofore been indecisive due to the fact that, despite the work done on the Assyrian monarch's reign, all reconstructions thus far must be viewed as tentative (cf. Luckenbill, ARAB I, 761 and Thiele, *op. cit.*, p. 156). Cf. Thiele's arguments for a date earlier than 738 B.C. (*op. cit.*, 156–163).

40. ARAB I, 770.

41. Cf. Albright, BASOR, 100, p. 18, n. 8.

42. AJSL, XLI, 1925, pp. 231–232.

43. Cf. Luckenbill, *op. cit.*, pp. 226–227.

44. Cf. Thiele, *op. cit.*, p. 161; H. R. Hall, *The Ancient History of the Near East* (9th rev. ed., London, 1936) pp. 463–464. That the Azariah and Menahem sections are very closely related in Tiglathpileser's annals and that the latter portion immediately followed the former is demonstrated by the fact that the last line of a fragment of one version of the annals, which was written across a group of figures (Plate XXI in Rost, *Die Keilshcrifttexte Tiglat-Pilesers* III) is the first line of a column of the twelve-line version (Plate XV in Rost).

45. Location " uncertain " (cf. Wright, Filson, Albright, *op. cit.*, p. 112).

46. II Kings xv, 19.

47. E.g. Usnu, Siannu and Simirra are mentioned as cities conquered at the time of Azariah's coalition, the date of which available evidence, as we have seen, places at 743 B.C. The same three towns are included in a group of coastal cities (ARAB I, 772) in which captives were settled when Menahem paid tribute (*loc. cit.*) Rost (*op. cit.*, pp. 24, 25). At the same time captives transported included people from Dur and Budu, places taken in Tiglathpileser's campaign against Babylon in his first year (ARAB I, 764). Captives are mentioned from Bit-Sangibuti taken in Tiglathpileser's second year (ARAB I, 772). A transfer of these captives to the West would logically occur the next year (cf. Thiele, *op. cit.*, p. 162).

48. Cities of Unki are noted in which transported captives were settled (ARAB I, 772). The conquest of Unki took place in 743, the third year of Tiglathpileser (*op. cit.*, p. 769). The logical procedure would be to transfer captives there the same year or soon thereafter (cf. Thiele, *op. cit.*, p. 162).

49. Rost, *op. cit.*, pp. 26–27, 11.150 ff.; ARAB I, 772.

50. Rost, *op. cit.*, pp. 12, 13, 11.61 f.; ARAB I, 769.

51. Rost, *op. cit.*, p. 16, 1.91; ARAB I, 769.

52. Whereas internal evidence definitely links the Menahem portion of the annals with the events of the third year, there is no such a connection with the occurrences of the ninth year narrated in the section immediately following.

53. Some early scholars yielded to the temptation to make Tiglathpileser and Pul two different Assyrian kings in an effort to solve the vexing difficulties which then existed in synchronizing biblical and Assyrian chronology of this period. I Chronicles v, 26

was frequently misused as documentary proof (cf. S. Cook, *Cam. Anc. Hist.*, III, p. 380, n. 1). However, as Horner has noted, the verse should be rendered, " And the God of Israel stirred up Pul, king of Assyria, *even* the spirit of Tiglathpileser, king of Assyria, and he carried them away". Since the verb "carried" is singular the " waw " introduces an epexegetical phrase. Thus, instead of countenancing the error that two different monarchs are referred to, it really becomes a valuable early documentary authority for the identification of Pul and Tiglathpileser (cf. Joseph Horner, " Biblical Chronology", in the *Proceedings of the Society of Biblical Archaeology*, XX, 1898, p. 237; also Thiele, *op. cit.*, p. 155, n. 34).

54. *Op. cit.*, I, 218 ff.

55. Cf. Thiele, *op. cit.*, p. 156 for the notations from the King List and Chronicle containing the pertinent evidence.

56. Thiele, *loc. cit.*

57. Albright, on the other hand, maintains that Menahem was still alive in 738, and rejects Thiele's terminal dates 742/741 (BASOR 100, p. 21, n. 24). Tiglathpileser's records do not seem to offer conclusive proof, however, that Menahem paid tribute to the Assyrians at so late a date, despite the fact that Julius Lewy places the end of Menahem's reign as late as 736 (*Die Chronologie der Könige von Israel und Juda*).

58. A thousand talents of silver required about 60,000 persons to pay fifty shekels apiece, since one talent equals three thousand shekels (cf. II Kings xv, 20 and S. Cook, *op. cit.*, p. 380). The amount equalled some 362,200 pounds sterling, or about 1,811,000.00 dollars.

59. Jepsen is doubtless correct in assuming that Rezin laid the first plans for concerted action against Assyria while Tiglathpileser was detained by affairs in the east of his empire in 737–735. It is reasonable that the Aramaic ruler, by virtue of the more exposed position of his country, should do so, and that Pekah's revolution effected by the aid of fifty Gileadites from east of the Jordan, should be thought of as being perpetrated with the secret or overt support of the Aramaeans to further a plan of union and collaboration against Assyria (AfO XIV, p. 171). That the Aramaeans of Damascus also took the lead in the advance against Jerusalem to attain a similar object there is also very probable. Cf. Jepsen's emendations and view of the original text of Isaiah vii, 1–9 in support of this hypothesis (*op. cit.*, n. 59). He maintains that verse one b is an addition; in verse two " Aram " is the chief subject; in verse five

the words " Ephraim and the son of Remaliah " are a gloss; that hence in verse four " Ephraim " is to be read before the clause " and the son of Remaliah ", which accordingly makes Aram the real instigator in verse five.

60. Evidence points conclusively to the fact that Ahaz entered upon the kingship between 737–734 (cf. Thiele, *op. cit.*, p. 167). He, of course, must definitely be in the picture during the years 734–732 when the eponym canon lists Assyrian campaigns against Philistia and Damascus, and his accession cannot be later than 734. The Syro-Ephraimite War is in all likelihood to be dated in 735, possibly 736.

61. Cf. II Kings xvi, 6 where " Syria " of the Massoretic text ought to read "Edom" and "Syrians", according to the Qere, LXX, and Targum editionis Lagardianae, 1872, ought to read " Edomites " (cf. Rud. Kittel, *Biblia Hebraica*, second ed. *in loc.*).

62. Cf. II Chron. xxviii, 17.

63. II Chron. xxviii, 5–15.

64. II Kings xvi, 7, 8.

65. Cf. ARAB I, 815, which is obviously a summary of several campaigns, including that of 734.

66. ARAB I, 776.

67. A. T. Olmstead, *History of Assyria*, p. 197.

68. Cf. the Aramaic inscription of Panammu II, the last part of which (lines 16–18) tells how the loyal Assyrian vassal gave final proof of the fidelity he asserts for Tiglathpileser by sacrificing his life in the Assyrian camp when the army was laying siege to Damascus (732). Cf. Kraeling (*op. cit.*, pp. 121, 125–127); Olmstead (*op. cit.*, p. 187).

69. ARAB I, 777.

70. *Ibid.*

71. II Kings xvi, 9.

72. The tablet recording Rezin's death, found and read by Sir Henry Rawlinson, has been irrevocably lost, and only the fact of its existence and loss remains (Schrader, *The Cuneiform Inscriptions and the Old Testament*, I, pp. 252, 257).

NOTES TO CHAPTER X

1. Cf. Ex. xxvii, 18.

2. E. Forrer, *Die Provinzeinteilung des assyrischen Reiches*, p. 62. Cf. G. E. Wright, F. W. Filson, W. F. Albright, *The Westminster Historical Atlas to the Bible*, p. 51, Plate VII: C; A. Alt, ZDPV, LII, 1929, pp. 220 ff. After Tiglathpileser's conquest of Galiliee, it was sufficient to dispatch a general to take Gilead, which Jeroboam II had recovered from Damascus (II Kings xiv, 25, 28; Forrer, *op. cit.*, p. 61). For Albright and Julius Lewy on Ṣubutu (*Ṣubite*) see Chapter III, n. 33 with references.

3. Wright, Filson, Albright, *op. cit.*, p. 49.

4. ARAB II, p. 437. Of course it is possible, but seems unlikely, that the Assyrians should have allowed native kings to rule at Damascus. Cf. S. A. Cook (*The Cambridge Ancient History*, III, 1926, p. 383), who speaks of "the kings of Damascus" as participating in Ilubi'di's rebellion in 720. An Assyrian governor would be expected. On the other hand if Assyria did permit native kings to rule, the circumstance would offer a natural explanation for the uprising of 727 and 720. But why should Assyria show any leniency in the provincial administration of a Syrian state which had caused so much trouble and had so consistently opposed Assyrian expansion in the West, especially after a new show of insubmission in 727?

5. A. Alt, *Die syrische Staatenwelt vor dem Einbruch der Assyrer*, ZDMG, 88, pp. 244 f.

6. Ilubi'di of Hamath is said to have "had no claim to the throne, was not of royal birth, who, in ruling his people, was violating the divine decree" (ARAB II, 5, 134). Thus he appears to be a usurper.

7. It is very probable that the revolts in Philistia and Hamath are to be correlated, rather than separated. See Kraeling, *Aram and Israel*, p. 135, n. 1.

8. ARAB II, 5; G. A. Barton, *Archaeology and the Bible*, 7th rev. ed., p. 468.

9. Barton, *loc. cit.*

10. Cf. II Kings xviii, 34; Forrer, *op. cit.*, p. 63. With Hamath constituted as an Assyrian province, the gap between the province of Manṣuate and Ṣubutu was closed.

11. Three hundred chariots, 600 cavalry, plus tribute and tax (the Cyprus Stele, ARAB II, 183).

12. *Sib'u* as Breasted suggests (*A History of Egypt*, p. 550), was probably simply the commander of the levy of Egyptian troops donated to the army of the southern allies, rather than another name for *Pi'anchi, Sô*, or some other Egyptian dynast. Egypt doubtless had a hand in the entire revolt of 720 (Breasted, *loc. cit.*). Sib'u is never called a king, but continually *turtan*, i.e. commander-in-chief of Muṣri (cf. Rud. Kittel, *Gesch. des. Volkes Israel*, II, p. 487). Olmstead equates Sib'u with Sô (II Kings xvii, 4) as " perhaps one of the Egyptian Delta kings " (*History of Palestine and Syria*, p. 454).

13. Breasted, *loc. cit.*

14. Olmstead, *Western Asia in the Days of Sargon*, pp. 57–60. Some five years later the Annals speak of tribute from *Pir'u of Muṣri*, that is, Pharaoh of Egypt, who now realized the peril of Egypt with a consolidated Syria-Palestine under Assyrian sway, and hastened to conciliate the Assyrian Emperor with gifts.

15. Olmstead, *History of Assyria*, p. 208; *Western Asia in the Days of Sargon*, pp. 58–60. A governor of Dimašqu is known for 694, for Samaria in 645 (Olmstead, *op. cit.*, p. 71, n. 35).

16. Alfred Jepsen, AfO XIV, 1942, p. 172.

17. II Kings xv, 29. Cf. Is. ix, 1, and Hosea's use of " Ephraim ", chs. 4–14.

18. Finegan (*Light from the Ancient Past*, p. 174) is likely incorrect in placing the taking of Damascus after Pekah's deposition and the accession of Hoshea. Although this event is undated in the Assyrian inscriptions, it is altogether possible (cf. also Thiele, JNES III, 1944, pp. 171, 172) that popular reaction upon the fall of Damascus and the death of Rezin in 732 may have brought Hoshea to the front as a pro-Assyrian candidate to fill the throne. This fits in perfectly with Thiele's date 732/731 and Albright's *c.* 732 (BASOR 100, p. 22) for the death of Pekah and the accession of Hoshea, although Lewy's date, 733, would place Pekah's fall before the taking of Damascus and Rezin's death, which is unlikely (cf. Julius Lewy, *Die Chronologie der Könige von Israel und Juda*, p. 32).

19. Although Pekah's actual reign could not have lasted longer than six years (*c.* 737–732), the twenty years of the Massoretic text

seems better explained by Thiele's theory that the usurper counted the years of the dynasty of Menahem, which he wiped out, as his own, and that the southern scribe, later working out the synchronisms for this period, accepted Pekah's unusual form of reckoning (*op. cit.*, pp. 168–170). This seems perhaps preferable to assuming the number originally came from oral tradition or that it grew with the passage of time (cf. Albright, BASOR 100, p. 19, n. 12; p. 22, n. 26). Thiele's adherence to both regnal years and synchronisms is essentially sound, and although it assumes an elaborate system of coregencies and variations in calendar, and other factors, this method, it seems to me, may yet prove the real key to the complex difficulties in the chronology of the kings of Judah and Israel. It seems evident no simple solution is possible, and the problems are conditioned by a multiplicity of factors.

20. ARAB I, 816. The evidence points clearly to Tiglathpileser's responsibility for the murder of the anti-Assyrian Pekah (S. A. Cook, *op. cit.*, p. 382).

21. II Kings xv, 30.

22. Hosea vii, 11.

23. Hosea xii, 1.

24. II Kings xvii, 3.

25. II Kings xvii, 4 f. Sewa (or Sô) is an otherwise unknown Delta dynast. Breasted offers the possibility that he was a ruler of a North Arabian *Muṣri*, but this surmise is to be rejected (*History of Egypt*, p. 549). Compare the theory of a non-Egyptian Muṣri, extending at least to south Palestine (S. A. Cook, *op. cit.*, pp. 383, 384 and 384 n. 1, for the origin and modification of this hypothesis).

26. II Kings xvii, 4–6; xviii, 9–11.

27. A. T. Olmstead, "The Fall of Samaria", AJSL, XXI, 1904–05, pp. 179–182; *Western Asia in the Days of Sargon*, p. 46, n. 9.

28. ARAB II, 4; Olmstead, *loc. cit.*

29. BASOR 100, p. 22, n. 27; J. Begrich, *Die Chronologie der Könige von Israel und Juda*, p. 98.

30. Thiele, *op. cit.*, p. 173.

31. *Loc. cit.*, cf. AJSL XXI, pp. 179 ff.

32. *Loc. cit.*

33. Babylonian Chronicle I: 28. Delitzsch first identified Shamarain with Samaria. (*Lit. Centralblatt*, September 17, 1887, 38, 1290). Paul Haupt accepted the identification (*Proc. Am. Oriental Soc.*, 1887, CCLX). Winckler's objection that the author of the

Babylonian Chronicle would scarcely have been concerned with such a distant place as Samaria (*Zeitschrift für Assyriologie* II, p. 351) is unsustained. Even if the author did not live in a time when Assyria was under Babylonian sway, Shalmaneser was at the time of the capture king of Babylon by the grace of Bel (cf. Olmstead, *loc. cit.*, p. 47, n. 9). Albright, however, notes that Shamarain (better *Shabarain*) is naturally Sibraim, while Samaria is Samerena, equal to Sameren. Note the reversal of sibilants.

34. The expedition is ruled out for 727 for " to (the land X) " precedes the account of Shalmaneser's accession, confirmed by the Babylonian Chronicle I, 24, where we learn he reigned only three winter months of 727. The year 726 is also eliminated, for there was no expedition that year, indicated by *ina mati*. 722 is similarly excluded, for Rm. 2, 97 reads for the year *karu*, referring only to building operations. The years 725–723 thus remain.

35. ARAB II, 437.

36. Cf. Olmstead, *loc. cit.*

37. ARAB II, 4, 55. Cf. A. G. Lie, *The Inscriptions of Sargon II, Part I, The Annals*, 1929, p. 5.

GENERAL INDEX